IN GOODE FAITH

by *W. Wilson Goode*
with
Joann Stevens

Judson® Press

In Goode Faith

Copyright © 1992
Judson Press, Valley Forge, PA 19482-0851

Goode, W. Wilson, 1938—.
    In Goode faith : Philadelphia's first black mayor tells his
story
   / W. Wilson Goode ; with Joann Stevens
      p.   cm.
   Includes index.
   ISBN 0-8170-1186-2
   1. Goode, W. Wilson. 2. Mayors—Pennsylvania—Philadelphia—Biography. 3. Philadelphia (Pa.)—Politics and government—1865–   . I. Stevens, Joann, 1951–   . II. Title.
F155.3.G66A3 1992
974.8′11043′ 092—dc20
[B]   92-17911

The name JUDSON PRESS is registered as a trademark in the U.S.
Patent Office.
Printed in the U.S.A.

To Velma Williams Goode,
My wife of thirty-two years,
My friend, my partner, and mother of our three children,
My most loyal and devoted supporter and constructive critic.

Contents

Foreword

A number of years ago I met a brilliant young man with an extraordinary desire to be of service to the people of his community and the City of Philadelphia. His name was W. Wilson Goode. I watched this young man develop into one of the most effective community development leaders in the city.

Most remarkable was his ability to bridge relationships between the many segments of the city: social, financial, political, racial, and religious. He was able to reach out and help people in a way seldom seen before. Accompanying his genius for working with people and doing good, was his ability to translate ideas into practical results. Wilson Goode came along at a time when people needed models for better housing and the improvement of communities, and as much as anyone I know, Wilson Goode translated activism into reality. He led the way for the construction of new and better housing for the poor and the needy; he organized neighborhoods to improve the quality of life for the people; and he was always in the forefront of movements directed toward the betterment of all the people.

Because of his unique management and development capabilities, he was selected to be the managing director of the

City of Philadelphia at a time when few African Americans anywhere in the country had assumed such roles. Before long the
entire city saw the magnitude of the capability of the man.

Within this book he describes some of his experiences, but
there are many unwritten stories about Wilson Goode that attest
even further to the great character and strength of the man.

I recall one occasion when he visited me at the Zion Baptist
Church, where I pastored, and informed me of his desire to run
for mayor of the city. I knew that this was the time for Philadelphia to have a leader like Wilson Goode. I wanted so much to be
of help to him that I changed my political registration from Non-
partisan and became a Democrat in order to vote for Wilson
Goode. I maintained that support for him to the very end of his
tenure.

In spite of some regrettable events, the Wilson Goode years
were good years. At one of the most difficult times in the history
of the city, Wilson Goode supplied Philadelphia with leadership
that will be hard for future mayors to match.

One of the most important parts of the life of Wilson Goode
is his religious fervor, commitment, and strength. He translated
his faith into daily action. One of the compelling and inspiring
statements in this book is: "Becoming a Christian was the most
important decision I have ever made in my life. It became the
glue that held me together during a time when there was little
consistency or joy in my life."

Over and over again when attending prayer meetings in city
churches, I would see Wilson Goode in the pew praying with his
people for their betterment and the betterment of Philadelphia.
Indeed, Goode is a good man, and his years were good years for
the city, and in many ways for the nation. The book tells of the
experiences of a remarkable individual whose legacy of leadership will live on for years and years to come.

In Goode Faith is a classic analysis of a Christian working in
the political world, a story that will be an inspiration to young
and old, black and white, and persons of all religious faiths. It is
our hope that this memorable book will be broadly read and
discussed for the lessons it teaches all of America.

Rev. Leon H. Sullivan

Preface

The rural South where I grew up was typical Tobacco Road country. Peanut, cotton, and tobacco farmers ruled the land while poor sharecropper families like mine worked for little more than peanuts in pay.

My family was one of thousands of black sharecroppers living in the tenant houses that dotted the countryside around Seaboard, North Carolina. We moved almost every year; sometimes it seemed like twice a year depending on whether or not the landlords tried to cheat my father out of his money. Some of the houses were pretty nice, with four or five rooms. Others were meager by standards even back then. None had indoor toilets, running water, or electricity. The houses were little more than a pile of weatherbeaten boards held together by nails and wire. But since this was all we had, we had no choice but to call it home.

Home. Even today when I think of my childhood in North Carolina I can smell the thick, acrid odor of kerosene lamps and feel the warmth of the big, potbellied wood stove that kept the room chilly on one side and burning hot on the other.

There were nine of us Goodes—my parents, my four brothers, my two sisters, and me. I was next to the youngest, which meant I always had clothes because I inherited my brothers' hand-me-downs. The only problem was, those clothes had passed through so many people that by the time I got them, they were just about worn out.

Daddy did the best he could to make a decent living for us, but because he was unable to read or write, much of the world was closed off to him. Mother had finished the eighth grade, so Daddy relied heavily on her to be the key that opened the world to him. She did what she could, but too often it wasn't enough to relieve the bitterness of segregation.

We lived in a world where colored folks rode in the back of the bus, used segregated drinking fountains and rest rooms, and sat in segregated sections of the local movie theater (as if we'd taint the screen with our blackness if we sat too close).

But what I hated most was the way white landlords talked to my father, as if he were less than a man. While he called them "Mister," they called him "Albert" and scolded him like a disobedient child if he questioned them about his share of the crop money.

Working the farm scarred my father's hands, but racism scarred his soul. I lived with what seemed like two fathers — one a hardworking, quiet, and gentle man Monday through Friday, the other a weekend boozer who used alcohol to unleash the pent-up frustration that churned inside of him.

I noticed changes in Daddy's behavior whenever he drank — the constant talking, angry looks, and the little fights he tried to pick with Mama and my older brothers and sisters. On those days when Daddy raged, I recoiled in fear, hating his anger even as I loved him. Then later, watching my "other" submissive father struggle in the white world armed only with the dull tools of illiteracy, my heart would break and I'd experience my own inner rage.

It wasn't fair. Watching Daddy mark his X on documents or seeing him struggle to maintain a little dignity when white men tried to cheat him, I pledged, "This will never happen to me." Over and over again, I promised myself, "I am not going to be like this. I'm going to learn all that I can and own my own land. I won't let anyone treat me as less than a man!"

I saw knowledge as a weapon that could fight bigotry. Along

with the realization of the power of education came an equally powerful lesson learned from my mother: With God all things are possible, if you believe.

The foundation of my Christian faith came from the example set by my God-fearing mother who taught me that "God can work anything out." There were times as I grew up when we didn't have enough to eat and times we had to put paper in the bottom of our shoes to cover the holes. Faced with a need, Mama would hum "Amazing Grace" or walk the floor, praying to her mighty God, who had never forsaken the righteous or allowed his seed to go begging for bread.

I was mystified and fascinated by the power of my mother's faith, especially since our lives were so hard. She would often tell us, "Even though today may be dark, tomorrow is going to be brighter." To Mama, God was no abstract religious theology or stained-glass icon. He was a near and dear Father whom she touched with her faith and talked to through her prayers. He listened too. And acted.

Through Mama I learned to trust in God because there were times when, frankly, there was no one else to trust in. During these times I waited anxiously to see what kind of miracle Mama's God would come up with to help us out of a jam. Whatever the challenge, Mama's God always proved to be as powerful as she said he was, even if he wasn't always as readily available as I would have liked him to be. "He may not come when you want him, but he's always on time!" the old folks used to say at our country church.

He was the God who came out of nowhere.

Education and the God who comes out of nowhere took me from the rural cotton fields of North Carolina to the seat of political power as Philadelphia's first African American mayor. Though Philadelphia is called "the City of Brotherly Love," it was neither love from other politicians nor the political machine that earned me the mayoralty. I believe it was the inner confidence and self-determination that I gained from lifting myself out of the degradation of poverty and racism. And, yes, I believe it was my faith in God.

How else can I explain rising above a stuttering problem so severe I spent much of my childhood in silence and many of my adult years struggling to compete? It seems like I've spent most of my life fighting. In North Carolina I constantly fought the inner feelings of hatred and inferiority that racism planted in my life. Going North to the "Promised Land" was my only hope for escape, but I found racism there too.

I fought feelings of inferiority when the counselor in my Philadelphia high school insisted that I be placed in an industrial arts program explaining, "Willie, you're from the farm. Therefore, you should know how to work with your hands." "And not your mind" was the unspoken message.

Eventually I was placed in an academic program, but not before my will was damaged and nearly broken. But the God who comes out of nowhere renewed me through the faith and support of my church, giving me the courage to apply to college and earn enough money to attend Morgan State in Baltimore.

Going to Morgan was like reentering the womb. My professors cared for, nurtured, and motivated me to dream and make my dreams come true. It was at Morgan that I gained a thirst for community service and captured the vision that maybe, one day, I could be the mayor of a big city.

The city that tried to make me a laborer swore me in as its 126th mayor on January 2, 1984. I went into politics with the vision of reforming government and creating a multiracial, multiethnic system that would respond to the basic human rights of all people. As I executed the duties of my office, I soon realized that I had trained for this position all of my life. Every humiliation I had suffered as a child on the farm, every racial snub I had withstood as a young army officer was part of a grand scheme directed by God to bring me to this moment. Every academic victory I'd fought for in high school and college, the wife I chose, every mountain I'd climbed to reach my career goals were all part of the preparation.

When I had refused to compromise my intelligence by allowing my high school counselor to push me into an industrial arts program, she called it defiance. Time showed me that my decision was the flowering of a growing inner strength that would later gain me a reputation as a political loner and maverick unwilling to make back-room deals that I felt compromised my integrity or the good faith of the people who had elected me.

My political career actually began in Philadelphia's grass-roots neighborhoods like the Paschall community where I grew up in West Philadelphia. When I headed the Philadelphia Council for Community Advancement (PCCA), a nonprofit housing agency that specialized in helping community agencies build low-income housing units, the black churches and community groups I worked with taught me about building neighborhood coalitions; where the power bases were; how to work with the local and federal government; and, perhaps most importantly, how hard-working and committed community people could literally fight City Hall and win when empowered to work for their dreams.

PCCA was a dying agency when I was appointed executive officer. By the end of my tenure I had raised more than $60 million in housing investments and built more units than any other agency in the city.

I believed then, and believe now, that with God all things are possible. Faith in God has unlocked many mysteries for me and has helped me to overcome amazing challenges and obstacles. I have learned that God can work through the faithful to achieve miracles. He gives them special insight, vision, and unyielding determination to accomplish the impossible. God does not do these things for us, but he gives us the ability to do for ourselves.

The negotiation and management skills I learned in my early career led to my appointment as the first black commissioner and first black chair of the Public Utility Commission.

I was politically unaligned, and critics thought my appointment a fluke that would never win Senate confirmation. The media called my chances at confirmation "a long shot." They didn't know me or my God.

I won Senate confirmation and was so successful during my tenure with the commission that I was appointed the first African American managing director for the city of Philadelphia, a landmark achievement that placed me in charge of a billion-dollar budget and more than thirty thousand city employees in ten departments.

My appointment as managing director came at a time when most large cities were reeling under serious urban pressures. Philadelphia was no exception. Escalating crime, federal budget cutbacks, and labor disputes were common occurrences. Yet as the city's chief labor negotiator with the municipal unions, I managed to negotiate every contract without suffering even the threat of a work stoppage while at the same time protecting the city's interests.

I faced many challenges in my political career: investigating the meltdown at Three Mile Island, establishing the city's first human-services crisis system, investigating police corruption, among others. But I believe the greatest challenge I faced as a politician came from the house that Rizzo built—the Philadelphia Police Department.

Frank Rizzo was a tough Italian cop who had maneuvered his way up the ranks from rookie officer to police chief to mayor. His greatest strength was coalition politics, built almost exclusively by appealing to the emotional fears of Philadelphia's ethnic neighborhoods. During his reign, Rizzo's cops made Philadelphia a police state where clashes between blacks and the city's predominantly white police force were legendary. A fateful confrontation in 1978 with an eccentric back-to-nature group known as MOVE set up a conflict that came to a head during my watch as mayor and epitomized the impact of Rizzo's force, even outside of politics.

To this day, the violent clash on May 13, 1985, between MOVE and the police haunts me, sickens me. I believe the decision to let the fire burn unchecked was a travesty of justice and a blatant act of racism. I question whether some police officers boldly murdered innocent children and adults. I am convinced that the police commissioner developed a secret plan a year in advance that resulted in the use of excessive force and the reckless destruction of a community.

I took the heat for the incident because it happened on my watch. I did not give the order to let the fire burn. The order came from the police commissioner. The question that haunts me the most is, How could there be a conspiracy of silence so strong that it kept me from knowing of the plans to destroy MOVE?

An investigation was held to ferret out the whole truth, but I feel that too many critical aspects of that investigation were handled superficially. As a result, I was left with only the same unanswered questions.

Now it is time for me to speak, to set the record straight about my activism as a political reformer, the MOVE incident, and the reason I feel I need to be out of local politics.

There are many people who feel they know who Wilson Goode is and why I ran my administration the way I did. A December 1991 news story in the *Philadelphia Inquirer* summed up that paper's view of me in a headline that proclaimed "Unwilling to Play the Game." In a way they were right. I'm not the kind of man to play games with this city's future. I've always tried to act in good faith, believing that acting out of a sense of basic decency and honesty would compel others to do the same. I was wrong, and I have paid dearly for my faith in others.

The traits that have characterized my career are simple: hard work, honesty, faith, and a practical approach to getting things done. No, I was not always the smartest person in the room, but I listened carefully and I knew how to cut through the red tape.

This book is my way of cutting through the red tape of all of the speculation, lies, and interpretations that have come out about my administration and the MOVE tragedy. I feel that I was a good, if too trusting, public servant who tried to be fair and just in dealing with the public, the media, and other politicians.

I was a public servant with a dream of helping shape and nurture a multiethnic political system that would serve the people and usher in a new era of politics for Philadelphia—an era that would eventually destroy the long history of political corruption and patronage that characterized Philadelphia politics.

We made some major strides in that direction, but in the process I was almost destroyed. This is my opportunity to set the record straight about the forces that shaped, influenced, propelled, and eventually ended my political career. And to tell you how my faith in God took me through. I stand today as committed as ever to those principles. I am determined to work from the outside to bring them about, determined to use my talents to help prepare a generation of African American males for the world around them.

Many people have asked, Why the African American male? Why not African American females? Actually, my real concern is the African American family. I have watched the African American family become weaker as a unit. I have watched women left alone to care for their children. I have watched children grow up without the benefit of a male role model.

Perhaps what crystallized the issue and challenge in my mind more than anything else was a beautiful, bronze African American woman who last year asked me, "Mr. Mayor, where have all the good black men gone? I can't find a husband." I could easily understand why. Responsible black men in our socity seem to be vanishing.

Based on my experience and analysis, I believe it is likely that seven out of ten African American males between the ages of seventeen and forty-four will, over the next five years, either contract AIDS, become addicted to drugs, become unemployed, be murdered in the streets, become homeless, or go to prison.

I know that if I am going to help the African American family, I have to first help the African American male.

Moreover, I know that if this statistic is going to change, I have to do more than talk about the problem; I have to devote my life to finding creative solutions to reverse the trend. After all, along the way, many have guided my path. Now it is time for me to give back.

Without knowing where I came from and what I stand for today, it's hard for anyone to gauge my public actions accurately. So let me paint you a complete picture by introducing myself, Wilson Goode.

Acknowledgments

My mother, Rozelar, and late father, Albert, who gave me valuable experiences to help me succeed in life. Percell and Gwen Stanford, longtime friends and supporters. Shirley Hamilton, Joan Woods, Catherine Boyd, Angell Keene, William D. C. Dennis, James Stanley White, Deborah Goens, Marge Staton, Lynn Fields, Karen Warrington, William O. Leggett, Cathy Weiss, Catherine Freimiller, Denise Goren, Lillian Ray, Betsy Reveal, Timothy Spencer, Sultan Ahmad, Clayton Carter, Patricia McKinley, who went beyond the call of duty while working with me. Willie Williams, William Marrazzo, Jane Malone, Harry Perks, Barbara Cox, Richard Gilmore, John Flaherty, David Fair, Angela Dowd-Burton, Kevin Tucker, Joan Reaves, Christine Murphy, William Hankowsky, Julia Robinson, David Brenner, Barbara Mather, who were the best of the best in city government. Dr. Bernard Watson, Dr. Maurice Clifford, and Judge Leon Higginbotham who were early role models. Christine Washington, Mamie Nichols, Alice Lipscomb, who changed the face of their communities. Henry Nicholas, Robert Sugarman, and Nolan Atkinson, Jr., who were early and consistent supporters of my candidacies for mayor. Donald Redcross, my campaign treasurer and one of the most courageous men I've ever met. Bill Batoff and Delores Brisbon who helped with fund raising in 1987.

John Cunningham, Melvin Ellis, Elizabeth Edoo, Mary Ann Colfer, Salvatore Giafaglione, Joanne Zmuida, Margaret James, and Henry Warner, loyal and dedicated security personnel.

Deacons Herbert O'Hagan, Theodore Thompson, John Rodgers, Augusta Freeman, John Roy Overton, William Allen, Sr., James R. Smith, Golden Cobbs, Ernest Walker, Walter Jones, Jr., Alex Harper, Ruth Freeman, Virginia Davis, Hazel B. Nelson, who gave me support throughout my developmental years at First Baptist Church of Paschall.

Prudence "Betty" Strickler, Steven Bishop, Camilla Scott, Lotelya "Penny" Overton, Nancy "Tina" Allen, who were inspirational friends at a crucial time in my life.

Vernon Odom and Maida Odom who along with relatives encouraged me to write this book.

Donald Billups who grew up with me and whose death as a homeless person deepened my resolve.

Rev. Sarah Potter Smith who prophesied that I would become mayor long before I thought it possible. She has been especially inspirational to me.

Alicia Christian, Chris Sprowal, Leona Smith, Rev. Henry Wells, Dr. Sylvester Outley, Sister Mary Scullion, and Chris Brown, who pioneered working for the dignity of the homeless.

Ned Wolf, Michael Churchill, Tom Gilhool, Shirley Dennis, Paul Vance, John F. White, Sr., Royal Sims, Clarence Farmer, Patricia Garrison-Corbin, Claudia Pharis, Shelly Yanoff, who have been systems change agents.

Graham Finney, former Mayor William Green, and former Gov. Milton Shapp who provided critical opportunities for me on my road to success. Bishop and Mother R.T. Jones, Rev. James S. Allen and the black clergy in their efforts to support my campaigns for mayor. Bishop Frank C. Cummings for his visionary leadership.

My deep appreciation to a group of people without whom finishing this book would have been impossible. They gave invaluable and unselfish service. Joann Stevens, who helped write the book. Kristy Arnesen Pullen who was dedicated from the very beginning. She took a personal interest in the quality of the entire publication. Pat Finn was absolutely super in her typing of the many copies of the manuscript. She, too, took a real personal interest. Mary Nicol and Kathleen Hayes provided their outstanding editing skills. Tina Edginton and Ife Nii Owoo put their most creative skills to work on the cover design. Ed Hunter enthusiastically assumed the leadership for the marketing of this book. My appreciation goes to each of them and the entire staff of Judson Press.

Karen Warrington, Pooneh Mohazzbi, Cathy Weiss, and Catherine Freimiller, who provided needed research.

And finally: Rev. S. L. Taylor, my pastor and supporter for eighteen years. My numerous nieces and nephews, but especially Ramona Cook-Browne, James W. Ellis, Jr., Alvin Ellis, Ronald John Anthony Cook, Javis Goode, Camilla Goode, Edward Goode, Jr., and Timothy Goode, who were great inspirations to me. And my ninety-two-year-old Aunt Maggie Tann for the love she has shown throughout my life.

CHAPTER ONE

Sharecroppers' Son

"Mama! Wilson's throwing rocks at the chickens again!"

I sent the next rock skipping towards my sister's ankles. She jumped just in time to miss it.

"Tattletale!"

"Mama! Wilson threw a rock at me!"

"Wilson, what are you doing?"

"Nothing! She's telling tales on me."

I could hear Mamie screaming as I ran towards the fields chuckling to myself. By now Mama would be at the kitchen door looking for me. I was long gone and had cheated her out of giving me a whipping this afternoon.

"Wilson, get me a switch off that oak tree there by the house," Mama would say when I got caught doing something. I'd try to find the smallest, weakest switch I could among the long, spindly branches that cut you like a whip! If the one I picked wasn't sturdy enough, Mama sent me back to get another one. Still, I always tried to pass off one of the puny ones.

My brothers and sisters claimed I was mischievous, but I was just trying to have some fun. It was boring living on a farm in the middle of nowhere. We moved so much that I had no playmates other than my brothers and sisters — and they usually had chores when we weren't working in the fields.

"All right, it's time to get up," my mom would yell as the morning light pushed the night away. We would all jump up and run for the wash pan. Mama had water warming on the stove. We washed our hands and faces and went straight for the table to get our regular breakfast, which consisted of hot biscuits, molasses, and fatback. We quickly gulped the food down.

"You children hurry up," Mama would say. "It's going to be a hot one today. Let's get as much work done as we can before the noon sun." By 6:30 A.M. we were out in the fields chopping the weeds from around the cotton and peanuts. Row after row we went, with the sun beating down on our backs. The wide straw hats shielded the sun from our heads. We would work till eleven o'clock and then stop until one or two o'clock, depending on the heat. And then we were back to the fields with our hoes until it started to get dark.

"You all got lots of work done today," Dad would say. "Now eat a good meal and go to bed so you can get up early tomorrow morning to beat the sun."

We would grab the wash pan, wash our faces and hands, sit down at the table, and enjoy our chicken and dumplings and hot biscuits. After supper we were off to bed. No bath, no shower.

Bathing was a luxury reserved for Saturday night. Once a week we would all line up and, one by one, take our baths in the big, round tin tub. When the water became too dirty, we would change it, but that was only maybe two or three times a night, because it was hard warming enough water for the tub.

There was Mamie, Mary Idonia, Alvestus, James Henry, Earn Lee, me, and the baby, Ed Louis. As the oldest, Mamie was the motherly type. She was left in charge when Mom and Dad weren't around. Mary Idonia, or "Donia," was the beauty queen, always primping and beautifying herself. We always said she was destined to end up in Hollywood. After my sister Mamie got married, Donia did leave home and actually moved to Los Angeles — to use her nursing degree, though, not to become a movie star.

Alvestus was the smart one and very adventurous. By the time I turned twelve, Al had joined the army and was serving in

Korea. Every day Mom eagerly went to the mailbox searching for a letter from Al. Whenever a stranger approached the house, she recoiled in fear.

"I wonder who that is?" she'd ask nervously. "I hope it's not about your brother."

Her anxiety was contagious, and I worried too, wondering when my brother would come home. For a year we lived on the brink of panic. Day after day, week after week, we cautiously eyed strangers and peered down the long, dusty road that led to our house—looking for Alvestus.

The day the strange car filled with black faces came down our road we barely looked—that is, until it stopped at our door. The door opened and out jumped Al.

"Hallelujah!" Mama shouted, throwing up her hands in praise. "My boy is home. Thank you, Jesus! My boy is home safe."

Tears welled up in my eyes. My brother was home safe from the war. Shortly after coming back home, Al got married and I didn't get to see much of him. Later in life he joined the Nation of Islam movement, becoming an avid follower of Elijah Muhammad.

"Why are you still going to church to worship that white man?" he would chide us. "You know the white race is nothing but the devil. They have mistreated black people ever since they came to this country."

Whenever Mom caught Al giving one of his lectures, she was equally as adamant in her response.

"Alvestus, get out of here with all of that Muslim stuff. We are Christians. You know I raised you better than that."

The rebuff would only cause Al to become more aggressive and animated. He could preach about Islam for hours, but our tolerance never lasted as long as his lectures. Halfway through his ranting we would drift out of the room, one by one, and retreat to other parts of the house. I usually stayed to listen the longest, trying to reconcile my Christian upbringing with my brother's revelations. I admired and respected Al. Curious, I even visited the mosque with him once. All I can remember is taking my shoes off and allowing a big security guard to search me at the door.

I admired Al and wanted to be like him, but my faith in Christ would not allow me to abandon Christianity for Islam.

James was the wild one in the family and "as strong as an ox"! Mama still tells the story about how James decided to teach himself to drive when he was eleven.

At the time, we lived on Harry Brown's farm near Skippers, Virginia. The farm had two houses that were joined together by a center porch. It was a Saturday afternoon. All of us were in the yard talking when James got into the car. We just laughed.

"Boot, you know you can't drive," Al said, calling James by his nickname. "Get out of that car."

Earn Lee jumped up and down shouting, "Look at Boot. He's going to drive!" Then he fell on the ground laughing.

The laughing and joking came to an abrupt halt when we saw the car move. Everybody started jumping out of the way, running for cover as James gunned the car into motion. Some of us ran around to the side of the house; some hid behind trees. I hid behind the biggest tree I could find as Mom headed for the porch between the two houses. She never made it. As Mom approached the corner of the house, the car slid into her, breaking open the skin on her knees and legs, exposing the bone and white tissue through a gaping hole.

"Oh God!" Dad exclaimed. "That boy done killed my wife!"

As concerned as I was about Mom, I was also surprised at Dad's reaction. This was one of the rare times I had seen him show any emotion but anger. He was visibly shaken.

It was comforting to see my father show his emotions. He was usually so quiet we never quite knew what he was feeling. This time, though, it was obvious he was as frightened as the rest of us.

Mom was hurriedly taken to the doctor in Emporia, Virginia. She had no broken bones, but it took several stitches to close the deep gash.

James was not the most careful driver, but he was one heck of a mechanic and handyman. He could fix anything around the farm and the house. We called James "Boot" because Dad played "boot jack" with him on his knee.

Earn Lee, nicknamed "C Boy" for no particular reason that I know of, was the mama's boy in the family. He seemed to get anything he wanted, and I thought he was Mama's favorite. In retrospect that was probably just my youthful jealousy. I'm sure it seemed like he always got his way because he was sickly with his notorious migraine headaches.

Ed Louis was the baby, and like most baby brothers, he was protected by all of us. He was a good little brother—always happy and affectionate. Johnnie Paul, Mamie's son, also lived with us. He was like a fifth brother to me.

Growing up I was a little devil, always into everything and doing what I shouldn't. I loved to pick on my sisters, calling them names, throwing rocks at them, teasing them, and doing my best to embarrass them. At times I was probably a young terror.

In 1943, we lived just across the North Carolina border in Skippers, Virginia. It was a year before I started school, so I must have been four or five. Mama and Daddy had gone shopping and as usual, Mamie was in charge. I thought I was big, so I decided I was in charge of myself. It was cold and I stood by the big, black, potbellied stove warming myself. The warm metal felt good brushing against my backside and I backed up some more. Before I knew it, I had burned my backside. It really hurt! But I don't think the pain in my bottom hurt as much as the blow to my pride. I had burned my backside, and I had no one to blame but myself.

For the next hour I cried and cried and cried. By the time Mama and Daddy came home, I had stopped crying, but as soon as I saw them I started crying again.

"Wilson, what's wrong with you?" Mom asked, her voice full of concern.

"Mamie and Donia pushed me against the stove," I fibbed.

"Mamie, Donia come here," Mama commanded. "Why did you all push Wilson against that hot stove? You both should be watching him, not hurting him. Bring me the switch."

Naturally Mamie looked bewildered.

"But Mama, we didn't do anything," she protested. "He did it to himself."

Before Mamie could finish explaining, Mama was on them with the switch. I stood back, a gleeful expression on my face, delighted at having them share my pain. But soon afterwards, I was sorry I had fibbed and gotten them the whipping.

Yes, I got into mischief, but mostly I just stayed to myself and daydreamed.

My favorite dream was that I lived in a big city, far away from North Carolina. Maybe Chicago or New York. I owned a big house with electric lights, running water, and indoor toilets. The best part was that I worked for myself. I was in control of my own destiny. No one took advantage of me.

In my dreams, life in the city was heavenly. There were lots of jobs and life was fair. People were treated the same. No one was looked down on for being poor and colored. In the city, you also could do important things with your life—get an education and even become famous like Ralph Bunche, the great Negro statesman, or baseball great Jackie Robinson, or Joe Louis, the "Brown Bomber." These were my first heroes. I read about them in school and dreamed of being like them—famous and looked up to by people.

I dreamed of being famous because I wanted to have the power to change things, to open up opportunities for people who were locked out. Jackie Robinson was famous; he was changing the face of baseball. Joe Louis's fame was changing the world of boxing. Ralph Bunche, well, he was changing the whole world.

If I were famous, I could change things. I could sit wherever I wanted at the movies. I could make sure colored kids could ride the bus to school. I could change the way the landlords treated my father. "By the time I become an adult," I vowed, "I'll be doing something different than what my parents do. I'll be in the city."

I knew I'd never become famous living in the country. All we had here was the farm and animals—cows, mules, hogs, chickens, and the squirrels, rabbits, possum, and coons we hunted to eat. Sometimes we got a deer. But the country held nothing much other than hard work and church.

Church was the second Sunday of each month. Rev. Frank Bullock, the circuit preacher in our area, tended four churches. So second Sunday was the only time he came through to preach at Mount Zion in our little community.

We always looked forward to that second Sunday because that's when we went to church and saw all our relatives and some friends from near our old farms. It was really one of those happy occasions.

For recreation, some Saturdays I walked into town with my brothers to attend a movie. Walking down the road, we always faced the oncoming traffic. We liked to throw rocks at the passing cars, but only after the car was long gone and we had no real chance of hitting it. Approaching town, we crossed the railroad tracks and headed for the sidewalks. When the sidewalks came into view, I started running.

"Wilson, come back here," Boot yelled. "You know those sidewalks are only for white folks. They're going to put your little black butt in jail if you don't get off there."

"But I'm going to Charlie Painter's store," I protested, stepping lightly on the sidewalk. Painter owned the grocery store as well as our farm.

"Don't matter. You just better get off that sidewalk before some white folks see you," Earn Lee chimed in. "Walk in the gutter. You know we're supposed to walk in the gutter."

Scared, I leaped off the sidewalk and walked in the dirty gutter. Walking into Charlie Painter's store, I stood silently to one side for about fifteen minutes, waiting for him to finish serving the white customers. When the last white person had left, Painter looked at me and smiled.

"Hey, Wilson Boy, what do you want?" he asked pleasantly. I knew that Charlie Painter liked me. He thought I was smart "for a colored boy."

"I want a Royal Cola and a bag of Planter's peanuts," I said.

Mr. Painter put the products on the counter. "That will be ten cents."

I handed him a dime and grabbed my purchases. Royal Cola and peanuts were my favorite. I opened the bag of peanuts and poured the salty nuts into the bottle. I was now ready for the movies.

At the movies, we sat way up in the balcony in the colored section away from the white folks. A western, *Lash Larue,* was the feature film. Sitting in that balcony drinking my Royal Cola laced with peanuts I thought I was in heaven! If this wasn't heaven, I knew it was the closest I would ever get down on the farm.

I loved the solitude of the movies because I was a shy, lonely kid who didn't talk much. From the time I was five or six years old, I stuttered so badly I could barely get some words out. Of course the kids in the little one-room country school I attended teased me unmercifully.

My first day of school I was so scared I refused to leave the house. I was to attend the Merry Oaks School, a one-room schoolhouse located about two miles from our farm. Mama spanked me real good when I said I was staying home. I cried my heart out.

"Unless you want more of that whipping, Wilson, take yourself on out of here with your brothers and sisters and go to school!" she commanded sternly.

My feelings hurt, all I could do was whimper. I was scared to go to school, scared of the unknown. What if they asked me to write? Or worse yet, speak? I thought. Why must I do this? Why can't I just stay home?

Everything had been all right up until now. I knew my parents and they knew me. It was all right with them that I talked funny. I was comfortable at home. Now I had to go to this strange place in the woods called school.

The schoolhouse was a sad, weather-beaten little wooden structure with huge white chips of paint peeling off the sides. Three teachers divided the eighty students into six grades. My early school years were miserable. Being around so many people was intimidating. I rarely talked because without fail, the kids made fun of my stuttering. The Colfax cousins were the worst.

"Come on, Willie Wilson, bet you can't count to ten," Norman challenged.

"Can too."

"Go on then," his cousin Charles chimed in.

I knew what they wanted, but I took the bait anyway, hoping to surprise them and myself.

I began slowly, "One. Two. Three. Four. Five. Si-si-si-si-six."

The cousins fell to the ground laughing. I could feel my whole body burn with shame.

As if stuttering wasn't bad enough, I also had trouble writing my *M*s and *W*s. For some reason I got them mixed up and wrote my name Millie Milson Goode instead of Willie Wilson Goode.

My classmates broke into gales of laughter every time I wrote my name wrong.

"Hey, Millie!" they teased.

"Little Millie Milson can't write his name!"

"My name's no-not Mi-Mi-Mi-Millie!"

My teachers encouraged me to practice, but I didn't like being laughed at. So I participated as little as possible and spent much of my childhood silently daydreaming.

I dreamed of becoming so famous that everybody would know my name, Willie Wilson Goode, and nobody would dare call me Millie.

Gradually I learned how to write my name correctly. The teacher was very patient with me, very caring. In time I learned to add, subtract, and multiply. I improved each day I was in school. I became interested. I was learning!

By the time I was eight years old, I had become a pretty good student, getting all A's and B's in my subjects, though I still had trouble speaking properly. By age fourteen, my love for learning had created a new dream in me—college. I wanted to go to college, learn about the world, and become a history teacher.

Among the few material possessions my family owned was an old radio that linked us to the outside world and its events. I loved listening to "The Shadow." And when the Brooklyn Dodgers played the Yankees for the World Series, we didn't miss a game. "Amos and Andy" was another favorite. Of course we also listened to every Joe Louis fight.

That radio broke up the monotony of country life and eased the frustrations I lived with daily. I didn't like the farm. Mostly I didn't like the fact that we broke our backs working and sweating to harvest crops for somebody else. It seemed like all we did was work like animals, only to have the landlord come and take most of the money, leaving us with practically nothing. We counted on hunting and canning the vegetables we raised to make ends meet. Without that, we couldn't have survived.

"Why do we do all the work and let the landlord take all the money?" I asked my father.

"You just have to do what you have to do in order to survive, Son," he replied wearily.

I couldn't accept that.

"Dad, I don't want to work like this when I get to be grown," I said. "I'm going to be different. I won't be down here working hard and giving someone else all the money I earn off the land."

My father never scolded me for my sassiness.

"Son, I hope you do make something of yourself," he said. "I hope you'll be better off than I am."

Born on Christmas Day 1903, my father was a quiet, hard-working man who let the lessons of hard work and obedience shape his life. He was a special gift to his mother, Babe Goode, who was just twelve when she conceived him. Babe had been raped by Henry Valentine, her sister's husband.

Because Babe had told everyone about the rape, Henry made life miserable for her, taunting her and beating her whenever he found her working alone in the fields. Babe often had to run and hide at a neighbor's house to escape her tormentor. Eventually though, she married a man named John Rodgers.

Dad's earliest years were made miserable by Rodgers, who never accepted Dad and beat him daily. From age five my father was forced to work in the fields and was not allowed to attend school. Finally, at age eight he went to live with his aunt in Seaboard, North Carolina.

From then on, Daddy lived in Seaboard, where Mama grew up. Both of their families were farmers. That's all he and Mama had ever known—farming and our little country church, Mount Zion. There was no organ or piano at that church, but to hear my parents tell it, that never stopped those country people from praising the Lord! They would just clap their hands and sing and shout the church down.

Mama and Daddy met at church, fell in love, and got married in 1925. There was never really any question that they'd become sharecroppers. It didn't provide a very stable life, but it became predictable. Each time they got cheated out of their money, Daddy and Mama moved the family to another farm, and the whole cycle would start all over again. I think we moved every year; sometimes it was twice a year.

Typical moves were from Seaboard to Skippers, Virginia, to Emporia, Virginia, and then to Pleasant Hill, North Carolina. Back to Seaboard, then on to Weldon, North Carolina, back to Seaboard and then over to Halifax, and finally back to Seaboard.

As the kids came, Mama worked the fields with a baby lying on the ground by her side. An older child was responsible for looking after the next youngest.

For the most part, the landlords were all the same—white, patronizing, and deceptive. Harry Brown was a little different. Harry Brown's farm was the one in Skippers, Virginia, about twenty-five miles from Seaboard. He, at least, treated my father with some semblance of respect, but my mother suspected he was sweet-talking us to hide the fact that he was also cheating us blind. Often as Harry Brown's truck passed our house, loaded with tobacco, Mama would yell out, "There goes our tobacco. Harry Brown is stealing our tobacco."

Despite our poverty, we had a pretty solid family, and our home was filled with lots of faith and love. My favorite time of year was winter. Christmas was in winter, and Christmas meant toys, fruit, raisins, walnuts, and Brazil nuts. About two weeks before Christmas, my brothers and sisters and I would go into the woods to find a nice Christmas tree to adorn the living room. We also gathered as much mistletoe and holly as we could find to make Christmas decorations to sell.

Wrapping the foliage into neat little bundles or wreaths, we would stand out on the main highway waiting for people traveling from the North for the holidays. With each approaching car, I'd hold out my hand to show off the Christmas bundles. Now and then someone stopped to buy.

"How much?" they asked.

"Whatever you think it's worth."

Most people gave me a dollar or two, but now and then someone only gave a dime or a quarter. The most we ever got was five dollars. But even a dollar was more money than we usually saw. Clutching my money, I would grin from ear to ear as I skipped along the highway looking for the next car. We sold holly and mistletoe until every bundle was gone or until darkness forced us back home.

Christmas Eve was the longest night of the year as I waited for Santa Claus to come. I really believed in Santa Claus then, and as I lay in bed listening to the night noises, every little sound heightened my expectation and excitement.

In my mind I imagined Santa flying his sleigh through the air, landing on our roof, and sliding down the chimney to bring a stocking for each of us. I wondered, though, how did he get down that chimney without being burned by the big fire we kept going? I soon dismissed such silly thoughts and slowly, reluctantly, drifted off to sleep.

Morning couldn't come quickly enough. During the night I had dreamed of getting a bike, a suit, and lots and lots of toys. I jumped out of bed and ran into the living room to look in my stocking. It was full of the usual fruit, raisins, walnuts, Brazil nuts—and a few small toys. No bike. No suit. But I was happy for one day. Besides, Daddy never drank on Christmas.

Daddy's drinking was a dark cloud that shadowed our lives. I felt like I lived with two fathers. One was a quiet, humble, hard-working man who was kind to everybody and loved his family. The other was a violent maniac who would turn on his own wife and children in a drunken rage.

Before they married, Mama hadn't known that Daddy drank. Little by little, he started coming home drunk. Money was real scarce in those early years. Sometimes Daddy made forty cents a day, one year Mama made fifteen dollars for a whole season of picking cotton. Daddy sometimes wasted it all on the corn whiskey he bought or by getting robbed after coming out of one of the juke joints where he bought liquor.

I must have been eight years old the first time I realized there was a problem with Daddy's drinking. It was a sunny Sunday morning in spring. Daddy had been drinking that morning, but liquor just seemed to make him talk more. Mama and us kids were walking out the door for church when Daddy announced that he would drive us. For a moment Mama's body tensed. She shook it off and smiled.

"Thank you, Albert. We'll manage."

"I said I'm driving," he growled.

My parents rarely argued, and I couldn't understand why Mama wouldn't just let him drive. In the end Daddy won out.

"I'm sitting by the window," I announced, as we piled into the old Ford. Being next to the youngest I usually got my way. The car lurched off in bumpy, little jerks before smoothing out.

It was nice riding with my family, feeling the cool morning air against my face. No one was talking, and I sat back enjoying the ride until I noticed that the car was picking up speed. Rows of tobacco plants now whizzed by in a dizzying blur. What's happening? I wondered.

"Albert, slow down," Mama said evenly. "You're going too fast."

Her words seemed to make the car go faster. I was scared now and holding on to my sister Mamie for dear life. Behind us a trail of dust rose from the dirt road as the car careened crazily around corners and down the narrow road. When we turned the next corner, Mama screamed. The car flew off the road and bounced along a grassy bank, crashing against rocks and fallen tree limbs. It felt like my insides were being shaken out. I knew I was going to be sick. When the car finally stopped, it landed upright in a ditch. Miraculously no one was hurt. Later I learned what had gone wrong. Daddy was drunk.

Nobody knows exactly why Daddy drank, but I'm sure it had to do with the frustration of living in the South. Landlords were mean, real mean, and they had no shame about taking more than their share of Daddy's money.

"If you don't like it, Albert, move! I don't have to explain it," they told him.

As I became more aware of my father's misery, I grew bitter and resentful towards the white men who mistreated him, especially when his misery caused him to mistreat us.

It was hard to watch my father being treated so unfairly. Sometimes as I watched white men talk to him like a child, I wanted to get my BB gun and shoot them. The only thing that stopped me was knowing that Mama would kill me if I even tried to do that. I never did accept white men calling Daddy by his first name while they were always "Mister." No human being should be treated like an animal and made to feel so small. I vowed to always treat people fairly and respectfully.

Once while living on Ellis Crews' Farm near Pleasant Hill, North Carolina, Dad got into a violent argument with Mr. Crews. Dad had been shortchanged and was really angry. Mr. Crews just laughed.

"Albert, you know you can't count anyway," he said in his

thick, slow drawl. "Stop putting up a fuss. You've gotten all you're going to get out of me this year. If you don't like it, then you take your family and move someplace else."

"I'm tired of moving, Mr. Crews," Dad said through clenched teeth. "I've been moving every year for as long as I can remember."

"Then take the money and shut your mouth, Albert," Mr. Crews concluded, as if scolding a boy.

I'll never forget the look of anger on my father's face or the smirk on Mr. Crews'. I was twelve years old. A few months later we moved again. Packing up my things, I wondered "Lord, is there fairness anywhere?"

The frustration of living in the Jim Crow South was enough to break any man's spirit, especially a poor black man's. It caused my father to drink, but that's not what made him violent. Mama said it was an accident that he had back in 1937 that made the whiskey affect him so badly. It happened on the second Sunday in May. Mama was dressing the children for church when she heard a crash. Running into the next room she found Daddy lying on the floor where he had fallen backwards off a chair. Doctors say he split a small section of his brain when he fell. After that, whenever he drank, the whiskey sent him into violent rages. Half the time he also couldn't remember things. Daddy lived a "Dr. Jekyll and Mr. Hyde" life. During the week he was quiet and humble. On weekends the alcohol made him a raging madman.

It seemed that almost every weekend some men — "friends" of Dad's — came to pick him up in a car. God knows where they went. But on those weekends two things happened: Dad returned home drunk and broke, and we knew food would be scarce for the coming week. Mama said the men helped get Dad drunk so they could steal his money.

Once during one of his drunken episodes, Dad got hit by a car and was nearly killed. I was thirteen and looking forward to my birthday. It was a hot Saturday in July. My brothers and I had walked into Seaboard to go to the movies. We'd just seen a good western, either Gene Autry or Roy Rogers, and I was going to Charlie Painter's store when my first cousin Buck Brown, Uncle Wilbert's oldest son, ran up to us with the news.

"Boys, don't you know that your daddy has been hit by a car? I think he was killed."

Buck then turned and walked away. For a moment we were stunned, unable to move. When I regained my senses, I didn't know whether to cry for my dead father or to pick up a rock and hit Buck for being so insensitive.

We all cried as we ran the three miles home. By the time we got home, Mama knew what had happened to us. She met us at the door to say Daddy wasn't dead, just bruised up a lot. Dad returned home after spending several days in the hospital.

I don't recall hating my father when he drank. I felt sorry for him. I also was scared. We all were. The worst feeling in the world came over me whenever I heard Daddy cussing and yelling as he staggered down the road home. Terrified, we kids would run and hide under the house or in the barn. Sometimes the whole family left home or locked ourselves in the house, leaving Daddy outside by himself to rage and scream.

During those early years I spent many days cowering under a bed or hiding beneath a bale of hay, praying, "Lord, why is this happening? Why do we have to live like this?"

Unable to get answers from God, I asked my mother, "Why this family? What did we do to deserve this?"

"Boy, stop asking why!" Mama snapped after I had questioned her one time too many. "You're always asking why, why, why!"

Mama probably had the worst to fear during Daddy's rages. More than once he had attacked her during a rage and started to beat her before my brothers and sisters could pull him off. I lived most of my adolescence afraid that he would kill her.

"Lord, don't let him hurt my mother," I prayed each night. "Don't let him hurt my mother."

Growing up watching my father's drunken behavior, I promised myself I would never drink or be like him. I realized he was a broken man, and I prayed constantly for him. I prayed that God would heal whatever was wrong with him so he could get well and we could live a normal life. I prayed for my family's safety. And I prayed for peace and happiness.

I was fourteen years old and had never known a stable home life. I had never had clothes other than overalls, cotton T-shirts,

high-top shoes, and one suit for Sunday. What kind of a world do
we live in, I wondered, where white kids ride nice, cool buses to
school and I have to walk? Why did life have to be an endless
cycle of poverty, cheating landlords, and violence for me, while
the white kids I saw lived in quiet, peaceful homes?

The only calm in my home was the peace that God gave us
and the example of Mama's faith. Often I stood in wonder as
Mama hummed "Amazing Grace" and prayed for God to take
control during one of Daddy's rages. Somehow God always
helped us. But more than anything, I wished God would just
make the misery go away.

CHAPTER TWO

Amazing Grace

During the second week of August 1950, Mount Zion Baptist Church held its annual revival, a special service designed to bring the unsaved to the Lord. Each year the church invited a visiting minister to conduct revival services. They always found a dynamic speaker who could make music with his words.

The summer I was twelve, the Reverend B. J. Byrd was the revivalist. Rev. Byrd was a fiery preacher who would start out preaching softly, barely above a whisper. Before long he'd be walking back and forth in the pulpit, his hands waving in animated gestures as his voice rose in a dramatic crescendo.

Church had never held any personal meaning for me. I went only because it was something my parents expected me to do, and I knew better than to argue. I grew up during a time when you obeyed your parents, did what you were told, and didn't ask questions. Children were seen and not heard. So I went to church and I behaved myself, too. But my good behavior in church was more out of fear of my parents than any reverence for God.

That summer Mama pulled me aside and reminded me about the upcoming revival. "Wilson, it's time for you to make your decision about Christ," she said.

My decision about Christ? I thought. What's this about? I don't have anything to decide about Christ.

There's a tradition in many Baptist churches that children reach spiritual accountability at age twelve. That's the age Jesus was when he met with the elders in the temple. When you reached twelve, there was no more riding on your parents' spiritual coattails hoping for salvation. You had to make a choice for yourself. That's what Mama meant when she told me I had to make a decision.

Over the years, I had watched my mother's faith in God take us through many difficult circumstances. Mama's faith was the strong cord that held our family together. When we doubted whether the canned goods and smokehouse-cured meat would take us through the winter, Mama's faith gave us the strength to believe that it would.

Sometimes all we had to eat was molasses and bread. No meat, no eggs, just thick, sweet molasses and bread. It was during those tough times that Mama's faith was strongest.

Walking through the house doing her chores, Mama would hum "Amazing Grace" with a passion that sent a chill through my soul. After she had hummed awhile, she sang "The Lord Will Make a Way Somehow" in a loud, joyous voice that always made me feel good.

Prayer usually followed the humming and the singing. Mama could pray anywhere, anytime. In the house, in the field, washing the clothes, her prayers surrounded us like a protective shield as she talked to her God wherever and whenever the Spirit moved her.

"Lord, we are your children. You promised never to leave us alone," she reminded God. "You promised to make a way out of no way. I don't have a way out of this problem, Lord. We need your help. I don't know where our next meal is coming from. The kids all need shoes and clothing, and they need a little something for Christmas. Lord, make a way for us. Thank you, Jesus! Thank you, Jesus! Thank you, Jesus!"

There was always a joyous expectation and peace after these prayers. We knew Mama's faith and Mama's prayers would make everything all right. It was as if God sat waiting, listening for my mother's prayers so he could be released to act. Somehow, some way, things always worked out right after Mama prayed. We had something to eat at every meal, and Santa Claus always came at Christmas.

The little I knew about God I learned from witnessing Mama's faith. I learned from watching her many unselfish acts of love for her children and her family, and I deeply believed in prayer — Mama's prayers — because I had seen prayer work so many times for her.

Now I was being asked to make a decision about God's Son, Jesus, for myself. I had always counted on Mama's God. Now it was time for me to find Mama's God for myself — to make Mama's faith my faith. And to have God's amazing grace that took care of Mama now take care of me.

My mother wanted me to go to the mourner's bench, which is another Baptist tradition that is true to its name. Anyone who wanted to "get saved" sat on the front pew of the church — the mourner's bench — waiting for the Holy Spirit to come down and lead him or her to salvation. Often during the service, the mourners sitting on the bench rocked back and forth, moaning to themselves in a kind of repentant ecstasy as they awaited the coming of the Holy Spirit.

Folks had always said no one can ever really explain what happens when the Holy Spirit touches you. You just feel it. And from that moment on your life begins to change and you're never the same again.

As I thought about the meaning of revival, I took my decision to go to the mourner's bench very, very seriously. I had always been a serious child and very inquisitive. Now, as I contemplated getting saved, I knew my life was about to change forever.

Revival week drew people to Mount Zion from all over the country. The week followed homecoming Sunday. That's when all the people who had left the South for a better life in the big city returned home to show off their big cars and fine clothes. Many stayed for revival week.

Mount Zion Baptist Church was an old wooden structure that looked like it had been around for a hundred years or more. Everything was made of wood, though the pews felt as hard as concrete. At capacity, Mount Zion seated about two hundred people. The simple wooden pulpit faced the center aisle. The choir sat directly behind the pulpit. Over on the left side of the church was the "Amen Corner," the special section of pews reserved for the church deacons. The Amen Corner was so named because when the emotions got high, you could hear the deacons, in loud voices, say "amen, amen," and the "amens" could be heard throughout the church.

The week I attended revival must have been the hottest week of the year. I sat on the mourner's bench, waiting expectantly for my salvation as streams of hot air blew through the church with the intensity of a fiery furnace. My clothes stuck to my body and sweat trickled down my neck.

Three others sat on the mourner's bench with me. There was Bennie Darden, who was so fair-skinned that most people thought he was white; Dayton Martin, my distant cousin and close friend; and another cousin, Alma Goode. We started out the week together, but by Wednesday Bennie, Dayton, and Alma had been touched by the Holy Spirit and had accepted Christ as their Savior. Only I was left behind. For a while it looked like I wasn't going to get saved that year, and Dayton teased me, saying, "You're going to be on the mourner's bench until you're an old man."

For some reason I couldn't joke about it. Nor could I contemplate going up front just to keep from being left on the bench. That would be playing with God. My mother had drummed it into my head many times that "God was not someone to play with. If something doesn't happen on the inside of you, Wilson, don't you dare get up and take that minister's hand!" So I waited for something to happen inside of me.

On Friday, the final day of revival, I took the front pew, alone. After an hour I shifted slightly to break the tension and the sticky feeling on my back as sweat plastered me to the pew. It was hot, burning hot, and my throat felt parched and dry. It got even hotter when Rev. Byrd's voice rose to a feverish pitch as he painted a graphic picture of a sinner's descent into hell.

"If you do not accept Jesus Christ as your Savior, you're going to die, go straight to hell, and burn in eternity!" he shouted, his hands waving and his voice rising. The Amen Corner responded with equal passion.

"Amen!"

"Well!"

"Have mercy, Lord!"

I squirmed in my seat scared to death! I'm going to die and burn in hell? I thought. Why? What have I done?

"Yet Jesus can open all doors and solve all of your problems. He can make a way out of no way," Rev. Byrd continued, his voice now a soothing whisper. "He loves you and wants to be your friend."

As Rev. Byrd talked about the friendship of Jesus, I felt myself calming down. I liked the idea that Jesus was not this big, bad man in heaven waiting to punish me for every little thing I did. Jesus was a good man, a good man who would do good things for me if I let him.

As the choir sang the invitation song, "I Surrender All," something stirred inside me.

"All to Jesus, I surrender. All to him I freely give."

My mind churned with emotion and questions. Is something really stirring inside me? I asked myself, or am I just embarrassed that I'm sitting here alone? If I get up, walk up there and take Rev. Byrd's hand, is God going to strike me dead on the spot? Am I going to die and burn in hell? What will my mother think if I go up there and I haven't really found Christ?

"I surrender all, I surrender all; All to Thee, my blessed Savior, I surrender all."

My heart pounded against my chest so wildly I could almost hear it. Thoughts continued to race through my mind. Then without warning, I jumped up and started walking towards the minister.

"Thank you, Jesus!" my mother screamed, rising to her feet.

The Amen Corner erupted in a chorus of amens and hallelujahs. Some of the sisters began to shout, and Mrs. Minisa Everett walked up and down the aisles of the church shouting, "Hallelujah!"

It just happened. I can't explain it even now. Something drew me up front with a movement that flowed naturally and spontaneously. Before I knew it, I was shaking Rev. Byrd's hand. This felt so good and so right. I felt good about myself. I had come to Jesus. But most importantly, I felt safe. Safe in knowing that God wasn't going to strike me dead and let me burn in hell. Safe being there with Rev. Byrd. Safe hearing the choir sing. Safe knowing that Jesus was now my friend.

"This is only the first step," someone was saying. "You have to go down into the water and be baptized."

I could hardly wait.

The month between my conversion and my baptism seemed like forever. Often while working in the fields I would stop, hoe in hand, and stare into the sky, wondering where God was and if he was watching everything I did. I wondered if God was reading my mind; if I thought something bad, would he take my conversion back?

Needless to say, I was extra good during that month, always very obedient and careful not to pick on my brothers and sisters. As I regulated my behavior, I also felt different. I felt better, cleaner, and more wholesome.

Sometimes I tried to share my feelings about God and my conversion experience with my baby brother, Ed Louis. We'd go out into the woods near the house and find a tree stump to use as a pulpit as we played church. We each took turns pretending to be the preacher. Standing on the tree stump, I preached, waving my arms dramatically in imitation of Rev. Byrd.

"I'm Rev. Willie Wilson Goode. I want to tell you that if you are not saved, you will burn in hell!" I shouted, pointing to Ed Louis. Ed Louis would leap to his feet and run towards the house screaming, "Mama, Mama, Wilson said a bad word."

"Come here, Wilson!" my mother called. "Now what did you say?" she asked as I stood before her.

"Mama, I just said what the preacher said," I explained. "I didn't say nothing bad. Ed Louis is just a tattletale."

My explanation would usually settle things down, and I would go back to my preaching.

I must have preached twenty sermons that month. The story of David and Goliath was my favorite text. Standing on the tree stump, I wove a sermon that resounded throughout the woods and mesmerized Ed Louis where he sat.

"David was a little bitty boy and Goliath was a big, big man as tall as the trees," I said, stretching my arms upward toward the trees to indicate Goliath's size. This always got Ed Louis. His mouth would drop open in awe, and his eyes would grow as big as saucers as he looked upward.

"But God was on David's side. David and Goliath got into a battle, and David took his little old slingshot and hit this big old man right between the eyes!" I yelled emphasizing the word "hit."

"Ain't God good? Ain't God good?" I shouted, waving my arms in the air.

"Yes! Yes!" Ed Louis shouted, leaping to his feet.

Ed Louis wasn't the only member of my little congregation. Sometimes my first cousins June, Willie, Lula, and Martha also came to play church. They were the children of my Uncle Wilbert, Mama's oldest brother.

Occasionally I got to feeling so good I tried to sing a solo. My brother and cousins laughed so hard I usually had to abandon my singing.

"Rev. Willie Wilson, you preach good, but you sure can't sing," they chided.

The month before my baptism was a tremendous time of change and discovery for me. I have never been the same since.

On the second Sunday in September, my family and I went down to our town's Jordan River for my baptism. Baptism was at 11:00 A.M., right before Sunday morning service. The new converts stood expectantly with their families awaiting the mystical moment. I stood by Mama, dressed in my old overalls, awaiting my turn to go down into the water.

The night before she had told me, "Don't worry, Wilson. The Lord's going to wash all of your past sins away. No matter what you've done wrong, Jesus will make you clean when you're baptized."

She also told me to hold my breath when the minister took me under the water; that way I wouldn't start choking.

As the new converts waded out into the river, the choir sang slowly and sweetly: "Take me to the water. Take me to the water. Take me to the water, to be baptized."

At my turn I stepped forward and waded out to where our pastor, Rev. Frank Bullock, stood waiting. The water rose to my waist. Rev. Bullock was the same minister who had baptized my mother thirty years before. I felt especially humbled at having him baptize me.

My body tensed at Rev. Bullock's touch. As he began the baptism ceremony, I sucked in my breath so tightly I felt like I was going to pass out. She tried to control it, but my Aunt Ann burst out laughing. She was my mother's younger sister and a big tease.

"Why is Wilson holding his face like that?" she whispered loud enough for everybody nearby to hear. I failed to see the humor in the situation. This was serious business. My expression grew even sterner, and my aunt's laughter even louder. A few minutes later it was over. Now baptized, I was a full Christian.

Becoming a Christian was the most important decision I have ever made in my life. It became the glue that held me together during a time when there was little consistency or joy in my life. Because of our constant moves, I attended a new school every year and my classmates were never the same. I had only temporary friends, except for the family members that I regarded as friends. We never stayed anywhere long enough for me to feel any real stability.

Jesus was the only stable factor in my life. He went with me everywhere, and that became very important to me. Knowing that I could count on Jesus to stay with me, to be my friend, I finally felt as if I didn't have to worry as much anymore. And I had worried a lot.

My conversion at age twelve started me on a faith journey that has continued through my life and was the beginning of my personal belief that my faith in God would enable me to do anything. I just had to trust him to take care of me and work out my problems.

The friendship of Jesus also made me more aware of the things adults around me said about him: "Keep your hand in God's hand. He'll never let you down." "Trust in the Lord." "Put God first in your life." I'd heard these sayings before, but now they were deeply meaningful to me. Hearing folks say these things was like listening to them talk about a personal friend. They were describing someone I knew—and someone who knew me.

I had always been quiet and a little different. A loner. But things would be different now. Jesus was my friend. He had made me and, of course, he understood me.

Things did begin to change in my life. I still stuttered and sometimes I had feelings of self-doubt, but my faith in God always turned these negative circumstances around. I was gaining a new self-assurance. As my faith deepened, I knew God was guiding my life and would not fail me.

My family circumstances also seemed to change after I accepted Jesus. They got worse.

In the years following my baptism, my oldest brothers and sisters drifted away from home. Mamie got married in 1949, and a little later Mary went off to nursing school in Philadelphia. She married also. Alvestus joined the army.

Only James Henry, Earn Lee, Ed Louis, and Johnnie Paul remained at home with Mama, Daddy, and me. The one thing that seemed to stay the same was that we continued to work as sharecroppers and moved every year.

Daddy continued to drink and to become more and more violent towards my mother. I prayed constantly that he wouldn't hurt her, but feared that he would. Some days were very peaceful, however, as we boys and Mama enjoyed each other's company working the farm together. This seemed to be one of those days.

It was August and the days were long, hot, and sticky. Ed Louis and I were working in the yard when we heard it. "Listen," my brother whispered, grabbing my arm to silence me. At first I heard nothing. Then I heard a faint voice in the distance, angry, yelling as if in a fight. I tensed as the voice grew louder and louder. It was coming our way.

"Yes, it's me! Here I come. I'm drunk! Get out of my way!"

My heart pounded wildly as fear rose in my throat. It was Daddy. He was drunk, again.

As if on cue, Ed Louis and I ran around the yard and through the house hiding the shotgun, hammer, gardening tools—anything Daddy might use as a weapon against us. James Henry was down at the creek fishing with our landlord Charlie Painter.

Daddy steadily proceeded down the road yelling at the top
of his voice. By the time he reached the house, I was looking
around for a place to hide. Too late. Daddy saw the hoe lying
halfway under the steps of the house and grabbed it before either
Ed Louis or I could reach him. Mama talked soothingly to Daddy,
trying to calm him down. He waved the hoe dangerously in her
face, and I watched in horror as he lifted the hoe to strike my
mother in the head.

"Mama, look out!" I yelled.

Mama screamed and raised her arms to shield her head. The
first blow hit her on the left hand, cutting her fingers badly. The
second never reached her. James Henry was on him now, having
raced up from the creek with Charlie Painter after hearing all the
commotion.

"Albert, come on and stop that," Mr. Painter yelled. "Look
what you done."

James Henry struggled and clawed savagely at Daddy to
wrench the hoe away while Daddy cussed and fought to hold on.
Finally James Henry managed to toss the hoe aside and went to
tend to my mother. Daddy rose to his feet and stood in the yard
looking dejected and pitiful.

Charlie Painter approached Daddy tentatively, obviously
fearing another outburst. The hoe lay on the ground several feet
from them, its blade stained with my mother's blood. I thought
I was going to be sick. Mama had slumped to the ground. Blood
poured from her hand, onto her dress, and was forming a small
pool around her.

"Albert, you done gone crazy?" Mr. Painter scolded. "Look at
this mess!" Mr. Painter continued scolding Daddy as if talking to
a wayward child. I don't know what came over my father. Maybe
it was the accumulation of the years of hardship and humiliation
or the final effects of bad corn whiskey. Before anyone could
stop him, Daddy hauled off and slapped Charlie Painter so hard
the blow nearly knocked him off his feet.

A fiendish expression of glee then twisted Daddy's face into
an ugly mask as he picked up the hoe and turned toward me and
Ed Louis.

"Now, I've got you!"

"Run, Ed Louis, run!" I yelled.

Ed Louis and I raced down the path from the house with Daddy chasing after us with the garden hoe. Charlie Painter stood by watching, gingerly rubbing his face.

Ed Louis was two years younger than me, but we were about the same size. I don't know if it was his size or fear that made it possible for him to keep pace with me, but I marveled at his speed as we tore towards the woods, running for our lives. Occasionally we'd glance behind us to find Daddy still on our heels, cussing and staggering in a dizzying run as he lurched toward us with the hoe.

"Come back here! Come back here!" he demanded.

We never stopped running, not until Daddy gave up and we saw him turn towards the road leading to town. Only then did we timidly sneak back to the house to see what was happening.

Everyone was gone. Ed Louis and I locked ourselves in the house. It was the worst day of my life as Ed Louis and I nervously paced the floor, worried about Mama. I learned later that James Henry had taken Mama to a neighbor who helped get her to the doctor. After having her hand stitched and heavily bandaged, Mama then went to spend the night with her oldest sister, our Aunt Maggie Tann. Daddy returned home late that evening only to find Charlie Painter and the sheriff waiting to arrest him.

I was numb, unable to believe what had happened just a few hours earlier. I had prayed so hard for my mother's protection, for peace, for security. Why was this happening to us? There was always turmoil, constant turmoil, in our lives. Turmoil with the farm. Turmoil with cheating landlords. Turmoil with a drunken father. Now Daddy had almost killed my mother. Why?

I prayed relentlessly that night: "God, why is my father acting this way? Why is he treating his family this way? What did we do to deserve this?"

After the accident I vowed even more solemnly never to drink. I never wanted to lose control like my father, nor did I want to be like him when I grew up.

Over the years, when people approached me with a drink, I always rejected them. I made that solemn vow when I was young to stay away from liquor, and I meant to keep it. I had seen liquor turn my father into a crazed madman, and I felt anything that could affect you in that way was not good for you.

Friends were always curious as to why I wouldn't even take a sip of wine. I guess deep down inside I've always had the fear that I might take a drink and not be able to stop. What liquor had done to my father it could also do to me. I was not taking any chances.

At the trial, Mama said Charlie Painter asked to speak to the judge in his chambers before the sentence was handed down. Daddy was convicted of assault and sentenced to a year in prison. Mama always said she believed Daddy was convicted because he slapped Charlie Painter, not because of what he did to her.

We were heartbroken. It seemed like our family was being broken apart beyond repair. Daddy left the local jail for prison that August. His prison job was walking the hot, dusty roads serving water to prisoners on the chain gangs.

In the months following the trial, my sister in Philadelphia convinced Mama to leave North Carolina before Daddy got out of prison. Mama and my brothers prepared to leave that January. I was doing well in school, and they said I should stay behind with Aunt Lonnie and Uncle Frank Brown to finish out the school term.

On January 3, 1954, Mama and my brothers left for Philadelphia. I tried to be happy as the moving van and car carrying my family headed North, but my heart was sinking. This was the first time I had ever been separated from my family.

Practically speaking, I knew it was only right for me to finish the school term, but I couldn't help thinking I needed to be with my family.

With my father imprisoned, I thought the days of violence and fear were behind me. That was before I found out about my cousin Joseph, nicknamed "Bunky." Bunky was Aunt Lonnie and Uncle Frank's son, their youngest child. I'd never spent much time around him, but it became clearer with each passing day that Bunky was one of those people who folks described as "not right." He was extremely violent and proceeded to make my life a living hell.

His mean little tricks were endless. Without warning, Bunky would sneak up behind me and pop me in the head. At other times he'd have violent outbursts and try to pick a fight with me.

The frightening thing about the fights was that Bunky never wanted to fight with his fists. He always had a knife, an axe, or a hoe nearby whenever he started talking loudly and making threatening gestures. I tried to act as brave as I could with a knife being waved in my face. Truth was, I was scared to death!

Aunt Lonnie and Uncle Frank were never around when the outbursts occurred, so I had to do the best I could to keep from hurting Bunky or getting hurt myself. Later when I told my aunt what had happened, Bunky always lied and tearfully accused me of telling stories on him. I felt trapped, especially when Aunt Lonnie scolded me for picking on my little cousin.

Life with Bunky came to a head the day he chased me into the field with a loaded rifle, threatening to blow my head off. Miraculously I got away, running across that field as fast as I could, while Bunky scurried behind me laughing and waving the gun. I knew then it was time to join my family in Philadelphia.

That night I wrote Mama, telling her I was ready to come to Philadelphia. Things were not working out at Aunt Lonnie's, I wrote, but I never explained why.

I don't know if Mama figured it out for herself or what. A few days later I received the money for a railroad ticket to Philadelphia and a letter telling me to come whenever I was ready. I made plans to leave immediately. It was March of 1954.

Years later my suspicions that Bunky wasn't right proved to be true. By then he was living in New York City and running with a wild crowd. After getting mixed up in some trouble, he allegedly killed a man. Today he is confined to a mental institution.

CHAPTER THREE

So This Is Heaven?

The night before I headed North I didn't sleep a wink. I was leaving the South for the first time in my life to join my family in Philadelphia and taking my first train ride. My cousin Bunky would have to find someone else to torment.

I was up before daybreak. I listened to crickets, cows, and chickens make their early-morning noises. Uncle Frank drove me to the train station in Weldon, North Carolina.

"I appreciate your letting me stay here for a short while, Uncle Frank. I am sorry things didn't work out."

"We enjoyed having you," Uncle Frank said. "You go up to that big city and you make something out of yourself."

"I am certainly going to try, Uncle Frank."

"Well, you are the smartest boy Ellar [my mother's nickname] has. I know you will make something out of yourself."

I didn't talk about Bunky, but somehow I got the feeling that he knew why I was really leaving early.

I boarded the train clutching a small suitcase and a greasy paper bag filled with chicken sandwiches and coconut cake. I was fifteen years old, and my young soul brimmed with hope for what I would find in the Promised Land. Over the years I'd done well in school, and my family had expressed high expectations for me.

"Willie is smart. Willie's going to do something with himself," Cousin Frances Jean Martin often declared.

"Willie is going to do something one day," other relatives agreed.

Now I had a chance. Up North, in the big city, a poor, colored boy can make something out of his life, I told myself.

I left North Carolina harboring a deep resentment for the white people who had kept my parents down all their lives. If I remained behind, they would keep me down too. The white folks I'd seen were unfair and unjust. I didn't know what racism was at the time, but I knew I had lived my whole life under a system of involuntary servitude. I never quite understood or accepted the double standard I lived with all my childhood. I saw whites as oppressors.

As sharecroppers, we had been forced to work for less than we were worth. We farmed the land, the same as our ancestors had, we did the same work and had the same struggles. The only difference between us and slaves was the little we got paid for our work and the freedom to move if we didn't like our wages.

Traveling north, I was confident that I could overcome the slave-like system I was leaving behind. Even the nagging questions from the old man sitting in the segregated car with me couldn't dampen my spirits or my hopes.

"Boy, ain't you scared to go on this train by yourself?" he asked for what seemed like the hundredth time. Each time he asked, I shook my head no, telling myself I wasn't afraid.

"Where you going?" he asked again.

"Philadelphia. I'm joining my family in Philadelphia."

"And you ain't scared to go on this train by yourself?"

I continued to deny being afraid, but I could feel the anxiety rising. Why wouldn't he be quiet?

"I'm going to New York," he continued. "New York ain't like people say it is. Lots of colored people up there. Lots of people gettin' drunk. Lots of people robbin' people there. Life in the city ain't gonna be what you think it's gonna be," he said knowingly. "It's not what you read about in the books. I don't know what you're expectin', Son, but it's not gonna be what you think it's gonna be. And you ain't scared to go on this train by yourself?"

As he spoke, I felt my dream crumbling. The city has to be the Promised Land, I had told myself. Now I wasn't so sure.

When I arrived in Philadelphia, my brother James was waiting for me at the station. I could barely walk for gaping wide-eyed at the scenes around me. I'd never seen such big buildings in my life! And the people! There were more people than I'd ever seen before. I had been to church services that a couple of hundred folks had attended, but Philadelphia had people everywhere! People coming, people going. People in cars. People coming out of buildings. And not just colored people, but all kinds of people. They were wearing coats, and some had ties and shirts on, and it wasn't even Sunday. How different from the folks back home who wore overalls, cotton shirts, and high-top work shoes all week long.

"What's that, James, over there?" I asked.

"That's the post office, the main post office," James responded.

"And what are all those buildings down there?" My mind was running a mile a minute.

"Oh, that's downtown. They have lots of big stores downtown, lots of tall buildings," James impatiently responded.

"What are those things? Are they little trains?" I asked, my mouth running a mile a minute, too.

"No, stupid. They're called trolleys. They go right near our house," James said, indicating I was getting on his nerves.

"What's our house like? How big is it? Is it pretty?" I asked, not letting him discourage me.

"Wilson, stop asking so many questions. You will see it when you get there."

I followed my brother in a constant state of awe about what I would see next, and I kept asking questions. Philadelphia was like a wonderland. As we passed house after house, I wondered, Is my house going to be like that? What is my house going to be like?

When we finally arrived home, I swallowed hard to hide my disappointment. We were living in a three-story row house with my sister, her husband, and two other families. A man by the name of Pop Fisher owned the house with his wife. It was worse than what we'd left in North Carolina. There was less space, no yard or privacy. And while it had running water and indoor plumbing, we all shared one bathroom. Deep down inside I said to myself, So this is heaven. Maybe Bunky wasn't so bad. But those thoughts quickly left me. I was glad to be home with my family.

The first time I took a bath, my brother-in-law John Cook was furious. I didn't know you were supposed to let the water out afterwards and wash out the tub. Down home we took baths in tin tubs and dumped the water out when the last person was finished. This thing of having a tub that you ran hot water into and emptied out while the water still looked clean was totally new to me.

Those first few days in Philadelphia were anxious, exciting, and disappointing. My third day there I registered for school at John Bartram High School and learned I had to repeat the tenth grade. I was crushed. Sitting on the front steps of the house thinking about my misfortune, I was confronted by a neighborhood bully named Kenneth Williams.

"You new here, ain't you." Kenneth stated more than asked.

I nodded yes.

"Everybody who comes to this neighborhood has to fight me," he said pulling me off the steps.

Within seconds Kenneth and I were going at it, punching and gouging like tigers. I don't think anyone had ever challenged him before because he seemed to be surprised at my willingness to fight him. Folks watching that fight also said I got the best of him. I was too scared and mad to tell. I just know that after that fight I never had another problem with Kenneth the whole time we lived in that neighborhood.

Soon after the fight I met Ronald "Nole" Blocker, a next-door neighbor who was about my age. We became fast friends, and Nole decided to take me on my first trolley-car ride into town. I was as excited as a child with a new toy. As we walked from Upland Street down Seventieth Street toward Woodland Avenue, my whole body was edgy with anticipation.

Sensing my fear and excitement, Nole was very friendly and supportive. He knew this country bumpkin was out of his element.

As we approached Woodland Avenue, we heard the clanging sound of the trolley and ran toward the noise. I had to hold back a little because Nole was slow. I was a good runner, having had lots of practice running from my father and chasing the chickens and other farm animals. When the traffic light changed in our favor, we ran across the street to catch the number 37 trolley on Woodland Avenue.

Boarding the trolley, Nole showed me how to put the money in the box, and we walked to the back of the car. I noticed that other black folks were sitting up front, so I knew we didn't have to go to the back of the trolley. I felt funny going back there and would have preferred to sit up front where I could demonstrate my new-found freedom, but Nole would have no part of it. We settled into our seats in the back and he started questioning me about life in the South.

"What was it like?" he asked. "Did you really have outdoor toilets? Did you have cars, or a mule and wagon? What about electric lights? Did you have those?"

We talked nonstop, enjoying each other's company and the grown-up feeling of riding the trolley alone. Deep in conversation, I didn't see the street disappear or feel the approaching darkness until it hit us.

"Oh my God, we're in a hole!" I cried, panic-stricken.

Nole laughed so hard he couldn't speak. I thought he was going to fall off the seat. But I was frantically searching for a way out.

"This is just the subway," he explained in between gulps of laughter. "We're going underground to the downtown area."

Eventually I settled down.

Later that afternoon when we returned home, Nole told all the neighborhood kids about the trip. After that, the kids on the block teased me about that trolley-car ride.

One little girl we called "Sissy" was unmerciful about it. Unable to take any more, I lost my temper one day and chased her down the street threateningly. But Sissy was not one to take threats lightly. Without warning she picked up a sawed-off broomstick and gave me three good whacks across the head, knocking me unconscious. When I came to, I decided to leave her alone. I had beat Kenneth Williams, but Sissy was another story.

We didn't stay at Pop Fisher's long after I arrived in Philadelphia. The house we moved to was even smaller, and we had to rent a room in someone else's home across the street for my two older brothers and my cousin Jessie, Bunky's oldest brother who was now staying with us. Heaven was not turning out the way I had imagined. And the cruelest part of all was the way I was being treated at John Bartram High School.

My first day at high school I felt like I was wandering in a foreign country. Bartram was 85 percent white. With three thousand students, it had more students than my hometown had people. I had never seen that many white folks before in one place and wasn't too thrilled about seeing that many now. Going to school at Bartram was also my first experience competing with white students. Consequently, I approached Bartram with a great deal of apprehension.

As I thought about this school and all of these people, I felt the way I did my first day of school years ago. This was a frightening, new experience for me.

On my way to school that morning I walked with Nole. "What's it like going to school with all those white folks? You know, down on the farm we went to different schools. What's it like, Nole?" I asked.

"They are just like you and me, Willie. Do your homework and you will come out all right. Things are different here," he assured me. "There's nothing to be scared of."

Despite his assurances, I was apprehensive.

My first stop was at the principal's office to see Dr. William Duncan, who for some reason failed to see me. Next I went to the vice principal, who assigned me a counselor, Mrs. Ann Hardigan.

Mrs. Hardigan was a stern-looking, portly white woman who had a way of ignoring you even as she spoke to you. She scanned my transcript and immediately assigned me to the industrial arts course, over my protests.

"I see here that you're coming here straight from the farm," she said.

"Yes, Ma'am."

"Did you do farm work?"

"Yes, Ma'am. I plowed the fields, picked cotton, pulled tobacco, shook peanuts, and milked the cows. I also gathered eggs from the chickens."

"Well, that seems like a perfect background for the industrial arts course. You seem to have done well with your hands so far."

"Mrs. Har-di-di-digan," I nervously tried to call her by name but stuttered terribly in the process. "I don't want to be in the industrial arts course. I want to be in the academic course." Nole had told me that I should be in the academic course.

"Well, you don't belong in the academic course," she replied stiffly. "You belong in the industrial arts course and that's where you are going. We know what's best for you."

As she talked, my mind drifted back to the conversation between my father and Ellis Crews. Here I was up North, and I was being told, "Boy, shut up, and do what you are told."

I tried to protest but was so angry and nervous I couldn't get the words out.

"Mrs. Har-di-di-digan. I-I-I- don't . . . "

She interrupted.

"It's obvious, Wilson, you can't even express yourself. How do you expect to compete in the academic course?"

I walked out of the office crushed. I was humiliated, angry and disgusted, but no less determined to get my way. How could she assume she knew what was best for me when she hadn't even tested my academic skills?

I was angry. I had come to Philadelphia in search of a better life. What I'd found so far was housing worse than what I'd left behind on the farm and a school system that wanted to rob me of the one thing I had already earned—the chance to use my brain. They wanted me to use my hands rather than my mind, and I resented it.

I knew I wouldn't give up. My faith would keep me from giving up. I entered the industrial arts program but visited Mrs. Hardigan often to ask for a transfer to the academic course. Whenever I grew discouraged, I would ask myself, What would Mama do? Would she give up? Or would she keep on fighting? I knew she would fight—and so did I. My faith in God would carry me through.

Time and time again I went back to Mrs. Hardigan asking to

be transferred to the academic course. Finally, either my persist-
ence or the wood and metal I wasted in shop class proved my
point—I had no aptitude with my hands.

In metal class I felt like a fish out of water. I couldn't get
anything straight. I don't know if that was because I didn't want
to learn the industrial arts or because I really didn't have the
aptitude.

"Willie, can't you cut this metal straight?" the teacher would
ask.

"I'm doing my best," I replied.

The teacher examined my work, shaking his head sadly.

"Willie, you really don't belong here. You don't seem to have
a knack for this at all," he said. I agreed with him, and if I could
just convince Mrs. Hardigan, I would be all right. I persisted, and
a month after I entered John Bartram High School I was transferred to the academic program.

John Bartram High School opened in 1938, the year I was
born. School work was more difficult here than it had been back
home in Gumberry High School. The course material was com-
parable but I found the teachers to be different. For some reason
it took me a while to adjust to my new teachers. They didn't seem
as personally interested in me as the teachers back at Gumberry.
Some teachers were especially difficult.

Algebra immediately became a problem. Math was never one
of my strongest subjects, and what complicated this class even
more was that the teacher refused to explain his technique to me,
no matter how often I asked.

"Please, can you take just a few minutes after class to explain
this algebra concept?" I pleaded.

"No! We don't provide private tutoring lessons to the students," he barked. "If you want a tutor, then you have to find
one. Who's your counselor? Maybe she can help you."

His refusal left me with no options. There was no way in the
world I was going to ask Mrs. Hardigan for help, especially after
she had already told me I didn't belong in the academic program.
I wasn't about to give her the satisfaction of going to her for help
so she could say she was right. I did my very best to adapt to his
teaching style, but it never clicked.

At the end of that semester I flunked algebra. It was the first and only course I ever flunked in school. By now I was beginning to doubt that Philadelphia was the Promised Land. I still struggled with speech problems. Mrs. Hardigan reminded me often enough that I had no aptitude for academic work, even though my grades steadily improved and I made the school's honor roll. I was working hard but seemed to be getting nowhere.

My dream of life in the big city had been far better than the reality. Day by day, my confidence about achieving greatness shrank as I looked at the people in my neighborhood and saw in them my future. Very few people in the neighborhood had gone to college. Other than my pastor and a few men in my church, First Baptist of Paschall, there were no visible role models. There were many with encouraging words, but few real mentors. The teachers at Bartram did not reach out to offer encouragement. There were none who went beyond the call of duty to take a real, personal interest in me.

So I struggled to make the most out of my experience at Bartram by reaching out to my friends. My friend Nole Blocker lived next door to me, and we walked to school with Sherman Coleman, Gordon Blackson, Butch Cook, and Donald Billups, and some other kids from the neighborhood. Another classmate, George Gough, was in most of my classes, and we used to pal around together too.

Among the white students I considered friends were Patricia Smith and the three "Roberts" — Robert Hammel, Robert Ballantyne, and Robert Herdlin. Most of these students had a positive influence on me, but one, Robert Herdlin, was a star basketball player and persuaded me to leave school for a couple of periods one day.

"Hey, Willie, how about going to get some jelly doughnuts and walk in the park for a while?"

"But, Bob, I have classes."

"Come on, Willie. They won't miss us."

"But, Bob, I should be in class."

"Willie, you are a goody two shoes. Loosen up; have some fun."

I liked Bob, so off we went to the pastry shop and then over to the park. I was scared. I knew what I was doing was wrong. But I did it nonetheless. That was my one and only time to play hooky. I learned a lasting lesson from that episode. Be careful even of your friends; they can sometimes lead you in the wrong direction. I'm glad that my childhood training had been so effective that my conscience whipped me even over small things. I never even thought of a repeat performance.

After a year, I had adjusted to attending school with white students and even felt comfortable with my white friends. My junior year I held elective office for the first time, becoming a corridor guard and a senator in the student government.

The Paschall neighborhood where I lived was an old, established, black, family neighborhood that lay nestled within the boundaries of a predominantly white ethnic enclave of southwest Philadelphia. But Paschall had been there since before the turn of the century. Needless to say it stuck out like a sore thumb, a black island in the midst of a white oasis.

Largely ignored by the ward politicians that served the district, Paschall had no recreation center or playground despite an abundance of kids. Nearby, the McCreesh playground boasted a beautiful sandlot and basketball court. Those of us who were brave enough occasionally ventured onto the playground to play baseball or basketball, despite the risk of being chased home by white bullies from the neighborhood. Most of the time we stayed in Paschall, where we played football between the cars in the street and strung plastic milk crates to streetlight poles to make basketball hoops. Our self-made playground was crude, but we were happy.

I was also lucky that William Neal and his wife, Lottie, took an interest in the kids in the neighborhood. We called them Mama and Papa Neal. They were kind people who opened up their home to us and encouraged us to do our best in school. The Neals also held social functions in the basement of their home and took groups of kids on summer outings to Ocean City and other places. We were organized into clubs, and I was president of the Hawks boys' group. I stayed under Mama and Papa Neal's guidance for more than two years. Papa Neal would get us in his basement and would lecture us on making something out of ourselves.

"You all are very fortunate," he would say. "There is no reason that all of you can't make something out of yourselves.

But you have to stay off those corners, listen to your folks, and for God's sake, do your homework."

You could tell that Papa Neal was sincere. You could tell that he was an unselfish man who was sacrificing much to help us.

His lecture came a few days after a group of us were standing on the corner of Seventieth and Greenway by Rose's store. Someone shouted as the police car rode by, "Does your father work?" And then someone else in the crowd yelled back, "No, he's a cop." The police car stopped, called for a paddy wagon, and came after us. Some ran away. I got caught. I was taken down to the police station and released. I knew then that I had to run faster the next time or stay off the corner with the wrong crowd. I stayed off the corner.

I matured steadily in Philadelphia, aided by my determination to work hard and by the good, God-fearing people who came my way. Steven Bishop, another neighbor, was one such person. Every Sunday evening I watched Steven leave his home about 6:00 P.M. and head toward the church, a Bible and book tucked underneath his arm. Eventually I mustered up the courage to ask him where he was going. Positioning myself on the front steps a little before 6:00 P.M., I watched Steve come out of his house and turn towards the church.

"Where you going, Steve?" I yelled.

"To B.T.U. at the church."

"What's that?"

"Baptist Training Union," he said and then explained. "It's like Sunday school, except we have more in-depth discussions on different religious topics. Why don't you come along sometime?"

"I think I might just do that," I said.

A few weeks later I accepted Steve's offer and went with him. After I joined the B.T.U., I became very active in the church and attracted the interest of some of the adults there. Mrs. Ruth Freeman got me involved in the junior missionaries and took me to the monthly missionary meetings for the southeast region of Pennsylvania.

As my involvement in the church grew, my faith deepened. I enjoyed working in the church and was inspired by the living examples of the faith-filled people who took me under their care.

My two Sunday school teachers, Ralph Overton and Judge Allen, took a special interest in me.

"Boy, you can make something out of yourself," they said. "Just stay close to the church. Don't let that foolishness out there in the world get hold of you."

Their sincerity touched my heart. I felt they really cared about me. Other mentors who entered my life were Virginia Davis, Hannah Cornitcher, and Ralph Overton's brother, John. They all played key roles in my life. Their lives weren't easy, but they seemed to have the same grace and spiritual confidence about themselves that I had witnessed in my mother for so many years.

My friends Camilla Scott and Steve Bishop and I took turns being president of various youth groups: the B.T.U., the young ushers, the young missionaries, and the youth choir (although I still couldn't sing).

Camilla, Steve, and I enjoyed each other's company, and deep down inside we competed with one another. Whatever one did, the others would try to outdo. In the midst of this great competition, Steve discovered that he had a real hidden talent— singing. Mrs. Murphy, our choir director, taught him how to bring the sounds from his stomach. He was *great*. I was jealous. And although she would never admit it, I think that Camilla was too. So when the opportunity came for me to sing a duet with Camilla, I jumped at the chance. Camilla at least had a voice and could carry a tune. We sang "I Come to the Garden Alone." I yelled my lungs out, made a perfect fool out of myself, and never tried to sing again publicly.

An added bonus to my church work was the direction my school work took. As my spiritual life deepened, my grades improved. Each year I did better and better academically, encouraged by my church mentors and faith in God.

My faith became important, too, for another reason. Less than a year after I arrived in Philadelphia, we learned my father had been released from prison and wanted to reconcile with the family. My mother broke the news to us in a family meeting.

"He's out of jail now and wants to come here where we are," she said.

"Is he still drinking?" I asked, almost certain that I knew the answer.

"He says he has learned his lesson and he'll never let whiskey drive him crazy again," Mama said. "Do you want him to come home?"

"Well, I guess it's all right if he has stopped drinking," one of my brothers said. One by one we all agreed.

I was skeptical, but like my brothers I was torn between the love I had for my father and the fear that his drinking would once again create violence and turmoil in our lives. We decided to have faith in him and take his promise at face value.

When Daddy came home that year, we were delighted to see him. He looked the same but seemed to possess a calmness that he hadn't had before. Daddy found a job with the Louis Sherman Box Company at Seventy-first Street and Grays Avenue. My brothers James Henry and Earn Lee both already worked there.

We were a family again, but life in the big city was exacting a harsh toll on the closeness we had shared in North Carolina. Because Pop Fisher's house was so small, there was no room for us to sit down and eat as a family as we had down South. But Mama still made the best meals. My favorite was always meat loaf, mashed potatoes, and gravy.

Mom and my sister Mary worked at the St. Vincent Home on Sixty-ninth and Woodland. The various shift hours and school obligations rarely brought all of us home together at the same time. So we never did recapture the special family feeling we had on the farm. Down home, each Sunday morning we would gather around the table and have Bible reading and prayer, and each one of us would have to repeat a Bible verse. In the midst of much turmoil and instability, I had found this time on Sunday morning especially meaningful.

We now enjoyed some of the luxuries of city life—electric lights, running water, an indoor bathroom, a telephone, and even a rented television set. We couldn't afford to buy a TV, so we leased one that we fed quarters to every few minutes to keep the shows running. We soon learned that for all the quarters we put in, we probably could have afforded to buy one. But we seemed to be paying a high price for these few luxuries in not having much family time.

Because my mother was such a forgiving person, our broken family was mended by her unselfish love. Admittedly I was skeptical about taking Daddy back, but in this case, as in so many others, Mama's faith proved to be right. After rejoining us, my father seldom drank. When he did, it was usually only a beer and it didn't affect him the way it had before. He worked diligently at the box company every day and remained employed there until his health failed at age seventy-five.

Daddy died on January 22, 1987, during my reelection campaign. He and Mama had been married sixty-one years.

CHAPTER FOUR

Morgan Man

In January 1957, I graduated from John Bartram High School, disappointed in the future that lay ahead of me. Mrs. Hardigan, my guidance counselor, had convinced me to give up any plans I had for college since I wasn't "college material." I didn't know what college material was, but I pointed out that I'd gotten good grades and was on the honor roll in a school that was 85 percent white.

"That doesn't mean anything!" she snapped, shifting her large body in her chair. "You don't have the background to make it in college. You're from the South, and college life is more than just knowing how to read and write and do your work. You would never succeed in college, if you made it in at all."

As she talked, I felt like my father must have when he was told by the landlords, "Keep quiet and do what you're told." Apparently, being on the honor roll meant nothing.

I was crushed. Most of my life I'd dreamed of going to college and becoming a history teacher. Now this white woman was telling me I didn't have the aptitude for college work, that I should face a new reality, the reality of becoming just another colored laborer in one of Philadelphia's factories, working for minimum wage with a once-in-a-lifetime shot at foreman—if I was lucky.

At graduation, Helen Gilmore, the class valedictorian, was one of a handful of black students to actually be going on to college. I sat through the ceremony disappointed and disgusted at the collapse of my dream. I had always thought I had the ability to go to college and that God would help me achieve that goal. On the farm, I'd spent hours dreaming about coming to the big city to fulfill that destiny. Now the dream had become far removed from the reality.

Though I despaired, somewhere deep down inside, I had the faith that one day God would see me through.

Contemplating my future, I gradually began to understand something about this whole issue of race and racism, about black and white. Racism wasn't just in the South; it was in the North as well. I had competed with white kids in a Philadelphia high school and had done well. But doing well wasn't enough for me to fulfill my dreams. There was still a difference between the way I was treated and the way white kids were treated. They could fulfill their dreams and I couldn't, no matter how hard I tried, or so it seemed to me.

Coming to Philadelphia had made no real difference in my life. The racial barriers were just as strong here as they'd been down South. The political and social system was controlled just as rigidly by white folks here as it had been down South. I wasn't farming, but I was still treated like a sharecropper in a world controlled by white people.

As I often thought about the plight I found myself in, I wondered what was happening to me. I sometimes doubted if my dreams would ever come true. My faith in God's provision for my life told me they would, but I just couldn't see how.

After graduation I got a job as a busboy carting tobacco from cigar maker to cigar maker at the American Tobacco Company on Sixty-eighth Street and Greenway Avenue. The American Tobacco Company was a red brick building that covered a whole block in the Paschall neighborhood where I lived. It was a major center of employment for the neighborhood and surrounding communities.

Twenty-seven years later, on January 2, 1984, I would return to my home at 6921 Greenway Avenue after taking the oath of office as mayor and stare at that huge building still on Sixty-eighth and Greenway. "Ain't God good? Ain't God good?" my soul shouted. I could see Ed Louis, his eyes getting big and round, cheering "Yes! Yes!"

Many of the people I worked with at the tobacco factory lived on my block. In the beginning it felt a little strange to be working with them because I'd always thought I'd be at college by this point. For years they had been the woman across the street or the man around the corner. Now they were co-workers and people I would come to know with a new intimacy.

Working at the tobacco company felt like one of the biggest ironies of my life. Just three years before, I couldn't wait to get out of the cotton and tobacco fields of North Carolina for a new life in the Promised Land of Philadelphia. Now the Promised Land had put me back in the tobacco fields. True, the work was different—but no less hard, boring, or tedious than it had been down South. In fact, it was more restrictive. I was eighteen years old, passing my days pushing around a cart full of tobacco. It was steady work, though, and I was grateful for that.

Not too long after I began working at the tobacco factory, Muriel Lemon, the pastor's wife at First Baptist Church of Paschall, pulled me aside to discuss my future. Nearly everyone liked Mrs. Lemon. She was a vivacious woman in her thirties who had graduated from college herself and possessed a zest for life and learning. I told her what my guidance counselor had said.

"Willie, I don't care what your counselor said to you. I don't care what they tell you. You are college material!" she said, trying to control her anger.

"But I-I-I stutter," I protested.

"I don't care!" she exclaimed. "Moses had a speech problem. He put stones in his mouth to speak properly. God used him."

Thoughts raced through my mind as Mrs. Lemon continued her forceful presentation. My self-consciousness about my speech problems had never left me. I found her arguments persuasive, but I was unconvinced that I would be one of the chosen few who could overcome my difficulties. I was still reluctant to speak in public. Even thinking about it conjured up the feelings of shame I had suffered when the kids laughed at me in school. I remembered their cruelty, and as I remembered, I couldn't help but contrast my own awkwardness with Mrs. Lemon's polished style and speech. She put words together beautifully. They rolled from her lips with a smooth, effortless grace that I knew I would never have.

I'll never speak like that, I thought. I still had trouble saying even the simplest words. Other times I rambled on a mile a minute, believing that if I talked fast enough I could get everything out before stumbling over a word. The speech problem was a nightmare for me. There was no way I could get through college without facing my speech limitations.

"You go to college, Willie," she pleaded. "Save your money and we'll help you here at the church. Don't let them tell you you can't go to college. You *can* go to college!"

Slowly I started to believe that maybe Mrs. Lemon was right. I thanked God for his faithfulness in bringing this Christian woman into my life. Her words were like salve to my ego. When others said I couldn't do something, God always provided someone to tell me I could. When others tried to tear down my hopes, someone always appeared to help turn my dreams into reality.

While I remained unconvinced that I could succeed in college, I knew I had to try—for the sake of all those in my family who had never gone to college. For all of those people who believed in me, had faith in me, I had to try. Those slaves who had made their way through the underground railroad to freedom never gave up. I wasn't going to give up either.

I began saving every cent I could. That April I applied to four colleges: Temple University, Morgan State, Penn State, and Lincoln University. Waiting for replies was like torture. I would rush home with high hopes about the applications I had sent, but ready to face bad news.

The first letter came from Temple. Looking at the envelope

lying on the table, I stared for a long time before finally working up the courage to open it. My hands shook as I tore open the envelope and tried to focus on the opening sentence. Who's right? I silently asked myself. Mrs. Lemon or Mrs. Hardigan? Silently I read: "We're pleased to advise you that you've been accepted . . ."

It took a few minutes for the meaning of the words to settle in. I was accepted! I was going to college! Shortly afterwards I also received acceptances from Morgan, Penn State, and Lincoln. I chose Morgan State because they gave me the best financial aid package. I was offered a job in the library, and they would assist me in applying for a National Defense Loan to help with my tuition and room and board. Morgan's overall costs were less than the others, too.

My whole life changed when I was accepted by those colleges. I now worked with a new enthusiasm and fervor because I had a goal to work towards. Sure, I might not succeed in college, I thought. I didn't know what the future held. But one thing was certain, I was leaving this urban tobacco farm for greener pastures.

By the end of summer I had saved enough money to pay my first year's tuition at Morgan State. Elated, I told my mother and Mrs. Lemon I could attend college that fall.

"Willie, I told you you could go to college," Mrs. Lemon exclaimed excitedly after hearing the news. "All you had to do was have faith in God. Now go down there, do your best, and your best will be good enough."

The Sunday before my last week in Philadelphia, my church held a special send-off for me, with the pastor and officers of the church appealing to the congregation for a financial gift on my behalf.

After the sermon, Rev. William H. Lemon stood before the congregation, his head held high, urging the congregation to give me a "love offering" to help with my college expenses.

Rev. Lemon was a handsome, older man with burnished bronze skin and wavy dark hair. His whole face seemed to glow when he smiled. He was also a forceful speaker who spoke with a graceful eloquence and a homespun common sense that had earned him the respect and love of his congregation. Hearing the pastor and officers of the church appeal for my needs brought tears to my eyes and a gladness to my heart.

When the offering time came, Deacon William Allen stood tall and erect before the congregation with Theodore R. Thompson, chairman of the trustees, at his side.

"Willie is one of ours," he said, his deep voice full of emotion. "And we like to see our kids make good. Give the boy some real money!"

"Amen!" a sister shouted.

"I agree with Deacon Allen," said Trustee Thompson nodding his head. As his head bobbed, the overhead lights cast a soft glow on his bald spot. "Willie's been a good boy. He ain't doing nothing bad, so we got to help."

When Trustee Golden Cobbs rose to speak on my behalf, I immediately got excited. Trustee Cobbs was a handsome, soft-spoken gentleman whose velvet voice and courtly manner made him the darling of all the women in the church. I knew his appeal would be effective. He was eloquent as he spoke, and I was very impressed with the simple sincerity of his presentation.

"This boy is trying to make something of himself, but he can't do it without our help," said Trustee Cobbs. "We need to help him. We must help each other."

After that, the money flowed like manna from heaven. The initial offering yielded $76.25. "We have $76.00," Trustee Cobbs said after counting the offering. "We need $24.00 more." One by one the dollars came in until the final collection yielded $100.00. (This would be equivalent to about $500.00 today.) The money was a big help in paying my bills at Morgan.

As those dear people poured out their love and money, I saw that moment as the fulfillment of God's promise to me. My faith in God had opened a door of opportunity for me to go to college, and now my church was helping financially, making a way out of no way.

Going to college was a major example of God's faithfulness to me. Though I never know which direction my life might take, I have learned to believe that God is in whatever situation comes my way, good or bad.

Life is often hard, with occasional highs that make the heart sing and moments of joy that make life worth living. My faith journey has taught me that God doesn't promise us a sea of smooth sailing or calmness. Nor does he promise a life free of problems, difficulties, or failures. What God does promise is that he will give us the strength to face life's challenges—to pick ourselves up from today's failure to face tomorrow with confidence.

I worked at the American Tobacco Company until the Friday before I left for college. James drove me to the train station. On the ride I was reflective and pensive as I choked back tears to hide my feelings. I wanted to cry; I was so happy—and so scared.

James dropped me off at Thirtieth Street Station, and I found myself suddenly alone. Though hordes of people milled around me, I felt terribly alone as I pulled my bags to the train platform.

The train arrived at 6:30 P.M., half an hour late. Pushing and tugging, I struggled to get my bags and an old steamer trunk aboard. That trunk held 90 percent of the clothing I owned. It contained my one good suit (perfect except for the small hole in the crotch, but no one would see that), a good pair of shoes, two sweaters, five pairs of underwear, six pairs of socks (only two of them had holes in the toes), and an overcoat with a missing button (I've always had problems keeping buttons on my coats).

I arrived in Baltimore at 8:00 P.M. For a few minutes I stood outside the station taking in my surroundings and looking for a cab. When none appeared, I dragged my belongings around the corner and waited some more. Still no cab. By now I was hungry, really starving. My stomach growled noisily as I looked around for someplace to eat. Across the street was a White Tower Restaurant.

I could almost taste the hamburgers as I dragged my bags and trunk across the street into the restaurant.

"Hamburger, please," I said, propping my belongings up against the wall.

The waitress was a thin, anemic-looking woman with an explosion of hair straining against a thin, mesh hair net. She looked at me as if I'd just committed a crime. Maybe she didn't understand me, I thought.

"I want a ham-mm-mmm-burger!" I said, stuttering slightly.

By now the waitress had regained her composure and fixed her face into a stony mask.

"We don't serve your kind in here," she said curtly.

Now it was my turn to look confused. My face was blank as I tried to figure out what she meant.

"What kind am I?" I asked.

Her next words were more forceful.

"We don't serve Negroes here. You have to go someplace else."

As the few customers sitting at the counter waited for my response, I felt my face heat up with anger. I was mad! Suddenly I realized I was down South again. For a moment I stood there flustered, unsure of what my anger would drive me to do. Regaining my composure, I turned and left, dragging my bags out the door with me. Baltimore in 1957 didn't feel much different from the North Carolina farms back home.

It was another half hour before I could find a cab to take me to my room off campus. I had applied to Morgan too late to get a room on campus, and I immediately hated the room and the long bus ride I took each morning to reach the campus. After a week of commuting, I convinced the dean of students to let me move on campus. Now I could settle down to become a "Morgan man."

Morgan was a small but beautiful black college with pretty, manicured green lawns and full, stately shade trees. It had about twelve buildings, which included four dormitories—two for men and two for women—a new Reserve Officers Training Corps (ROTC) center, a library, gymnasium, and administration and classroom buildings. It was possible to walk from one end of the campus to the other in about ten minutes.

My first roommate was Brian Estrada from Salem, New Jersey. With his handsome, dark looks, Brian was a smooth ladies' man who had some of the prettiest girls on campus interested in him. We got along well despite the fact that some of his friends teased me about my quiet demeanor and the way I talked.

"You are a quiet one, Willie. Do you do anything but study?"

one friend always asked. "You're always in this room with your head buried in a book. Don't you have a girl?"

Another, who teased me about my speech, decided "Man, you must have just come from Africa!"

If the teasing became too harsh, Brian always stepped in. He had a crude but funny way of putting people in their place. His friends always got the message that it was time to back off. I liked Brian, but it was clear to both of us that we lived in different worlds.

Dorm life provided me with some valuable lessons about tolerance as I learned how to deal with different kinds of people. I'd always lived in a big family, but this was different. These students didn't know me or my values and, of course, I didn't know them. At first I tried to accept them based on how I wanted them to be. I quickly realized how narrow that perspective was. They were who they were, just as I was who I was. I wasn't going to change my habits or values to accommodate their preferences any more than they were going to change for me. My responsibility and challenge was to learn to accept them where they were, not where I wanted them to be.

That semester I signed up for a full course load, taking Freshman Orientation, World History, English, Writing Composition, and Math. World History made the deepest impression on me because of the instructor, August Meier, and the challenge it provided.

Professor Meier was German-born and seemed to be a perfect example of the wacky professor. He wore thick, wire-rimmed glasses and talked a mile a minute in his strong German accent. I'm sure he was a brilliant man, but his teaching style was so scattered I had difficulty understanding him as he tossed thoughts and concepts into the air like confetti. It became the student's responsibility to pick up whatever he or she could catch, and at first I couldn't get much.

Those first few weeks in World History went by in a blur as I struggled with Professor Meier's accent and his unique approach to lecturing. By the time our first exam was scheduled, I was in a panic. There was no way I was going to pass this course.

I started classes at Morgan deathly afraid of failing and having to return home an embarrassment to my family and church.

Despite all the encouragement I'd received from folks back home, I still didn't have the confidence that I could succeed in college.

As I struggled in classes like World History, Mrs. Hardigan's words haunted me: "You don't have the background to make it in college!"

What if she was right? What if I wasn't college material after all?

During those first few weeks at Morgan, I approached each class tentatively, feeling my way through them to see how much I really knew. Afraid of stuttering, I didn't talk much or ask too many questions. Instead I took a "watch and learn" approach to discovering how college operated.

When I shared my fears about World History with a sophomore who lived next door to me, he assured me there was nothing to worry about. He had a solution, a stolen copy of Professor Meier's exam.

"A lot of people cheat," he explained. "You won't make it here at Morgan unless you find a way to take some shortcuts."

I couldn't believe what I was hearing. I had to cheat to succeed in college? All my life I'd been warned about taking shortcuts or the easy way out. Now I was being told my success in college depended on how well I could cheat.

I knew this sophomore seemed to be more sophisticated than I was. He appeared to be smart, too. Now I wondered how much of that intelligence was earned and how much was the product of creative shortcuts.

I was confused, caught between my fear of flunking out of school to return home an embarrassment and my desire to give myself a fighting chance to succeed this first year. I needed at least a solid foundation to get me started, I reasoned. And besides, who back home would know?

As I wrestled with my conscience, I was assaulted by Sunday school lessons that ran through my mind like spontaneous newsreels, warning me of the danger of making the wrong choice. In my head, I heard the booming voice of my Sunday school teacher Judge Allen as he intoned, "Stay on the straight and narrow, children. Walk that straight line. You will succeed in life only if you don't try to take the shortcuts."

I had respected Brother Allen as well as the Reverend Ralph Overton as they taught us kids about living a godly life. They were Christian role models for us as well as mentors who gladly provided an encouraging word or some fatherly advice when needed.

They had warned us that life's temptations would come our way and we shouldn't fear. Temptation is not a sin, they taught. Even Jesus was tempted. It's what you do with the temptation that makes the difference.

"Whenever you have a problem, just leave the problem in God's hands. Let him guide you. He will never lead you wrong."

Now temptation was staring me smack in the face, and I didn't know what to do, other than pray. Unlike some of my classmates who didn't seem to have second thoughts about using the stolen exam, I agonized over this decision, wondering how they could be so unconcerned about doing the wrong thing when I was so miserable even thinking about it. They didn't seem to think cheating was wrong. Why?

Suddenly the answer hit me—the Holy Spirit. I had the Holy Spirit in my life, and he was telling me that cheating was wrong. The values and lessons that I had learned from my parents and Sunday school teachers were not the ramblings of old-fashioned adults; they were the word of God. The guidance that I'd gotten from my pastor and his wife was not religious mumbo jumbo. It was the word of God. God's word was guiding my life and the Holy Spirit was reminding me of that.

I sighed with relief as I realized God was helping me decide what to do. No matter what the consequence, I had to follow the godly teachings that had directed me all of my life, first through my mother's faith and now through my own relationship with God. "If I flunk out of school and return home an embarrassment, at least I will be an honest embarrassment," I chuckled.

After that I settled down to study for the exam. My classmates who planned to cheat prepared by devising ingenious crib sheets and little cram cards with the answers written on them. Sometimes I got tickled at how hard they worked to hide the answers on different parts of their bodies when they could have put that energy into studying.

On exam day I entered Professor Meier's class trembling. It

was up to God and what little brains I had to get me through this situation. But despite my concern, I felt a deep inner peace at knowing I had done all I could. Two hours later I left the classroom drained but sighing with relief at knowing that whatever happened, I could still hold my head up high.

I passed! When I learned I had passed on my own skill, I couldn't stop patting myself on the back and thanking God. The cheaters, however, failed miserably. Professor Meier had found out about the stolen papers and switched the exam.

That experience at Morgan was probably my first confrontation with outright deception. It wouldn't be my last. But the moment marked a turning point for me. From then on I was convinced that I was able to do college work. I was going to make it as long as I held on to my faith in God and worked hard at my assignments.

My first year at Morgan held one memorable experience after the other. We had the biggest snowfall I have ever seen when what seemed like two feet of snow was dumped on the city in just a few hours. Classes were canceled, and the students had a great time with snowball fights and dorm parties.

That first year I also had my first blind date. Her name was Alberta Rice, and the evening was a disaster. We just didn't hit it off well. I jokingly complained to Alberta's girlfriends about her clumsiness. Alberta had been my date for a school dance. While I am no Fred Astaire, I couldn't imagine anyone being a worse dancer than I—until I met Alberta.

After telling her friends about the date, I was startled when Alberta later confronted me about what I had said.

"What did you say about our date?" she asked, cornering me in the hallway.

"I don't remember precisely what I said," I replied sheepishly, ashamed that I had been caught.

"You know what you said. You ought to be ashamed of yourself," she said angrily. "That's the last date you will ever have with me!"

I took the tongue-lashing silently, knowing I was wrong. But

Alberta wasn't content to just bawl me out.

"Willie Wilson Goode, I will get even with you. You had no right to embarrass me with my girlfriends the way you did. Believe me, I will get even."

Alberta was as good as her word.

Later that semester, I ran for sophomore class president and was deadlocked in a tight election. I was counting on Alberta and her friends to generate the votes I needed to take me over the top. Instead, Alberta and her "Maryland Bloc" voted against me. I lost the election by two votes.

Alberta and I eventually made peace and remained cordial friends throughout my years at Morgan. I never mentioned the election episode or the word "date" to her again.

During their first two years in school, Morgan's male students were required to take the ROTC program. I enjoyed the initial experience and thought it might be fun to be commissioned a second lieutenant in the U.S. Army if I remained in the program. I opted to stay in for that and two other reasons.

I was grateful that ROTC helped stretch my meager wardrobe. The program provided a uniform that cadets were required to wear on ROTC days. We also earned sixteen dollars a month. That four dollars a week was enough to provide snack money and take care of my laundry.

Between my freshman and sophomore years at Morgan, I met my wife, Velma. A cousin, Bennie Frank Brown, had introduced me to Velma's two sisters, Mavis and Norma Williams. They were joyful, wholesome young women who seemed to possess a special quality. When they told me about their baby sister, Velma, I reasoned that she had to be the same kind of person.

"You ought to meet her, Willie. She's real nice," Mavis teased.

"Maybe I will."

Mavis gave me the telephone number where Velma was staying with their aunt in Darby, Pennsylvania. I decided to call her when I went home that weekend for summer vacation.

"Hello, this is Willie Goode. I know your sisters, Mavis and Norma," I began nervously. "How are you?"

"I'm fine," Velma said shyly.

"Look, I'm just finishing my first year of college, and I thought maybe you'd like to go out with me."

Click! I listened to the dial tone in amazement wondering what I had said wrong. What did I do? What did I say? I asked myself.

I called back prepared to get to the bottom of this.

"Why did you hang up on me?" I blurted out.

"If you want to talk to me, Willie Goode, talk straight," she said. "I don't want any jive city talk." Then she hung up again.

I was shocked—and a little pleased that this seventeen-year-old country girl was putting this nineteen-year-old college man in his place. I called back, putting on my most gentlemanly behavior. This time the conversation went better, and she began to relax. Later she explained that she'd hung up because I'd sounded like I was trying to impress her by mentioning college. From then on I knew Velma wasn't easily impressed.

Velma had graduated with high honors from high school in North Carolina just a few months before. There was a sweetness and innocence about her that I immediately liked. She was different from the Philadelphia girls, more refreshing and wholesome. Yet she was smart and very independent. I convinced her to go out with me.

The day of our date I took the bus from my home at 6026 Locust Street to Fifty-eighth and Woodland, where I caught the number 11 trolley for Darby. It took another half-hour from there to get to Ninth Street in Darby, but I arrived on time for our date. In fact, I was fifteen minutes early. Velma wasn't home.

"She'll be back shortly," her Aunt Mattie Harmon reassured me. "Just wait out here on the porch."

While I waited, my mind raced with thoughts about Velma. What would she look like? Had she forgotten about the date? Did she just say yes to get me off the telephone and was now standing me up?

A few minutes later my thoughts were interrupted by this pretty girl approaching me. I knew by the way she looked at me that she was Velma. I stared back speechless, grinning from ear to ear.

Her face still had the smooth, sun-browned glow of the country. She was wearing shorts, and I noticed what nice big legs she had. Her eyes were also big and brown.

"Hi, I'm Velma," she said approaching the porch. She had a light, bouncy walk that exuded youth and energy. "I was down the street watching the fire. Come in and have a seat."

Silently I followed her into the house.

"This is my Aunt Mattie. Please have a seat. I'll be ready in a minute."

As Velma disappeared, I settled back in a chair to face Aunt Mattie. She was a stately, handsome lady who was the matriarch of the Williams/Peters family. She looked me over carefully while Velma got ready. I could feel Aunt Mattie's eyes piercing through me, taking in every detail. She spoke first.

"What do you do?"

"I go to college," I replied meekly.

"Which one?"

"I go to Morgan State in Baltimore."

She nodded approvingly.

"What are you going to be?"

"A history teacher. I'm going to be a history teacher," I repeated uncomfortably. The answer seemed to please her.

"Well, you take care of my little girl," she instructed. "I don't want any slick stuff out of you."

"Yes, Ma'am. I'm a nice boy."

Velma and I left and took the trolley back to Philadelphia, where we caught the show at the Benson movie theater on Woodland Avenue. The film playing was a love story, *A Farewell to Arms*. It was a good movie. Afterwards we took the trolley back to Darby, and I walked her home.

By this time I was holding her hand. We had gotten off to a rocky start with that first phone call, but now the chemistry was flowing. She was someone special, and I knew this would not be our last date.

Walking towards the house, I kept wondering whether I should try to kiss her goodnight. Would she let me? I felt very comfortable with her and could sense that she was comfortable with me. And we were holding hands. Should I steal a little kiss before we got to her house? What if her aunt was still up and sitting on the front porch? This might be my only chance.

As we approached her front door, I said, "I want to see you again. May I call you?"

"Yes."

Suddenly we were in each others' arms, embracing and kissing. Reluctantly we pulled apart. I said goodnight and made my way home in a fog of emotions.

I called the next day, and the next, and the next. By the time I returned to school in September, we had developed a serious relationship following numerous dates, hours on the telephone, letters, and a love poem I'd written.

> A phone call, a conversation, a movie date,
>   and a new life with you;
> A kiss on your lips and my own
>   private world became a reality.
> I have found in you the happiness
>   that can only be found with one you love dearly.
> I have discovered in you what love is,
>   its true meaning and the effect it can have on one's life.
> For where love prevails, happiness finds its place
>   and hatred and unhappiness die.
> The clouds of doubt and despair fade;
> The sun soon shows its face
>   and the entire world is happy.
> Love has found its place in their hearts,
>   and now it has found its place in mine also.
>   *Willie W. Goode*

Being with Velma reminded me of my deep appreciation for southern women. She was very southern and also very mature and outspoken for her age. I never had to guess what was on her mind—she told me.

A lot of the city girls I knew wanted a guy who had a good line, sharp clothes, and a nice car. That impressed them. Not Velma. She was more concerned about my dreams and my values. One of the things I enjoyed most about her was her insight as we discussed future plans for my life. I came to depend on her wisdom.

Also like me, Velma had had a pretty tough childhood. Her

parents had separated when she was a child, and her mother had raised the children alone. That early abandonment caused Velma to mature early and, I believe, also become a little distrustful of men. I felt honored that she trusted me. By the time I came home for the Christmas holidays, Velma and I were going steady. I invited her home for dinner to meet my parents. She soon became a regular fixture around the house.

By my junior year I knew that I wanted Velma to be my wife. I didn't plan to propose until after graduation, but an incident with a neighbor changed the timing.

It was 1960, and I was home for the Penn Relays. A neighbor, Veronica Roberts, wanted to go to the relays, too. I told her I already had a date but she could come along if she wanted. To my surprise, Velma didn't like the "competition." She was very polite the entire afternoon, but after we were alone, she let me know how inappropriate she thought it was to invite Veronica. Anxious to demonstrate my love for her and only her, I proposed.

"Velma, I'm not interested in any other woman. I want you to be my wife. Will you marry me?"

Before Velma could answer, I had to ask her mother's permission to marry her. She said yes—and Velma did too. We set the date for August 20, the day after my twenty-second birthday. Velma began planning the wedding.

I was happy as I returned to school to finish that semester. Life was grand. I was engaged to be married, and school was going well. Each semester at Morgan I had applied myself more and more and had been rewarded with better grades. My self-confidence was improving, and I was more active in extracurricular activities, such as the sports column I wrote for the school paper under the heading "Goode Sports."

Most satisfying, however, was my involvement in the student civil rights protests. Throughout my early years at Morgan, Dr. Martin D. Jenkins, the university's president, frequently told students that it was our responsibility to change the world around us.

"If you don't like what you see, don't just talk about it. Change it! No one is going to give you anything in this life. You must earn everything you get. Prepare yourself here; then go out and change the world."

I was energized and ready to act whenever I heard one of these speeches. Dr. Jenkins's words engendered a spirit of impatience among the students about the segregated shopping center in town. Students who shopped at the Northwood Shopping Center were treated like second-class citizens. We couldn't go to the movie theaters or eat in the restaurants. Now we were tired of waiting for Baltimore's Jim Crow policies to change.

I still smarted from the blow I had received trying to buy a hamburger at the White Tower Restaurant. So when student activists marched to desegregate the shopping center, movie theaters, and restaurants near the campus, I was one of the first recruits. We had read about the Montgomery Bus Boycott and the sit-ins at North Carolina Central University. Black people throughout the South were protesting for their freedom. We would too.

I joined the sit-ins at the Northwood Shopping Center with glee, relishing the chance to fight against the Jim Crow policies in Baltimore. A few times I was arrested and jailed. It didn't bother me because I was fighting for something that was politically, and personally, important to me—the right to be accepted as a human being and enjoy the same freedoms and services that white people already enjoyed in this country.

While the student protests were going on, two significant people arrived on campus as students: Phillip Savage, an official with the National Association for the Advancement of Colored People (NAACP), and Clarence Mitchell III, the son of the NAACP lobbyist in Washington. Both of them joined forces with us to lead in the student protest.

The protests were emotional and exciting. We would march along Cold Spring Lane and turn up Hillen Road to the Northwood Shopping Center, our target for the day a restaurant or the movie theater, or sometimes both.

A student approached the cashier of the movie theater to ask for a ticket.

"We don't serve your kind here," the cashier said, blushing.

"I want to go to the movies," the student responded.

"No. You can't go to this movie theater. We only serve whites here."

"But I'm a student at Morgan State College."

"I don't care where you're from," the cashier would yell, annoyed. "You can't come in here."

We would then sing "We Shall Overcome."

Almost immediately the police would arrive. They were some of the meanest-looking people I have ever seen in my life. Some of the officers had dogs that they left barking and snarling near their police vans.

"All right, all right. Let's break this up," the officers said, pushing through the students. "These people have put up with your foolishness long enough. Break it up and go home or we will have to arrest you."

"Who wants to be arrested?" a student leader would shout.

A few hands shot up, mine among them. We were the volunteers. As I rode in the police wagon, my mind went back to those whites who had systematically kept my family down by stealing crop money from us.

My mind went back to those big yellow school buses that passed me loaded with white students riding to schools that were located nearer than the school I walked to. I would walk, holes in my shoes, shivering from the thin clothing I had on.

My mind went back to the segregated water fountains marked "colored only" and "white only." By the time I emerged from that police wagon, I was glad to go to jail for my freedom. At least now I was fighting back, and somehow, deep down inside I knew things were going to change.

The police took us down to the police station, but no charges were filed against us. We sat in jail for a few hours before being released.

The student protests lasted several months and succeeded in desegregating the restaurants and movie theaters near the school. Morgan was teaching me the power of civil disobedience and the landscape of politics.

With each passing year I realized that going to college was one of the best things that ever happened to me. It not only fed my mind but nurtured my soul, as black scholars taught me how to see different sides of an issue and to think outside the narrow confines of some of my long-held opinions. Dr. G. James Fleming, a political science professor, invited me to become a scholar in the Institute for Political Education, a Ford Foundation project aimed at giving minority students a practical working knowledge of the political system.

The scholars were required to read newspapers daily to analyze political stories and discuss their views in class. A lecture series featuring visits by elected officials was another part of the program.

One of the highlights of that course was the mock Democratic National Convention we held on campus in 1960. We chose delegates, simulated the electoral process, and selected candidates to run on the Democratic ticket. Paul Butler, the Democratic National Committee chairman in 1960, was the keynote speaker for the convention. This was my first real opportunity to be involved with a political campaign close up, and I learned a great deal about how the system worked.

Morgan was a nurturing environment for me, a cocoon that I entered as a caterpillar and emerged from as a butterfly. All of my teachers seemed to take a personal interest in me and provided the support and encouragement I hungered for, while also presenting the challenge I needed.

Dr. Benjamin Quarels was a case in point. A history teacher, Dr. Quarels bragged that "no one has ever gotten an *A* in my class." I was determined to become the first.

For two nights before taking his first exam, I stayed up studying, living on NoDoz. I reexamined every concept, principle, set of dates, and historical movement that we had ever covered in class. The day of the exam I was ready. Ninety minutes later, Dr. Quarels and I were the only ones left in the exam room, and I was still writing.

"As long as you stay, I'm staying too," he said.

I wrote for another half-hour. He gave me an *A*.

Another favorite professor was Dr. Robert Gill, a political science teacher. I loved Dr. Gill's class and delighted in taking copious notes as well as writing long essays on his exams. The only problem was, Dr. Gill could never read my handwriting.

"Wilson, your penmanship is not good," he said sympathetically. "It's no better than mine. So you're probably going to become a professor of political science one day if you keep writing the way you write now."

We had a lot of fun talking and joking about our penmanship.

Something that was no joke was my discovery of how poorly my southern childhood and education had prepared me for the real world. At Morgan, I found that I lacked some basic, fundamental writing skills as well as full command of proper verb structure. I had always thought stuttering to be my worst verbal problem. Now I found that I was also deficient in such things as sentence and verb structure and proper syntax. Eager to learn, I signed up for remedial writing and speaking courses. My short time in these classes gave me added confidence and hope.

Morgan quenched the thirst I had for knowledge and instilled in me a hunger for public service. A philosophy that was a hallmark of the school was the Promethean Principle, named for the Greek mythological figure Prometheus. In the myth Prometheus, a mere man, risks his life traveling to the home of the gods to bring the gift of fire back to humankind. The principle encourages a life commitment to public service or any endeavor that will serve humanity and improve humankind. I took that challenge seriously and harbored a dream that I would find some way to enter community service.

That dream crystallized at a student assembly in recognition of Morgan's Second-Mile Award winners. Second Milers were those students who had made the extra effort, gone the second mile, in scholastic achievement and participation in campus activities. The speaker for the event was the mayor of Baltimore.

As Dr. Jenkins, Morgan's president, introduced the guest speaker, he presented a challenge, an almost prophetic message, that I have never forgotten.

"Mr. Mayor, this is an assembly for Second Milers," Jenkins said, "and, in a sense, for other students as well. Mr. Mayor, I want you to know that out there in this audience are future mayors of Baltimore and other cities around this country. Their time will come, and they are being well prepared here at Morgan."

I sat there awe-struck. Here we were living in a time when black people throughout the South were fighting for the right to vote and for basic human dignity. This black man was standing here telling a white mayor that black students were being prepared to take his job. I said to myself, This man is either crazy or prophetic!

The auditorium burst into thunderous applause. It was a rarity even in those days for students to appreciate something the university president said. But we did. We appreciated Dr. Jenkins's courage, his guts and, most importantly, his challenge. Listening to Dr. Jenkins, I began to believe that those dreams of being famous I had back on the farm might actually be possible. He certainly made it seem so.

College represented a personal triumph over my insecurities and poor self-image. I had started at Morgan as a scared, timid kid from North Carolina and learned that I would probably end my last semester of my junior year there with straight A's. I looked forward to my last year at Morgan with joy and excitement. ROTC training camp and my wedding were both scheduled for August. As I anticipated a busy summer, I knew I was approaching the flowering of my youth and a new chapter in my life.

ROTC had been a good experience for me, teaching me leadership skills as well as giving me the chance to supervise a company of cadets. The last ROTC camp was held at Fort Meade, Maryland, the week before I got married. Students from Morgan and big white schools all over Maryland and Pennsylvania participated. Big military powerhouse schools like Pennsylvania Military College and Bucknell University sent their spit-and-polish cadets who looked like they'd been weaned on hardtack and C rations.

Each day a new cadet was designated company commander. When I was selected, I was both honored and surprised. My turn as company commander would occur right before camp ended. That gave me extra time to watch, listen, and learn from the instructors and other cadets who preceded me.

Throughout the week I made hundreds of mental notes as I absorbed the dos and don'ts of command leadership. By the time my turn came, I was ready.

The night preceding my command I was restless. I tossed and turned for hours, unable to sleep as I worried about the next day's exercises. My biggest fear was being unable to speak clearly. You can do this, I told myself. Just concentrate. You can do this.

Still, I worried. What if I stuttered? What if the white cadets gave me a hard time and refused to follow my instructions?

The day dawned bright and sunny with low humidity. At daybreak I was the first one up. I spit polished my shoes for an hour, shining them to a high gloss before the other cadets even stirred. My khaki uniform was laundered and creased to military perfection. Nothing was out of place, except for the fear that knotted my stomach.

My command fell on the first day of mock military exercises, and it was my responsibility to engage my troops in combat with the enemy. I approached the cadets with a mixture of excitement and anticipation, delivering orders with an authority that even I didn't know I had. Surprisingly, I didn't stutter, nor did the cadets balk at my command. The troops cooperated willingly under my leadership, and the exercise was performed to perfection. That day was the highlight of my ROTC career. Walking across the grounds, I was on top of the world as friends and other cadets rushed up to pat me on the back and congratulate me on a job well done.

A boisterous cadet from Bucknell approached me, his hand out and a grin reaching from ear to ear.

"You are really pretty good for a Negro," he said pumping my hand in congratulations. "I must confess that I am surprised. You did real good!"

For a moment I was taken aback by the back-handed compliment. It was a few seconds before I could regain my composure and murmur a reluctant thank you. The best recognition, however, came from the command instructor. He commended me for my leadership and organizational skills and awarded me a special commendation that helped rank me near the top of the class.

The commendation was a real confidence-booster. It proved that I could perform at a higher level of authority than I'd ever expected and that I could cross racial barriers to succeed. Elated, I went home to get married that weekend.

Our wedding was a beautiful, modest affair held at the First Baptist Church of Darby. Percell Stanford, a Morgan classmate and ROTC buddy, was best man. Malcolm Boykins, another classmate, was also in the wedding party.

I wore a white formal coat and black pants. Velma was radiant in a traditional wedding dress. The pastor of the church, Rev. Willie W. Williams, was an old man bordering on senility. All went well until the exchanging of the vows.

"Do you William Wilson . . ." neither Velma nor I understood a thing he said after that. Poor Rev. Williams stumbled through the entire ceremony but seemed encouraged as we gave what we thought to be the proper responses at the appropriate time. Neither Velma nor I remember Rev. Williams asking me if I took Velma to be my wife. After the ceremony we joked that we really weren't officially married because we never knew if Rev. Williams had asked us the right questions.

The reception was held in the basement of Velma's family home at 5842 Pemberton Street. My mother refused to attend the wedding, objecting to the marriage on the grounds that I should have waited until I graduated from Morgan.

"Wilson, you're jumping into this too early," she scolded. "You don't have a job. How are you going to take care of a wife?"

"Mama, Velma's working, and I get a small check from ROTC and from working in the library at school. It's going to be all right."

She didn't say anything more; she just didn't come to the wedding. I felt bad about Mama not being there. Mama had been a part of every important decision in my life. To have her absent on this special day in my life was disheartening. But I respected her views. She was right that I was taking a risk, but it was a risk worth taking.

During the reception, various people came up to me to inquire about the honeymoon.

"Where you going on your honeymoon, Wilson?" my brother-in-law Alja Porter asked.

"I haven't made plans for one," I responded.

"Man, are you crazy?" he exclaimed. "You better take this girl somewhere. You can't just stay over at Oscar's house." Oscar was Oscar Clark, our new landlord.

"I haven't made any arrangements to go anywhere," I said, annoyed. "Besides it's too late now. I don't have a car, and you know I don't drive."

Alja shook his head sadly.

"Wilson, listen to an old-timer. Take your pretty wife on a honeymoon."

"But, Porter, I don't have any honeymoon money."

"One night, Wilson. You can go for one night. I'll drive you wherever you want to go."

I was cornered. The only place I'd ever been outside of Philadelphia, besides Baltimore, was Ocean City, New Jersey. Papa Neal had taken a group of us down to his summer home in Ocean City for a weekend. That was the most exciting place I'd been, so I immediately decided on Ocean City.

"That's where we want to go, Porter. Ocean City."

"Do you know where in Ocean City?"

"No, I told you I didn't make any arrangements," I said, my annoyance returning. "Maybe we can just drive around until we find a place."

My brother-in-law looked at me with an expression of bemusement. I wasn't smiling.

"Wilson, Ocean City is a crowded place this time of the year. And it's Saturday night, too. You'll be very lucky to find any vacancies."

By now I was ready to be finished with the whole thing.

"Look, Porter, first you tell me to take my wife away, and when I tell you yes, you find all kinds of reasons why I can't do that. We will either do it now or not at all!"

"Come on, Wilson, get Velma and let's go, but I'm not making any promises to you."

When we arrived in Ocean City, we went from hotel to hotel, motel to motel, and rooming house to rooming house. The story was always the same.

"No vacancies. Try us tomorrow night."

"Doesn't this guy know it's my honeymoon?" I said after being turned down after hours of looking.

Finally we found a vacancy. I paid for the room and happily led my bride into it. To our amazement the room was secured by an accordion door with a safety lock. Anyone with a strong hand could just pop the handle and slide the door open. Moreover, the bathroom was a common bathroom way down the hall. Some honeymoon.

But we really didn't mind. I had grown accustomed to common bathrooms in college, and the room we'd rented to live in together at Oscar Clarke's had an accordion door. This room was just practice for what lay ahead.

We were married, in love, and beginning our life together. That Sunday we took the bus back to Philadelphia and our one-room home at Oscar's place. For the remainder of the summer I worked at odd jobs before returning to school that fall.

The first time Velma saw Morgan State was during ROTC weekend when she came to attend the ROTC ball. I had arranged for Velma to stay with a student from Philadelphia, but there was some confusion and it didn't work out. We ended up spending the night in a car on Cold Spring Lane. By now Velma must have thought I'd never provide a decent place for us to stay. But the car was nice, and we managed to find a place inside a house for her to dress the next morning.

My last semester at Morgan I learned I would graduate *cum laude* and ninth out of a class of 223 students. That knowledge, along with the fact that I was making straight *A*'s that semester, was enough to send me home to find someone I had avoided seeing for years—Mrs. Hardigan, my high school counselor.

She looked grayer than I remembered, and sterner. Showing her the graduation program, I reminded Mrs. Hardigan of my first week at John Bartram High School and our conversations, how she had told me I wasn't college material and would never succeed in college, if I got accepted at all.

"I hope you never tell anyone else they're incapable of doing college work," I said. To my surprise she was very gracious and apologized.

"Sometimes I make mistakes, Willie," she said. "You were very different for me."

I was puzzled.

"How?" I asked.

"We didn't have many country boys coming to school here. I guess I had some prejudices I didn't know about. But I've learned something from this."

I had learned something too. Having faith, I achieved my dream despite obstacles like Mrs. Hardigan.

CHAPTER FIVE

The Goode Lieutenant

By the time I graduated from Morgan, I was ranked as one of the top cadet commanders in my senior class; for graduation we received new tan uniforms with gold bars. I couldn't have been a prouder soldier in the U.S. Army. Graduating commissioned as a second lieutenant, I returned home to work until September 12, when I had to leave for my command post at Fort Gordon, Georgia.

I got a job selling paint that summer at the MAB Paint store at Sixteenth and Columbia Avenue and worked there until the Friday before leaving for camp. I bid my friends farewell, and that Sunday I left for Georgia.

Lt. Percell Stanford, the best man at my wedding, and three other officers from our class had made plans to meet in Washington, D.C., so we could take the train together to Georgia.

My back ramrod straight, my military uniform fitting just right, I thought I cut a pretty handsome figure. No one could tell any one of us that we weren't the perfect picture of authority. We were college educated, twenty-two-year-old black men, commissioned as second lieutenants in the U.S. Army. Our gold bars gleamed on our shoulders and our shoes were spit polished to a high gloss. Not a stitch or seam was out of place. We were immaculate and professional as we boarded that train in Washington, D.C. in September 1961.

When the train arrived in Sumter, South Carolina, the conductor walked through the cars announcing, "All coloreds move to the rear of the car."

Surely he doesn't mean us, I thought, settling more deeply into my seat.

Seeing the motion, the conductor scowled and spoke a little louder.

"All coloreds move to the rear of the car."

"Come on, Willie," Percell said, tapping me on the shoulder. "We have to move."

"But we're lieutenants in the U.S. Army," I protested.

"Willie," Percell said, looking me squarely in the eye, "down here you're still a nigger. If you don't want to lose those gold bars before you serve in the U.S. Army, just mind your business and move to the rear of the car."

Reluctantly we gathered up our belongings and moved.

Army life awakened me to new degrees of American racism. Somehow it never seemed to get any better. It was just different from what I had encountered as a child.

One night while Percell and I had dinner on base, we were joined by a white lieutenant from Salt Lake City. It was a pleasant meal, and afterwards we enjoyed an amicable conversation before turning in for the night.

"You know, Willie, Percell, I never had a chance to meet any colored folks before," Lieutenant Stahl said pleasantly as we rose to leave. "I've heard all kinds of tales about you all, and I want you to know, you're just like people."

He wasn't even aware of what he had said.

"What did you expect?" I asked.

"I don't know. Maybe that when you took your uniforms off you'd have tails," he confessed. We all laughed at how ridiculous this was. Despite the humor, all of us had learned something.

We spent two months at Fort Gordon before receiving our assignments. I was assigned to the military police division at Fort Carson, Colorado.

After basic training, I went home to be with my wife for a few weeks before making the two-thousand-mile trip to Colorado Springs and then Fort Carson. While I was home, my brother-in-law Alja told me he would be driving to Texas soon and offered to coordinate his trip with mine so he could drive me part of the way.

December 4 came and Alja and I headed down the Pennsylvania Turnpike, the car loaded to the brim. Velma was expecting our first child any day and couldn't make the drive. I regretted how far away from home and family I had to be during this very important time of our lives.

Alja and I arrived in St. Louis late that night. To relax, Alja took me to a night club to see the famous black tap dancer Peg Leg Bates, so named because he had one wooden peg leg. It was my first time in a night club. The next day Alja dropped me off in Omaha, where I boarded a train bound for Colorado Springs.

After arriving in Colorado, I found I could have gotten an extension until after the baby was born so that Velma and I could have been together. With no house, no furniture, and a pregnant wife back in Philadelphia, I was lonelier than I'd ever been in my life. As if the loneliness wasn't bad enough, the first day at my duty station presented a problem I hadn't expected.

"Where is your car?" the duty officer asked.

"I don't have a car," I said.

He looked up at me with a slight look of disbelief.

"What about a driver's license?"

"I don't have a driver's license either," I replied.

"Do you know how to drive?" he asked with mild annoyance.

"No."

The duty officer looked puzzled.

"In order to work in the military police unit, you have to know how to drive," he said. "That's one of the requirements. Why don't you know how to drive?"

"During my teen years there was no car available for me to learn how to drive," I explained. "I didn't even have a bicycle."

"All right then. We'll have to get you situated."

Sgt. Blocker, who seemed to be sixty years old at the time but was probably much younger, took me under his wing.

"I will drive you back and forth to town, Lieutenant, until you find a place," he offered.

With the help of the sergeant, I found a house and got a few pieces of furniture so Velma could be comfortable when she joined me later. My next task was to learn how to drive. Lt. Joe Burke assigned the motor sergeant to teach me.

"Another one of these college kids," he mumbled after we met. "Don't even know how to drive, huh?"

He was a demeaning, arrogant cuss.

"All right, I'll teach you how to drive," he said.

We went out on the highway.

"I want you to drive this straight road," he ordered as I slid behind the wheel. I spent a few hours driving before he was satisfied. The next day I was given new orders.

"I'm going to take you up on this mountainside," he said pointing to a bank of steep peaks behind us. "I'm going to drive you up, and I want you to drive down, but I'll be in the jeep with you."

This was only my second day of driving. The sergeant took us into the mountains near Pikes Peak. Snow covered the ground, and deep canyons yawned like gaping mouths on both sides of the road, ready to swallow us up if I made a wrong move. I'd only had two driving lessons. Naturally I questioned the wisdom of his methodology.

"The only way you're going to learn how to drive is to understand that your life depends on the decisions that you make," the sergeant explained.

"If you make the right decisions coming down these peaks, you will have learned how to drive. If you make the wrong ones you'll kill us. Let's go!"

Coming down that mountainside I learned as much about driving and survival as most drivers learn in ten years. By the time we got to the bottom, my instructor's complexion was flashing like a neon sign, alternating between beet red and ash white. I was fascinated.

"Tell me something," I said. "Are you turning red and white from my driving or the cold?"

He never answered my question.

"I think you're ready to go out on your own," he responded

quietly. "Just take the jeep and drive around the base. You're a military police officer. No one will bother you."

I took that jeep and drove half the day. The next day I went out and bought a 1957 Nash Rambler, took the driver's exam and road test, and got my license. The very first day I drove off the base in my new car someone rear-ended me.

"Why did you stop so suddenly?" the other driver asked, irritated.

"The light turned yellow," I said, explaining that I was a new driver. He seemed to understand.

"Well, out here, you ought to be running through those," he said.

I was assigned to the Nineteenth Military Police Company and directed 223 men. Only six or seven blacks were in the whole military police division. I was the highest-ranking black officer, and many of the white enlisted personnel didn't like being outranked by a black man, especially one who had earned his bars through college ROTC.

My first confrontation came a short time after I arrived and I was serving as duty officer for the evening. The ranking sergeant and I had a dispute.

"Listen, Goodie Boy," he said, spitting out the word *boy* as if it left a nasty taste in his mouth, "I know you have those bars and I know you got them by going to college. See these stripes here?" he said tapping his left arm. "I earned them through hard work. So from my point of view, Sonny Boy, these stripes outrank those bars."

Throughout his little speech I fought to control my temper. When I did speak, my voice was low and even.

"I may be young," I said, "and I may have gotten my bars through ROTC. But one thing I understand is authority. And after today, I don't think you're going to be a sergeant."

His eyes widened in surprise. For a moment he stood speechless, his mouth gaping open.

"You . . . you can't bust me," he stammered.

I was still calm.

"I can, and I'll prove to you that I will," I said.

"But you just got here! I've been here two years. They won't let you do that."

"Watch me."

Later that day I went to see the provost marshal, Major Killough, and told him what had happened.

"I insist that this man be demoted one rank," I said, concluding my story.

The major leaned back in his chair and thought a moment before answering.

"We don't demote people," he said quietly.

I had expected this reaction and was prepared.

"I feel very strongly about this," I continued. "He was totally insubordinate, and I don't want to think that he's only insubordinate with blacks and that *you* would tolerate him saying something to blacks that he wouldn't say to whites."

The major shifted ever so slightly in his seat.

"Lieutenant, let's not be racial about this thing."

"I don't want to be, Major, unless I'm forced to."

The sergeant was not demoted but was given a strong reprimand. After that it wasn't long before I had a problem with another sergeant. I also had my first experience with the unwritten military "brotherhood" code that says you protect a military brother regardless of the infraction he commits. It gave me a good understanding of the "code of silence" among police personnel as well.

I was duty officer for the evening, and a sergeant and another soldier brought in a civilian for some infraction. During the evening, they took the man into the cell block and proceeded to beat him up. I had heard about things like this happening but had never been so close to an incident before. After roughing the man up, they let him go. Normally it would have ended right there, but the civilian wrote his congressman and filed a complaint. The sergeant who participated in the beating fabricated a story and asked me to sign his report. I refused.

"I'm not going to sign that," I said tossing the report back to him. "That's not what happened."

He turned beet red but managed to hold his temper.

"Listen, Lieutenant, if you want to survive in this military—survive in this company—you have to support your men."

I agreed with him.

"You're right. I will support my men when they're right, but

I won't support them when they're wrong. You used unnecessary force. I was there and saw what you did. I asked you to stop and you wouldn't. I'm not signing that report."

All hell broke loose after that. The congressional investigation continued, and some of the men on that shift branded me a traitor. None of them would come near me. If they saw me walking towards them, they turned their backs to avoid giving or returning a salute.

Military life was teaching me about the harsh realities of the social pecking order. In any kind of structure—the military, politics, or corporate America—there is a code of conduct among colleagues. In a bureaucracy you're expected to protect your peers and play the game the way it has always been played. Don't change the rules. Don't have your own standards. Just play the game. And if you refuse to play the way your peers want, you'll be marked for destruction, isolation, or identification as a troublemaker.

As I became more and more isolated from the men on that shift, I remembered thinking, Why am I feeling as if I've done something wrong because they refuse to support me? Why am I being ostracized for their bad behavior? It was hard being on the outside. Still I stuck to my guns.

Things returned to normal when the sergeant who beat up the civilian retired. Most of the other men in the unit were transferred. For a while it looked like the rest of my stay at Fort Carson would be smooth sailing.

Then I got wind of an upcoming raid on a downtown night club on the evening when, as duty officer, I was responsible for any events that occurred, including raids scheduled with my division. I went to the officer who was to lead the raid and told him I was taking over the command that evening.

"No way!" he exclaimed. "I've got orders from the provost marshal that we're not to take any colored personnel down there. This is a white club in Colorado Springs."

The provost marshal was in charge of the entire military police operation and clearly outranked me. Still, there was no way I was going to be duty officer for the evening and take responsibility for a raid I couldn't even monitor.

"I will be the officer in charge of this operation," I repeated.

"Fine, Lieutenant! However, I think you ought to call the provost marshal."

I did.

The provost marshal was a "good ole boy" like most of the other white officers on base.

"Lieutenant, this is a segregated club and they don't allow coloreds to go there," he explained pleasantly. "Surely you understand."

I took a deep breath.

"What I understand, Sir, is that it's my duty to be there with my men. I'm responsible for what happens while I'm on duty. Now, if you are going to absolve me of all responsibility while—"

He cut me off before I could finish.

"Lieutenant, what I understand is that I am instructing you to go into your office, sit in your chair, and mind your own business while these men do their job as they have done it before you were assigned out here. My best advice for you is to keep your mouth shut. Then, maybe, maybe you might go somewhere in this army."

Once again, I felt I was being told to be a "good boy." Don't rock the boat or you'll be sorry.

I had lost another battle but not the war. After that encounter I began talking to other blacks in local civilian and military communities about my experiences.

"Do you have a chapter of the NAACP out here?" I asked.

"No."

"Then why don't you organize one?"

"We don't know how."

Quietly I worked with the black people in Colorado Springs to form their first chapter of the NAACP. I don't think the army ever found out.

By now Velma and I had been in Colorado for a year. I was homesick. We both were. Muriel Lynette, our first child, was the joy of our lives, and we wanted our families to have some time with her before she was much older.

Muriel was named in honor of Muriel Lemon, the pastor's wife who had had such a profound influence on my life. She was gorgeous, a beautiful, happy baby who had a disposition like sunshine. People used to stop us in the supermarket when we went shopping to comment on her beauty and sunny disposition.

"Come, look at this beautiful baby," the women cooed. "Isn't she gorgeous!"

I wasn't sure whether the fuss was because they rarely saw a black baby or if Muriel was truly that special. Of course to me she was the most beautiful baby in the world.

After a year in Colorado, I applied for a month's leave. We drove two thousand miles cross country to Philadelphia, stopping only for gas and rest-room breaks.

Home never looked so good, and I was never before so happy to see my family's faces in my life. As I crawled into bed that night, I made mental notes of all the people I would see that week. My head had barely touched the pillow when the phone rang.

"Lieutenant, the base commander is ordering all personnel back to the post immediately."

The next day the three of us piled back into the car and headed back to Colorado. We had three days to get back, so this time we didn't drive through the night. After arriving on base, I learned why we had been called back. The United States had invaded the Bay of Pigs in Cuba. When I got back, two-thirds of my unit had been shipped out.

Of the many assignments I had in the army, one of the most interesting was my service as defense counsel for enlisted men who were being court-martialed. While I had had no legal training, I felt my education as a political scholar at Morgan would help me conduct fair investigations and formulate a reasonable defense for my clients.

My first defense before a panel of senior officers involved a prison break. I read the case, researched the Court-Martial Manual, and found I had grounds for acquittal.

As the court got underway, almost immediately I announced, "I move for acquittal."

The panel looked as if they'd been slapped.

"On what grounds?"

"On the grounds that the prosecuting attorney has not proven the crime was committed," I said. "We don't have any evidence on record that a prison break took place. We don't have any witnesses."

The guy was acquitted.

Three other cases like that followed, and I was able to get the cases thrown out on technicalities. Suddenly, enlisted men from all over the base were asking me to defend them. Following my fifth consecutive acquittal, the deputy base commander asked to see me. It was extremely unusual for the deputy base commander to see a low-ranking lieutenant like myself. I couldn't imagine what he wanted.

I walked into his office, saluted, and took my seat.

"Lieutenant, we don't have any Perry Masons on this base," he began.

I was puzzled.

"Sir?"

"From this moment on you are relieved of all authority to ever defend any enlisted personnel for crimes committed while you are on this base. That's all I have to say. You may close the door when you leave."

I saluted and left. Until then, I didn't know that my position as defense attorney was merely a formality. I thought I was supposed to really try to enforce the law. Instead, the army just wanted to show, for the record, that they had provided counsel. Later the provost marshal schooled me on the procedure.

"You know, Lieutenant, no one is ever brought up on charges unless they are guilty. Your role there was a perfunctory one and you got all serious about this thing."

"Major," I said, "I'm serious about everything I do. If I can't do my best at performing a task, then I don't do it. That's my nature."

He looked at me in disbelief and said simply, "Lieutenant, you are living in a dream world. Wake up."

Maybe I was living in a dream world. Yet I knew there was only one way I could do things — what I believed to be the right way. I spent two years at Fort Carson before my army tour was up. Relieved, my family and I headed home for Philadelphia.

CHAPTER SIX

New Beginnings

When my tour at Fort Carson was completed, I looked forward to civilian life again. It was September 12, 1963, and new careers were opening for blacks as a result of the civil rights movement.

I applied to some of the school districts down South and seriously contemplated going back to North Carolina to teach. I even thought about joining the Philadelphia police department, but changed my mind. I took the civil service exam, was placed on the register, and was hired as a probation officer in the West Division of the juvenile section of the probation department.

I had a case load of about thirty kids to work with. Reviewing my cases, I found these kids had committed a wide variety of crimes: purse snatchings, assault, burglaries, as well as petty theft. Weapons charges were rare, but occasionally I got a case involving a kid with a zip gun, a homemade gun that wouldn't kill you but could inflict serious damage.

Most of these juvenile criminals were about fourteen years old. Many were repeat offenders. I was dumbfounded to find that kids under eighteen would routinely be involved in such serious crimes. My job was to see that they stayed out of trouble.

One of the first clients I visited was a fourteen-year-old

named Bobby Smith. Bobby lived on North Preston Street near Fortieth and Market in West Philadelphia. His case was representative of most of the juveniles I would meet through the probation department.

Bobby lived in a run-down row house with his mother—a woman in her late twenties who had three younger children. The front walk to the house was gouged with deep cracks, and the window in the front door appeared to have been broken ages ago. The other windows were covered with dull, thick plastic to keep out the chilly October air.

I knocked on the front door and was greeted by one of the wildest-looking women I have ever seen. She was probably pretty once, but her face had a hard edge to it now and her voice a raw bitterness.

"What do you want?" she demanded before I could explain who I was. "My son didn't do nothing. Why do you all keep bothering him? Leave him alone!"

"Miss Smith, I'm Mr. Goode from the juvenile probation department. You know I have to see Bobby for my report." She sucked her teeth and spewed forth a stream of profanity as she opened the door to let me in.

As I entered the house, the sharp stench of neglect and poverty took my breath away. The smell was a combination of urine, stale food, and must. The house badly needed cleaning and airing. I fought hard not to gag.

The sparsely decorated living room held a ragged couch, a coffee table, and an armchair. I shifted uncomfortably on the couch, trying to find a spot with enough padding to protect me from the hard, steel springs poking through the cushions. A long crack ran the length of the glass-topped coffee table like an ugly scar, and dirty cotton padding spilled from the arms of the armchair.

"Bobby! Come in here!" his mother yelled.

A slightly built, timid child walked into the room. He was short for his age, about five feet two inches, and weighed little more than one hundred pounds. His clothes were dirty and he appeared frightened. This hardly seemed like the kind of kid who would snatch an old lady's purse and knock her down so hard she had to be hospitalized.

Bobby cowered by the door like a frightened puppy.

"Miss Smith, can I talk to Bobby alone?" I asked.

"Why you need to see him alone?" she protested. "I'm his mother. I need to be here."

"Miss Smith, I need to talk to him alone."

She left the room in a huff, mumbling something under her breath. I turned my attention back to Bobby, inviting him to sit down. Reluctantly he slunk over to the armchair facing the couch. His small body was nearly swallowed by the old cushions.

"Bobby, how you doing?" I asked trying to sound upbeat.

"All right," he mumbled.

"Have you had a good day?"

"Yes."

"Is there anything I can help you with?"

"No."

I was rapidly getting nowhere. I shifted my tactics.

"Tell me about what's written here in this report."

We sat in silence for a few minutes; I stared at Bobby while he focused on some imaginary object on the floor. His eyes never glanced upwards. With each passing moment I grew more and more frustrated with the futility of the conversation and the oppressive stench.

"Do you feel like talking?" I finally asked.

"No, I don't feel like talking," he said giving me a quick glance. It was the most interaction we'd had.

"Is there any reason?"

"No, I just don't feel like talking."

"But you have to talk to me so I can fill out this report." A slight smile fluttered across his lips, then faded as suddenly as it had appeared.

"That's *your* problem," he said. "I don't want to talk."

One thing Bobby didn't count on was my stubbornness. I could be as persistent as he was sullen. It took most of the morning, but I continued to talk and cajole until Bobby loosened up. I learned that he didn't even know who his father was. He had no adult to confide in other than his mother.

"They made me do it," he finally blurted out.

My heart pounded with the realization that I had broken through.

"Who are they?"

"The gang down here. They made me snatch the purse."

"How did they do that, Bobby?"

He fought back tears as he spoke. His voice was steady but little more than a whisper as he poured out his grief.

"They told me if I didn't snatch the purse and bring them back the money, they would beat me up. Every time they saw me, they would beat me up." He sighed miserably. "I was scared. So I snatched the purse while they stood on the corner and watched."

I believed him. In the short time I had spent with Bobby, I knew he was more a victim of his surroundings than a bad kid who couldn't be controlled. Without help, though, it wouldn't be long before Bobby crossed the line where he couldn't be reached.

Bobby's background was typical of most of the cases I encountered during my first two weeks of work. Filling out my reports, I poured out their sad stories and told how I had worked with them to win their confidence. One day after I turned in one report, my supervisor, Joe Stank called me into his office. Joe was a quiet, unassuming man who had already spent some ten years in juvenile probation. Waving me to a seat, he got right to the point.

"I want you to know, Mr. Goode, that you are not a social worker. You're a probation officer."

He must have read the quizzical look on my face.

"Your reports," he said, tapping a thick sheaf of papers on his desk. "We don't want you getting involved with these kids. Your job is simply to report what's going on, not to try to solve their problems. You don't have the time to spend as much time as you do on them."

As he talked, I knew that I'd made a mistake in taking this job. There was no way I could stand by and watch kids suffer without getting involved. What was the use of making sure they stayed out of trouble if I didn't try to give them some hope or goals to shoot for? I tried to explain this to Joe, who responded by becoming even more agitated.

"Look, we want you to process five of these cases a day." I'd done only five in two days.

"Cut out the social work and keep up with your case load. We're not social workers; we're probation officers. We're not going to solve any of these kids' problems or turn them around. Our job is to make sure they're not out there violating the law. Doing anything beyond that takes too much time."

I gave the job a few more weeks, but basically I knew I couldn't spend my time watching kids throw their lives away. For a while I tried to detach my feelings from the job. But every time I met another kid and heard his story, I couldn't help but empathize and get involved.

My fourth week on the job earned me another summons to Joe's office. This time he was really angry. "This is the second time you've been in here in a month," he pointed out. "You're spending too much time working with these kids!"

I tried to protest, but he cut me off.

"Maybe you need to work for the welfare department rather than here. This is the probation department, not child welfare!"

As he bawled me out, I decided to resign. There was no way I could ever be happy on this job doing what Joe expected. Soon after that meeting I submitted my resignation, and Joe informed me I had to meet with Dr. Leonard Rosengarten, the head of the probation department, to resign.

A few days later I sat in a government office facing a huge desk where a heavyset, scowling man in shirt sleeves and glasses was seated.

"Mr. Goode, I understand you are wasting taxpayer dollars," he said. "We've had you here a month, and now you want to quit."

"Dr. Rosengarten, I think it's better for me to leave now than later," I said humbly. "I don't feel this is the place for me."

It was as if he had never heard me.

"I don't appreciate the fact that we invested all these dollars to train you and get you on the civil service list and now you want to quit!" he bellowed.

"Sir, this job isn't working for me. I feel that I have to resign now."

"You can do whatever you want to do. I just want you to know I don't like it."

Before resigning, I had called a man named Milton Clark to

ask if the job I had interviewed for before joining the probation department was still available. Luckily it was.

Milton Clark was a black entrepreneur who had opened his own window-washing company with a squeegee and a bucket back in 1947. Sixteen years later he was a financial success and a management wizard operating various enterprises. I spent what were probably the most educational two-and-a-half years of my life under his tutelage, learning all I could.

Clarkie, as I came to call him, had many traits that I admired (as well as a few that I didn't, such as his rude treatment of women). But more than anyone else, Milton Clark taught me the relationship between hard work and success, and the principles of good management.

He showed me that if you put the effort into a project, the dividends will return to you in the end. He emphasized that a good manager knows what's going on in his organization at all times because he's accountable for what happens. If you're assigned a task, go out, do the job, and make sure you do it right, he advised. If you don't, you haven't earned your pay. Also, don't ever expect to get something for nothing.

I admired Clarkie's sage wisdom and business techniques. He had some tried-and-true methods that at first I thought were rather odd but later came to respect. He had one practice, for example, of bringing all employees into his office at the end of the day to assess what they had done. He took fifteen minutes with each person to review their phone calls, asking what each caller wanted and how the employee had responded.

The first few times we went through this exercise I thought it odd. Later I realized this was how Clarkie kept abreast of everything that went on in the company. In this way he monitored the daily activities of the entire operation.

The process was overly thorough, but the principle was sound. A good manager must have some method of gathering information daily so as to be able to hold staff members accountable for their actions.

Shortly after arriving at the company, I attempted to streamline Clarkie's employee-management process.

"Mr. Clark, I think you have some real good management instincts and habits," I told him in a private meeting, "but you need to update your system so that it takes less time."

He was suspicious, but agreed to hear me out. I told him that I had discussed some ideas with one of his board members, Thacher Longstreth, who was president of the Philadelphia Chamber of Commerce and a leader in the Philadelphia Urban League.

"Talk to him and see what he has to say," I suggested.

After several conversations, Clarkie was persuaded to allow an outside firm to install a new management system in our office. The system took two-and-a-half months to design and lasted two-and-a-half weeks before Clarkie threw it out and returned to his old system.

Clarkie had the exterior gruffness of a Marine drill sergeant. One of the few things he couldn't tolerate was sloppy work. If he felt a task was done poorly, his wrath would send employees scurrying for cover.

"Harry, I got a call from the store on Fifty-second Street, and they are not satisfied with the floor you did," he bellowed one afternoon. The poor employee cringed. "How many times have I told you to strip the floor before trying to wax it? You didn't do a good job. If you want to get paid, you will go back and do it right. If you don't, I will send someone else."

Harry knew better than to question Clarkie's judgment. He redid the floor. The client was satisfied, Harry got paid, and Clarkie was happy.

Despite his tough exterior, Clarkie had a heart of gold and was an easy touch for the needy. "Mr. Clark, I'm running a little short this week. I need to borrow some money to feed my babies," one of the female workers pleaded.

Clarkie had a way of whining, but the workers knew that there wasn't anything he wouldn't do for them. This woman knew his basic decency would win out. She got the money and Clarkie kept whining—everyone was happy.

Incidentally, it was at this time while talking to one of my colleagues at Clarkie's, Elizabeth Seamon, I was complaining about people calling me "Bill."

Elizabeth said, "Well, you know they do that because of your first name—"Willie."

"I know," I said. "But my family all call me 'Wilson.'"

"Why don't you just call yourself 'W. Wilson'?" she suggested. From that point on, I did.

By the time I left Milton Clark's employment, I was twenty-six years old and had learned all that I felt I could from him. Those of us who knew him wondered what would lead to his downfall, his hot head or his soft heart. In the end it was his soft heart.

Twenty years later, I was mayor of the city when I got the news. Marge Staton, my secretary, buzzed me one morning with a call.

"Jim Jamison is on the phone. He says it's urgent."

"Marge, what does he want?"

"He says it's about Milton Clark."

I picked up the phone not knowing what to expect.

"Mr. Mayor, this is Jim," a tearful voice said, "Uncle Milton was killed last night. We tried to reach him this morning since we couldn't get him all night. When we couldn't reach him at his office, we called the police. They went in and found his body. He had been beaten to death, probably with a hammer."

"Oh my God!" I cried. "Oh my God! He was such a good man."

"Yes, he was, " Jim agreed.

My mind recalled how good Clarkie had been to me and the many lessons I had learned from him. I wanted to remember him as he had been, so full of life, so strong, so forceful, and so much in control. I couldn't imagine him dead.

I collected myself and thought about Thacher Longstreth. I wondered if he knew.

Thacher was now a Republican city councilman-at-large. Our paths had crossed again in politics. I picked up the telephone, dialed Thacher's number, and waited while his secretary connected us.

"Thacher, this is the mayor," I said when he answered.

"Yes, Mr. Mayor. It's good to hear from you."

"Thacher, I have some bad news. Milton Clark was just found murdered." The silence that followed felt like an eternity.

"Mr. Mayor," he said choking back the tears, "I loved that man. He was one of the finest men I ever knew. I told him to be careful. Why wouldn't he just listen and be careful?"

We both knew the answer. As long as Milton Clark was alive and there was someone in need, he was going to help. Later I learned that an ex-drug offender he had hired had asked if he could sleep in the office. The man didn't have a home. Clarkie readily agreed, not knowing that the man was back on drugs. Clarkie returned to the office unexpectedly one night and surprised the addict as he rummaged through the office looking for money. When Clarkie refused to give him money for drugs, the addict beat him to death.

Sometimes the events of life can take a strange twist. If you truly give your life to helping people, you always run the risk of being hurt. There's no real sacrifice without the risk of pain.

Milton Clark's life taught me much about community service. He taught me that those of us who have been blessed with special talents must give those talents back in an unselfish and uncompromising way. Those of us who hide behind a hard exterior must sometimes be guided by a soft heart.

Life offers many challenges for getting involved with others—be it in the church or in our neighborhoods working with troubled youth and adults. Those to whom God has entrusted many riches and talents are expected to give much back. God blessed Clarkie with many gifts, and Clarkie gave back just as much as he received.

The funeral for Milton Clark was held at the White Rock Baptist Church at Fifty-third and Chestnut Streets. The Rev. William Shaw was the eulogist. He gave a fitting tribute to this fallen warrior. I was recognized but did not speak. It had been twenty years since I had worked for Milton Clark, but it seemed like yesterday.

On August 9, 1965, my wife gave birth to a handsome, healthy son—W. Wilson Goode, Jr. With his birth I thought it was time I found a job with more potential for advancement. I needed to think about my future. Working for Milton Clark had been a great experience, but it was time to move on.

I found a job with the Allstate Insurance Company, becoming

the first black claims investigator to serve Montgomery County. I stayed with Allstate for about two years. I might have floundered in jobs that weren't right for me for the next ten years if one of the officials at my church, First Baptist Paschall, hadn't decided to intervene in my career. Unbeknownst to me, Mrs. Nettie Taylor had monitored my progress for several years. By now I was a trustee in the church, and she and her husband decided to give me some friendly advice.

"Wilson, you really have to start making a contribution to the city in a more direct way," Mrs. Taylor said.

In response to my "How?" Mrs. Taylor got me a job working with the Philadelphia Council for Community Advancement (PCCA). The council, a forerunner of the antipoverty programs, was funded by the Ford Foundation, and Sam Dash, a professor of law, was the first director. Sam ran PCCA and also assisted with the founding of the Opportunities Industrialization Center (OIC) and the North City Congress.

Despite his best intentions, Sam's efforts to have PCCA launch the antipoverty effort in Philadelphia never came to fruition. He and most of the people who worked for him eventually left the agency.

Its director after Sam, Graham Finney, hired me in 1966 as a program designer to create, develop, and implement community programs while surveying what community services were already being provided by other agencies.

For a year I researched every conceivable community service in Philadelphia, compiling volumes of information about community service organizations throughout the city. Unfortunately Graham and his assistant, Yvonne Perry, left the agency before I finished. A man by the name of Tom Burress was then brought in as executive director.

By now I had moved up the ladder to become housing director and was writing programs on fair housing issues. Tom Burress lasted at PCCA for about six months. He was replaced by William Cameron, who stayed a year.

By 1969, the agency had had three executive directors and several staff turnovers. The board then appointed me executive director and asked me to phase out the program. The $1 million we had left was to be systematically given away in small grants to community projects. The board had asked me to give away as much of the money as possible and then close the agency down.

That hardly seemed to be the best approach for me in my first executive job. So I looked for ways to save the agency.

Tony DeVito, an architect who served on the PCCA board, provided the first clue. "I don't want to tear this agency down, Tony," I confided one afternoon. "What do you think we can do?"

"Why don't you go back to the Ford Foundation and ask for more money?" he suggested.

"But they told us not to come back to ask for money," I replied.

"Well, then, think of something else that will earn money. You need to spend as much time thinking about ways to save the agency as you are thinking of ways to put it out of business," he advised.

He was right. I was putting too much effort into watching PCCA die. I began to wonder what I could lose in trying to get the Ford Foundation to see the benefits of its survival.

After talking with Tony, I got in touch with the Ford Foundation program director, David Carlson, who headed the housing division. The foundation had become interested in developing low- and moderate-income housing in urban areas. That became the key to our solution: PCCA would assist church groups, non-profit agencies, unions, block groups—virtually anyone who wanted to develop housing.

My job would be to take the developer by the hand from concept to completion as I found architects, FHA (Federal Housing Authority) and HUD (Housing and Urban Development) financing, and contractors to develop rental and single-family housing units. In concept, it was perhaps the most complete and innovative housing program of its time.

Ford liked the idea and began funding us in 1969. I suddenly found myself executive director of a major community housing agency committed to rebuilding deteriorated areas in Philadelphia and surrounding communities. All I had to do now was learn enough about housing to really do it.

This was certainly a critical time in our nation. The Kerner Commission had just issued its report on the causes of and recommendations following the 1960s riots. There were many social problems, and they needed to be attacked.

In the civil rights activism of the late 1960s, Americans willingly engaged in a domestic war against poverty and racism, while protesting U.S. involvement in the Indochinese jungles of Vietnam. Groups like the Urban Coalition and the National Urban League promoted visionary community-service programs that symbolized the rebirth of the inner cities. A new generation of young black men and women discovered "Black Pride" and "Black Power" in their African ancestry and wooly hair, as well as in a new community fervor that energized them to create free breakfast and lunch programs for hungry children, African heritage community schools, and biracial political coalitions.

It was in the midst of this climate of change that the renewed PCCA opened its doors in 1968. I had hired an in-house consultant, Donald Reape, to spend one year nurturing and guiding me through the rudiments of housing development. Working up to sixteen hours a day, I learned about architects, contractors, FHA guidelines, bank financing, mortgage packaging, and anything else I needed to succeed. By the end of that year, I had absorbed the mechanics of the housing development business. What I didn't know, experience would teach me.

As community groups applied for PCCA's help, I stepped through the looking glass of grass-roots politics and discovered a Philadelphia I didn't know. The Advocate Community Development Corporation in North Philadelphia, a nonprofit group directed by Episcopalian priest Father Paul Washington and his wife, Christine, was our first client. One member of the group, a slim, black Sun Company employee named Barbara Harris, would one day rise to the pinnacle of leadership in her church by becoming the first female bishop in the Episcopal church. None of us knew that at our first meeting, but that fateful April day remains etched in our minds for another reason.

The meeting was about to wind up when Father Washington walked into the room and solemnly announced, "Dr. King has just been shot. They don't think he's going to make it."

His words hit us like a shock wave. For a long time no one moved or spoke. Father Washington stood there shaking his head in disbelief. It wasn't too long afterwards that I found myself heading for the subway to go home. By the time I transferred to the trolley heading for Woodland Avenue, the disturbances had already begun. I reached Forty-ninth and Woodland Avenue to find people running amuck — breaking windows, throwing rocks and bottles, and shooting at cars.

In weeks to come, black people across the nation would unleash a flood tide of frustration in riots. They destroyed homes, businesses, and neighborhoods and recklessly claimed lives. Largely locked out of the political arena, America's disenfranchised children had taken their voices to the streets where they shouted their complaints against racist America and the untimely death of a black hero.

The lootings, shootings, and mayhem swept the nation, scarring communities from Los Angeles to Philadelphia. As neighborhoods were reduced to ashes, PCCA's job to help rebuild the city and surrounding communities became a Herculean task.

Not too long after King's death, I received a proposal from the West End Ministerium, Inc., in Chester, Pennsylvania. They had tried for years to get the Martin Luther King, Jr., Homes built. Now with King dead, completing the project had passed from the realm of dream to obsession. I worked with them to find new contractors and new financing, as well as to cut through the bureaucratic red tape that kept the houses from being completed.

I got a great deal of satisfaction out of listening to these grass-roots activists weave their dreams. It soon became clear, however, that housing contracting not only harbored dreamers but also hustlers and crooks.

Of the fifty or so projects that PCCA completed, half a dozen stand out in my mind for various reasons. The West End Ministerium Project in Chester is one of them.

Chester's city government was legendary for its history of political corruption. Illegal payoffs and kickbacks to city officials were the norm rather than the exception.

The West End Ministerium was directed by Rev. Daniel G. Scott, a tall, lanky man with thinning hair. He had invited me to speak to his coalition of ministers to explain how PCCA worked. The ministers were surprised but gratified to find that all of my services from concept to completion were free of charge. My job was to help the ministers build single-family homes in a low-income, black neighborhood on the west side of Chester, where most of these pastors had their ministries. The building project had been mired in red tape for years. Nevertheless, Rev. Scott seemed to count the mayor and several city officials among his friends.

I knew about Chester's history of political corruption but was determined to do all that I could to keep it from affecting my project. Accepting or distributing graft to get building permits would have no place in my organization.

I was scheduled to make a site visit the next day when Rev. Scott called and asked if he could see me the next morning. Curious, I agreed to the meeting.

I arrived at Rev. Scott's second-floor office early the next morning. Knocking lightly on the door, I responded to his "come in" and found him sitting in a swivel chair, eyes closed, lightly tapping his fingertips together to form a pyramid. He appeared to be in deep meditation and looked stern, very stern.

"Mr. Goode, please sit down."

I took the nearest chair, which was next to the door.

"Mr. Goode, I have watched this housing process move for a long time now. You have done a magnificent job," he said opening his eyes. "I want to congratulate you."

For a moment I looked at the outstretched hand unsure of what to do. We shook hands and I waited.

"I do have a concern though. I want to discuss it with you because I don't understand how your process works."

"That's fine with me," I said.

"Last month I saw the architect get paid. I saw the builder get paid. I saw the surveyor get paid, and you are getting your salary through your agency. Everybody seems to be getting something out of this. I just want to know, as a point of protocol, who takes care of me?"

I could barely believe what I was hearing. The president of the religious coalition that had fought so hard to build affordable housing for poor people wanted to know where his kickback was. I was disappointed in Rev. Scott's behavior. I met his gaze and stared deep into his eyes.

"Mr. Goode, do you understand what I am asking?"

"Yes, Rev. Scott, I understand. And I just want to say to you, the good Lord will take care of you." I stood up and walked out.

Rev. Scott got a very clear message from me. Neither of us mentioned the incident again. We proceeded with the business at hand—completing the houses.

We completed the West End Ministerium Project using a black architect out of Cleveland and the C. White Construction Co., a black contractor from Philadelphia. The two businesses worked well together, and I was satisfied with the results.

In its enthusiasm to win the job, however, C. White Construction had underbid the project and was making very little profit. I held them to their contracted bid. When they saw they wouldn't make much profit on the project, they tried to sue me for "involuntary servitude." The judge laughed that one right out of court.

I have learned that housing development, like politics, is unpredictable. There's no telling who you might find in the housing business or the kind of creativity you might have to use to make a project work.

The Ardmore Community Development Group in Ardmore, Pennsylvania, submitted a proposal for us to help them build twenty-four row houses. The only problem was that Ardmore had an ordinance against building row houses. Cooperatives and condominiums were acceptable, as were single-family or semidetached and detached houses, but not row houses.

I met with Nolan N. Atkinson, Jr., the group's attorney, to see if we could find a solution. Searching the town's housing laws together, Nolan and I gradually became close friends. We read housing codes, talked to housing officials, and searched neighborhoods to find a solution. I met with the group's housing contractors every day. We also did a lot of thinking out loud as we tossed suggestions back and forth and tried to work out the problems. Finally someone hit on what sounded like a workable solution.

"Why not build twenty-four row houses under one roof and call them condominiums?"

As crazy as it sounded, the idea fit the town's housing codes. We filed a condominium application to build twenty-four houses, side by side under one roof, and it was approved. Ard-Spring Condominiums were born.

To comply with the condominium license, we sold shares in
the corporation and hired a housing management agency to take
care of common areas such as the parking lot and sidewalks.

Helping community groups build and renovate houses
honed my management skills to a razor-sharp edge. Often I had
to be financial manager, diplomat, administrator, architect, contractor, and community organizer to translate dreams into realities. I think I was successful largely because I approached each
project as a sacred mission. It was common for me to work from
early morning to midnight until a project was completed. I also
believed that every project was possible to achieve.

There is perhaps nothing that requires more faith than to
look at a trash-strewn lot and imagine it landscaped and filled
with rows of new houses. You have to envision families living
there and kids playing happily on green lawns, with nice cars
parked in the driveways. You have to envision taxes being collected to run a city, people working, and a community living
together. If you can't get excited about the potential of a garbage-
filled lot, housing development can be a difficult career.

Among the many challenges I faced as a developer was finding creative ways to finance the development of multiple-family
dwellings. The Reverend Cecil Gallup of Holy Trinity Enterprises
Project offered such a challenge. It was difficult, if not impossible, to find financing for multifamily units. Searching the federal
housing regulations, I discovered a little-known HUD program,
235(j), which financed the development of duplex housing for
low-income families. That meant we could develop the units we
needed for seven families as well as seven income-producing
units to help the families make money to pay for their homes.

The program worked extraordinarily well. We found a row of
old brownstones located in a rundown area of the 2200 block of
Fitzwater Street. The block had decayed, but the brownstones
were sound. Once renovated, they would be large, elegant
structures.

Again we used a minority contractor to turn the units into
duplexes. Today those homes are in a neighborhood that has
become one of Philadelphia's trendiest middle- and upper-in-
come areas. The families who invested in those houses still own

them and will make hundreds of thousands of dollars profit whenever they sell.

I believe it was faith—my faith and the faith of those families—that made Rev. Cecil Gallup's development so successful. Many people, including some in the Gallup organization, never believed the homes would amount to much. We worked two years before they began to blossom. But when they did, it was like watching a child grow up. First it was a baby, dependent and often messy. Then it was a toddler, frustrating but with lots of potential. As the renovations advanced, the homes blossomed into a bright adolescence. Finally they emerged fully grown with their own charm and personality.

I experienced a similar feeling of satisfaction as I worked with tenants in the Dorothy Nelson-Brown Homes Housing Project, even though the process wasn't quite as smooth.

Three women, Jerri Williams, Margaret McMullen, and Yvonne Cross headed the group. A fourth person, Dorothy Nelson-Brown, died before the project was completed. The women were all single mothers, with four or five children, living in a city housing project. My guess is they ranged in age from their late twenties to early thirties. The oldest might have been forty.

None of the women had college degrees or professional careers, if any jobs at all. What they did have was an unwavering determination and vision unlike any I had ever seen.

Their dream was to build eighty-eight single-family homes on land they'd won in a settlement with Temple University. In the 1960s, Temple University had expanded to the point that the community began to resent the university's encroachment. Neighbors protested, blocked traffic, and picketed to stop the expansion.

Round-the-clock meetings were held between Temple representatives and the community until an agreement was reached. It was agreed that a tract of land would be turned over to the community for a housing development. I'm sure Temple thought the residents would never do it, but Temple didn't know these women. I never doubted from the minute I met them that they would keep going until the houses were built.

The women would then sell the houses to low-income families in their housing project as well as to people from throughout the city. My job was to turn their dream into reality.

My first task was to get the group incorporated. Jerri became president. The other two were made vice president and secretary-treasurer. I wanted to expand the corporation, but they protested, arguing, "No, the three of us work well together, and we don't want to disrupt that communication. We're in charge of this. This is our corporation and we know what we want to get done. But we'd like you to work with us."

Working with those women proved to be the most instructive, though difficult, learning experience in my housing career. While they had the best intentions in the world, they were probably the most mistrusting souls you could find. They had to know everything.

Sometimes I met with them six or seven hours a day to review the details of a project or something that had happened earlier that day. We often met at Mrs. McMullen's house. We'd get there at 6:00 P.M. and leave around midnight. She never offered us food or a glass of water. We were there to work!

I understood, though, and was just as determined as they were to see the project completed.

Looking back years later I remembered that building the houses had not been without mishaps in the three years it took to complete the project. One architect we hired moved to Colorado and abandoned us halfway through the project, and a minority contractor was in over his head with the size of the development. At one point, we needed special approval from the city to complete the project. This time I turned out to be the hindrance. Goldie Watson, the deputy mayor at the time, called me into her office to explain.

"The mayor does not want you involved in his project in any way, Wilson," she said. "He won't give it any money as long as you're connected with it."

The word was that Mayor Frank Rizzo resented my involvement in groups such as the American Civil Liberties Union (ACLU) and Americans for Democratic Action (ADA). He had

pegged me as a "bleeding-heart liberal." I told Goldie I wasn't
getting any money from the project.

"Then just make sure your name doesn't appear on any
document that comes in here," she warned. "Otherwise he won't
approve it."

The style was typical Rizzo. There was no way he would let
any of his real, or perceived, enemies benefit from "his" government. He didn't care that his malice might destroy the dreams of
some innocent people. It was his government, and those who
were against him shouldn't receive any city benefits in any way.

It was on this point that Rizzo erred most. The government
doesn't belong to any elected official. It belongs to the people.
And in a democracy you must be able to disagree, have different
viewpoints, and still fully participate in the fruits of democracy.

We celebrated when the Dorothy Nelson-Brown Homes became a reality. The three women succeeded in selling the homes
to between 10 and 20 percent of the tenants in their housing
project. The remaining buyers came from throughout the city.

The determination of those three women didn't stop with the
housing project. One went to college and became a teacher. All
three became homeowners. I don't think you'll find anywhere
else in this country an example of three public-housing tenants
building a housing project of this size.

Jack Kemp now talks about tenant management, but these
women set the standard twenty years ago. The difference then
and now is that the federal government took away the tools to
develop these kinds of homes. And if state senator Chaka Fattah
is interested in a model for his American Cities Project, the Nelson-Brown Homes is the best example anyone could find. All
that is needed now are the tools to duplicate it.

Three other projects stand out: Lipscomb Square developed
by Alice Lipscomb in South Philadelphia, a sixty-five unit cooper-
ative; Mount Carmel Gardens headed by Rev. Albert Campbell, a
forty-eight-unit apartment complex adjoining the church on a
piece of ground where a vacant warehouse once stood; the Reverend Robert Johnson Smith's development of a seventeen-unit
apartment complex in Jenkintown, Pennsylvania, in a burned-

out apartment complex. These unique leaders took long-de-
ferred dreams and turned them into reality.

PCCA marked the awakening of my political career. As a
housing activist, I gained citywide recognition for my achievements as I networked with business leaders, politicians, and
grass-roots organizations throughout the city. At the same time I
earned a master's degree in governmental administration from
the Wharton School of the University of Pennsylvania. I attended
at night, finishing in two-and-a-half years. At the time it seemed
like a huge sacrifice, but it prepared me for many things to come.

Long before set-aside programs and other affirmative action
programs, PCCA was pushing the concept of using minority contractors, architects, and engineers in the development business.
At a time when city and federal contracts awarded to minority
contractors were practically nil, 90 percent of the builders I used
were minorities. I believed that to rebuild our minority communities we should use the skills of our own people, so I strongly
encouraged the nonprofit groups to use minority contractors and
management firms. It was another way I felt I could contribute
to the civil rights effort.

I loved community service. As that love intensified, I felt the
need to make a choice to either spend my life helping people
through public service or start climbing the corporate ladder to
have a platform from which to serve others. As executive director
of PCCA I had attracted the notice of grass-roots activists, local
politicians, and ward leaders who held a vision of developing a
multiracial coalition of political reformers to counteract the old
system of party politics and patronage.

In 1972, the Jaycees civic organization named me "Outstanding Young Leader of the Year" for my work with PCCA and other
organizations. I beat out Congressman Bill Green for the honor.

Another finalist was Lynne M. Abraham, the executive director of the Redevelopment Authority. She is now Philadelphia's
District Attorney. I had not known Lynne well before the ceremonies. As I was standing in line to go in for a photo session,

someone slapped me on my backside. Stunned, I turned and saw it was Lynne Abraham.

"I hope I didn't shock you too much, but I'm a butt slapper." She had this devilish look on her face, and I knew she felt comfortable. So after my temporary shock, I laughed and we proceeded to the photo session. I could see why they called her a "tough cookie."

In accepting the award as the Jaycees' outstanding young leader, I could have said all the right things and graciously accepted the award, but I was moved to do more than that.

> I am pleased at the recognition, but sad because my son and daughter are, even while I speak, being denied the right to a quality public education in our school system.
>
> I am sad because the poor are still ill-fed and ill-housed, and while I speak, the abandonment of our city increases. I am sad because even with all the ill-housed and even with all the abandonment, the president has announced a moratorium on *all* solutions to these problems.
>
> Things will not change. Things will not get better until and unless an aroused and intolerant public gets involved. The time for action is now, by me, by you, by all of us. Let's not fail our city. Let's not fail ourselves, and for God's sake let's not fail our children.

Recognition as the Jaycees' outstanding young leader increased my public image and stature. Immediately afterwards I was approached to run for city controller. I felt the timing was wrong and said so. I didn't want to use my award as leverage to launch a political career though supporters asked, "What good is that award if you can't do something for yourself?"

I didn't see it that way. I had won the award because of my work with the neighborhood groups. My immediate goal was to finish those projects. I felt that God was using me to help some of the groups who had struggled for years to rebuild their neighborhoods. Without my help in cutting through the layers of bureaucratic red tape, they may not have gotten the government loans or city licenses to rehabilitate broken-down buildings or build new houses. PCCA helped build over two thousand housing units in Philadelphia. At no time before, or since, has any agency come close to matching that feat.

As PCCA was beginning to move to help rebuild neighborhoods, other significant efforts were under way to help change the plight of poor and minority residents. At the forefront of this were ministers and reform-minded community activists.

Ministers helped pave the political path that many black elected officials tread today. Beginning with the Reverend Leon H. Sullivan's successful boycott of the Tasty Baking Company to force the hiring of black drivers and leading up to the founding of the Black Political Forum in 1968, churches have been at the forefront of community activism in Philadelphia.

The founding members of the Black Political Forum (BPF) were twenty-five men led by John F. White, Sr., chairman of the deacon board of the Nineteenth Street Baptist Church. Early members included Hardy Williams, a ward leader in West Philadelphia; Dr. George French, assistant school superintendent; businessmen, educators, white-collar workers, and laborers. Our goal was to build a political coalition of reformers who would help put in office black politicians who were accountable to the people who elected them, not the Democratic party. There could be no real empowerment among black voters until more blacks entered the political process and we chose our own candidates.

The BPF's vision was ambitious. No black elected official had ever won public office in Philadelphia without the endorsement of the Democratic party. Put bluntly, the Democratic party had always selected the black leadership for the black community. No one won without their support.

We aimed to change that by successfully running Hardy Williams for state office. I was selected to be his campaign manager. Hardy appointed Paul Vance, a middle school principal, as co-campaign manager with me. Paul and I worked well together.

The founding of the BPF also coincided with the election of Richard Nixon as president of the United States and an upcoming mayor's race in Philadelphia. Talk was that Frank Rizzo, the swaggering, loud-talking police commissioner, would be the next mayor. Rizzo was promoting a law-and-order campaign that he boasted would make "Attila the Hun look like a faggot!"

As police commissioner, Rizzo had helped turn Philadelphia into a police state where charges of police brutality by black citizens were commonplace. No black person was safe from Rizzo's troops as illustrated by a November 17, 1967, demonstration where police officers attacked a citywide coalition of black students. The students were marching to the school board to demand that black studies courses be included in their curriculum. Several people were beaten, including state representative David Richardson. Throughout the attack on the youth, Rizzo allegedly yelled, "Get their black asses! Get their black asses!"

Locked out politically by machine politicians such as Rizzo, black reformers had historically used boycotts and nonviolent protests to draw attention to their causes. Among the most successful activists using these methods was the black church. The black church was, and remains, one of the most significant grassroots political forces in Philadelphia politics.

The BPF understood the power of independent politics and was counting on it to propel Hardy Williams to victory. If we meant to change the complexion of Philadelphia city government, we knew we had to do it by uniting the black and liberal white vote.

One of our first efforts to build community unity was to hold a dinner at which Richard Gordon Hatcher, the newly elected black mayor of Gary, Indiana, was the guest speaker. Hatcher came and explained how he had built his coalition over a period of five or six years, moving from fighting the political system to petitioning it to finally controlling the system by capturing his city's highest office. He encouraged us to recognize we could not build a political base overnight. It would take time. But if we charted our course, he said, we could win state seats, top congressional seats and even the office of the mayor.

The dinner was a turning point for the Black Political Forum. More than a thousand people attended. Hatcher's speech energized us and renewed our hopes for political empowerment. I would remember Hatcher's words and gain much strength from them as we worked to create a new political reality in Philadelphia.

Hardy's campaign got underway in 1969. He was running for state representative against an entrenched incumbent named Paul Lawson, a labor leader who had the party's endorsement as well as labor support. We put together a door-to-door campaign that operated six days a week. Although political nay-sayers and the media predicted our doom, we were determined to succeed.

On election day we combed the district to get out the vote—
knocking on doors to remind people to vote and providing cars
and buses for transportation. To the media's amazement, we beat
the machine two to one. Hardy won the primary and went on to
become the first black official elected in Philadelphia without
Democratic party endorsement.

The state house seat was only the beginning. We felt we had
to attack the system citywide. In 1971, Hardy decided to run for
mayor. No one who had worked on the earlier campaign believed Hardy could win the mayor's office. It just wasn't time. But
we agreed that it was time for people to recognize that a black
person could run for the mayor's office and be considered a
serious candidate. In the primaries, Hardy ran as Democratic
candidate for mayor against Democrat Frank Rizzo and Congressman Bill Green III.

I was selected to be election-day coordinator and co-campaign manager. We followed our old formula, launching another
door-to-door campaign. On primary election day Hardy captured
12.5 percent of the votes, receiving support from fifty thousand
voters. Green won 38 percent of the votes, though he captured
more than 50 percent of the votes in black wards. Rizzo won 48
percent.

The process was a victory for the black voters of Philadelphia
as they exercised their voting muscle and political savvy. They
sent two strong messages. The first was that black voters were
more willing to support a white liberal like Green who could win
the mayoral election than a black candidate who was relatively
unknown to white voters. The second message was that black
voters would do anything to defeat Frank Rizzo.

In the general election, black voters joined white liberals in
supporting Republican candidate Thacher Longstreth, executive
vice president of the Philadelphia Chamber of Commerce, and
came close to defeating Rizzo.

In a polling of ten wards in which 90 percent of the registered
voters were black, Rizzo won only 23 percent of the vote. Citywide, 64 percent of the registered black voters went to the polls,
and of that number 77 percent voted against Rizzo.

With the support of black voters, the liberal white and black
reform coalition was becoming a formidable contender in Phila-

delphia politics. After running Hardy Williams, the coalition put its strength behind David P. Richardson, whom we successfully ran against a white incumbent in his district. (We literally had to register Richardson to vote before we could run him!)

A year later Bill Gray came to me to ask for help in running against the incumbent Democratic party candidate for Congress. Gray came within a few hundred votes of defeating the incumbent. He ran again in 1978 and won.

Throughout the late sixties and most of the seventies, BPF flexed its muscles and sent a powerful message to the Democratic party. The forum was not a black social club but a formidable political entity. Our goal was not only to try to legislate which candidates would win but also to educate the grass-roots community about the political process, the candidates running, and their records in supporting black causes.

Without the Black Political Forum and the kind of groundwork we laid over a decade, I don't think it would have been possible for me to have been elected mayor in 1983.

CHAPTER SEVEN

Fighting City Hall

My job in the probation department had whetted my appetite for working with kids. So I looked for volunteer work or something I could do in community service to help children. My search led me back to my old neighborhood and the Paschall Betterment League.

The Paschall Betterment League was comprised of a dozen neighborhood people who did some of the work and made all of the decisions about activities in the community. Almeta Gross was the president. Mrs. Gross was a member of the Murphy family, an established black clan that had lived in Paschall since the turn of the century. Between Mrs. Gross and her two sisters, the family ran the whole neighborhood.

As president, Mrs. Gross was also the most vocal of the league members and the most visible community leader. She was not college educated but possessed uncanny energy and drive as well as a practical intelligence that folks called "Mother Wit." My involvement in the community and subsequent election as Paschall Betterment League vice president had obviously threatened her. Immediately after I was elected vice president, Mrs. Gross began querying neighbors about my involvement in the community.

"What is he trying to do?" she asked neighbors, attempting to raise suspicion about me. "Why is he trying to take over? He doesn't even live in this neighborhood."

The past decade had been hard on the Paschall community. Velma and I hadn't lived there since I'd gone into the army. My family had moved out a few years earlier, after several of the businesses had closed. The businesses that remained rarely hired local black residents, claiming they couldn't find qualified workers. Police brutality against blacks in the neighborhood was also a common complaint, as was poor city services. The kids in Paschall still lacked a playground or recreation center. And whites in the surrounding communities were as hostile as ever to their Paschall neighbors; incidents of black children being beaten by whites as they walked to school continued to occur.

Mrs. Gross was understandably suspicious of why I would want to return. She didn't realize how deep my emotional roots were in Paschall. The community had been my first home outside of North Carolina, and many of the residents who remained were mentors and friends who had helped me become the man that I was. I felt I owed that community something.

After discussing Paschall's problems with Velma, we agreed in 1964 to move into a new Paschall development of single-family houses located in the 6900 block of Greenway Avenue, the closest block to the adjoining white neighborhood. Our daughter Muriel was about four years old at the time.

The 6900 block of Greenway Avenue turned out to be the battlefield for blacks and whites in the two neighborhoods. Fights usually erupted after a group of white kids attacked some black kids as they walked through the white neighborhood on their way to school. Blacks would retaliate by beating up a white youth.

With an unsettling frequency, large bands of white teenagers and adults from the white sections of Greenway Avenue would march onto our street shouting racial epithets and looking for trouble.

"Niggers go home!"

"Niggers go back to Africa!"

"We're going to get us a nigger tonight!"

I had heard words like that my whole life. On one of these

occasions, I got so mad I grabbed a monkey wrench and ran outside, shouting back at the angry mob. Harry Brown, a neighbor and a police officer, stopped me.

"Look, Brother Goode, you are a leader in this community. These folks are looking to you for leadership. You can't lead when you're angry and acting like the mob. Give me that wrench and go on down there and cool these people off."

I wanted to strike back, but I knew Mr. Brown was right. I reluctantly took his advice but said very little to him at the time. Later when I saw him on the block, I said, "Thank you, Mr. Brown. You were right. I don't want to be acting that way."

After I had calmed down, I walked down the street and confronted the mob. In a few minutes it was over with. I guess all those years of being put down by white people had brought me to the boiling point.

The racial confrontations were always ugly. As word got out about the white mobs on the streets, blacks from Seventieth and Seventy-first Streets banded together to form a countermarch. Meeting on Sixty-ninth Avenue, they fought until the police arrived. Such fights occurred frequently until the late 1970s.

Two years after I moved into the neighborhood, I was elected president of the Paschall Betterment League. Years of hard work and loyalty to the league had earned me the community's respect and Mrs. Gross's support. She willingly stepped aside as president to let me take over and remained a strong supporter.

My first task as president was to assess the community's needs and decide what the league could do about them. Finding problems was easy. The community needed everything! But housing, jobs, and recreation were the most pressing issues.

In my work with the PCCA, we had guided community groups like the Paschall Betterment League in rehabilitating and developing housing. Through PCCA I helped the league apply for and receive a federal housing grant to rehabilitate a row of abandoned houses in the 7000 block of Upland Street. I then went to work to find jobs for people.

General Electric was located on the edge of the community at Sixty-eighth and Elmwood. George Branch, one of GE's black executives, was assigned to talk to me about why GE had hired so few black people from the neighborhood. I was delighted to find Mr. Branch to be an open-minded man who was very much concerned about GE's standing in the Paschall community.

"Mr. Goode, work with me," he said. "We'll put people to work who are willing to work, but you must help me find them."

George Branch was as good as his word. Over the next year, GE hired about fifty people from the neighborhood. A year later many of these same people were laid off and there were no new hires, but some of the neighbors hired by GE held on to those jobs for years. It was a bittersweet victory.

Between my job with PCCA and my community work with the Paschall Betterment League, I gained a better sense of how the federal and local bureaucracies worked. I learned that it was true that the wheels of justice turned exceedingly slowly. Our effort to get a playground built in the community was proof of that. After months of appeals to politicians and agencies, we were no closer to getting a playground than before we began.

"We can sit here all day long waiting for the city to help us, or we can go out and do something for ourselves!" I complained to anyone willing to listen.

In the midst of my complaints, I stumbled across a newspaper article announcing that Gino's fast-food chain was willing to help communities develop playgrounds. The Gino's office in Valley Forge, Pennsylvania, had already funded several community projects.

Two vacant lots in the neighborhood, one at Seventy-first and Paschall Avenue, the other at Seventy-second and Yocum, were ideal sites for playgrounds, I thought. We might be able to get one of those lots through the city's beautification program, which awarded city lots to communities who could provide the resources to beautify them. If the city could give us the lot, maybe Gino's would finance the redevelopment.

The playground project was a major eyeopener for me. I suddenly realized that being a neighborhood activist was a pretty big deal in many people's eyes. As I pulled the business and political power brokers together, I was seen as someone with clout and influence in high places. People started coming out of the woodwork to offer help in getting the playground built.

Gino executives visited the neighborhood to tour the lots and awarded us a fifty-thousand-dollar grant. The city eventually gave us one of the lots, and we used the Gino's grant to do the construction. Watching the transformation of that vacant lot into a playground was like witnessing the miracle of birth. Slowly it changed from a barren plot of ground into a fertile, green playground. An elegant, cement sprinkler pool rose from the center of the field, which was bordered by a ring of lush trees. Finally Paschall had its own playground.

The dedication ceremony was a festive event with food, balloons, and appearances by politicians who hadn't been to the neighborhood in years, if ever. Councilman Bill Cibotti and Congressman Bill Barrett joined Gino executives, Paschall residents, business leaders, and other friends to applaud the community's success.

I was on "cloud nine," basking in a warm glow of achievement that lasted throughout the day and into the next morning. My telephone rang at 6:00 A.M..

"Brother Goode, you up?"

The caller was Mrs. Ethel Manuel, an elderly woman who served as treasurer of the Paschall Betterment League. Most people knew me to be an early riser, so I wasn't surprised by the call.

"Yes, Mrs. Manuel."

"Got some bad news for you."

"Who's sick, Mrs. Manuel?"

"No one's sick. Those doggone kids done tore down every tree in that playground!"

My heart started to pound wildly, and I could almost feel my blood pressure rising.

"What are you talking about, Mrs. Manuel?"

By the time she finished her story, I was furious. I ran outside, gunned the engine of my car, and tore down the street to the playground about three blocks away. I got out and approached the field slowly, unable to believe what I saw. For a few moments I stood quietly shaking my head and blinking back the tears. Every single tree surrounding the playground lay on the ground, mangled and torn.

Who would do something like this? I asked myself. We had worked so hard, so hard for this neighborhood, and in one day it was practically ruined.

It was Saturday, and I spent the rest of the day walking

around the neighborhood asking kids and adults if they knew anything about the trees. Almost everyone I asked came up with the same answer—the Lloyd boys.

The Lloyd boys were three brothers who lived in the 7100 block of Greenway Avenue. They ranged in age from eight to eleven years old and were neighborhood terrors. I'd heard of other Lloyd boys' escapades that had made my skin crawl, but the tree destruction seemed to be even beyond them, or so I hoped.

When I got back to the playground, I was surprised to find the youngest of the Lloyd boys standing there. Without thinking, I hurried over to him.

"Did you tear down those trees?" I asked, trying to control my temper.

His face knotted into a snarl of contempt.

"None of your business!" he snapped.

Before I knew what I was doing, I grabbed his arm and started shaking him as I questioned him about the trees. The child screamed at the top of his lungs as he kicked and clawed to get free. Before long, something hit my back as his brothers came to his defense, clawing and screaming as they fought.

"Leave our little brother alone! Leave him alone! You're a grown man picking on our little brother!"

Still I wouldn't let go. I don't know if I was holding on in self-defense or anger. I just refused to let these little demons have their way.

Before long the boys' mother and aunt arrived at the scene with a host of neighbors. Embarrassed, I was able to settle down. The youngest Lloyd boy stood behind his mother, whimpering and wiping his eyes.

"Mr. Goode, what's wrong with you, picking on my boys?" Mrs. Lloyd asked angrily. "They're just children."

"Your boys tore down those trees."

She looked puzzled.

"My boys never did anything like that."

"Then why is everyone in the neighborhood telling me that they did?"

That afternoon was probably one of the worst days of my life. I had gotten frustrated and angry beyond reason. Why else would

I grab a child's arm like that? True, he was a terror, but he was still a child.

The tree incident remained a sore point between the Lloyd family and me for months. At least we still have the sprinkler pool, I thought. With time the whole ugly memory will fade away. I got some people to help me clean up the mess and replant the least damaged trees. Two months later we set a date to turn on the sprinkler pool.

The day of the sprinkler ceremony dawned hot and sunny. As I approached the playground, I saw that a large crowd of people had arrived ahead of me. I could tell by the expressions on some of the faces that something was wrong. I glanced at the trees; they looked okay. The grounds looked fine. Then I saw it. In the center of the pool the iron rods leading to the sprinkler pool system rose twisted and curled beyond repair. Someone must have taken a sledgehammer and worked half the night to destroy them.

I could feel the bottom dropping out of the pit of my stomach, but I kept my composure as eyes watched to see what I would do. I'd already learned the hard way that if I was going to be in the business of helping people, I had to control my temper.

I had originally gone into community service to help families and children. That's why getting the playground had been so important. The incident with the Lloyd boys showed me how easy it is to lose sight of one's priorities. In my zeal to keep my beautiful playground nice, I had missed seeing that maybe a child was deeply troubled and crying out for help. The Lloyd boy might have been using his anger to send out a plea for help, but in my anger I failed to hear.

The playground lesson also taught me some powerful dynamics about community organizing. I learned that no group of ten or twelve people can speak for a whole community. To be truly successful, community activism must empower the people who are being served by involving them in the decision-making process. Otherwise, even good ideas, like building a playground, become problematic. Everyone needs to feel ownership in a decision that affects their lives. From the senior citizens on down to the children, the total community must be included. If not, the people of that community will rebel.

Again, I got a crew to help me clean up the lot. With their help we also put in a homemade sprinkler system, which the children enjoyed for six or seven summers.

We renewed our efforts to get a community recreation center when we learned that the Fels Naptha Soap Company was scheduled to close sometime in 1969 or 1970. The company was located in a huge building on Seventy-third and Saybrook Avenue.

For months, on behalf of the league, I wrote to state representative James O'Donnell, the Democratic ward leader in the Paschall area, requesting that he intervene on our behalf. He promised over and over again that he would act, but did nothing. I now knew that it was time to try another method, especially after we learned that O'Donnell supported having the Fels building turned into a halfway house for prisoners.

In July 1970, I called a meeting of the league and showed them my letters to O'Donnell and his responses. I wanted us to go on the offensive, to picket the facility or hold some kind of public demonstration to have our complaints aired.

"If we don't do something as a neighborhood, they're going to put a halfway house here," I said. "We're concerned about preventing people from going to jail, not taking care of them while they are there! We want to build a facility that will make a halfway house unnecessary. I don't understand Mr. O'Donnell's response."

To my surprise, the vote to demonstrate was not unanimous.

"You can't fight City Hall. You can't fight the state," a league member declared. "Why do you want to start all this trouble out here, Wilson? We've never had any trouble before. Just keep writing the people, and maybe we'll get what we want."

I was relentless, believing if we gave up now there was no telling what they would put in the neighborhood. Today it was a halfway house. Tomorrow, a prison? Or perhaps some other kind of facility that would destroy more of the peace of our already embattled community. No! I wouldn't allow it. Besides, O'Donnell had promised he would help.

"To get what we want, we must take it by civil disobedience," I said, pounding my fist on the table. "No one's going to give us anything if we aren't willing to fight for it."

By the end of the meeting, half of the league supported me and the other half thought I was just asking for trouble by picking a fight with City Hall. As I saw it, the politicians had thrown the first punch by lobbying to put a halfway house in our community. I wasn't about to walk away from a fight.

I was fired up! Ready to take on Goliath! And when the first demonstration planning meeting was held at the First Baptist Church of Paschall, I explained our cause with an intensity and fervor that had people leaping to their feet. Word spread rapidly throughout the community: We were going to demonstrate to block a halfway house from coming into our neighborhood.

Women, children, senior citizens, and a handful of men helped make picket signs that read "Down with O'Donnell!" "Recreation Not Prisoners!" "O'Donnell Lies." "We Want a Recreation Center, Not a Prison."

The plan was to begin picketing on Island Avenue in front of the Fels building that July. Our protest would be made most effective, we decided, if we blocked the flow of traffic leading out to the airport and created a scene in front of the site in question. The television cameras would love it.

Picketing commenced on a hot July evening after work when the flow of traffic was heaviest. The first night brought out about thirty neighbors, mostly women and children, to form the picket line. Drivers blared their horns and cussed the picketers as tempers flared from frustration and heat.

Bernard Lee, a sixteen-year-old junior in high school, joined me at the front of the line. Bernard was president of a youth group that met in the basement of my home.

Our second night out George Fencl, head of the police department's civil disobedience unit, arrived on site and ordered us to stop the protest or face arrest.

"Mr. Fencl, Mr. O'Donnell can stop this problem immediately by withdrawing his support for the halfway house," I told him. "Otherwise we're not leaving."

"If you're here tomorrow, we're going to arrest you," Fencl threatened.

That night the protest got a brief mention on the evening news. The next night fifty people showed up on the picket line. An irate driver nearly caused an accident, ramming through the picketers at a high rate of speed. The line parted like the Red Sea as screaming women and children jumped out of the way of the vehicle. But no one left the line, and just as quickly as the sea of people had parted, it came back together again to form a human fortress.

The protests continued every evening from six until eight. We never got a lot of media attention, but the few media mentions we got buoyed the determination of the strong corps of neighbors who kept the demonstration going.

A week after the protests began, George Fencl returned to make good on his promise. I was arrested and taken to the police station six blocks away as the remaining demonstrators hoisted their signs high, chanting, "No! No! No!" We'd made plans even for this, appointing a list of people as alternate leaders as each one of us was arrested.

At the police station Fencl pleaded with me to stop the demonstrations.

"What will it take for you to end this thing?"

I thought for a moment before answering.

"It will take a meeting with some high-level city officials who can do something to halt that halfway house," I said.

Fencl looked pleased.

"All right. I'll arrange everything."

I left the station house that evening with a deep sense of satisfaction that we were on the verge of something powerful if our little protest could attract the attention of City Hall. The picketing continued for several weeks and several more arrests. Fencl returned to see me and said that he could arrange the meeting at City Hall if the picketing stopped.

"No, arrange the meeting first, and then I'll stop the picketing."

"I want the picketing to stop first," he said.

"Mr. Fencl, we have been out here too long to give up now."

"Please trust me, Mr. Goode. If you stop the picketing, you will get the meeting. But I can't arrange a meeting before then."

I thought about our options and decided to give it a try.

"All right, Mr. Fencl. We will trust you for forty-eight hours. If we don't have a meeting by then, we will resume with double the people. They're not going to put a halfway house in our neighborhood."

"Believe me, you can trust me," Fencl said. "I'll be back to you in a day or so."

Forty-eight hours later the meeting date was set.

I called a special meeting of the Paschall Betterment League five days before the meeting to discuss our strategy. The group decided I would be the spokesperson and go to City Hall. Our defense against the halfway house would be the preservation and improvement of our neighborhood for our children.

"We care about keeping kids out of jail first," I was to tell the city officials. "We can serve more kids by giving them a recreation center than a halfway house."

I arrived at City Hall later that week, excited and nervous. This was the first time I had ever been in the municipal services building, and as I walked through those hallowed halls, I couldn't help but be impressed by the ornate architecture and police security force that stood like palace guards on duty. I was to meet with managing director Fred Corleto and police commissioner Frank Rizzo. I knew the names, but had never met either one of them. I prayed silently that I would conduct myself well in this meeting. We had fought so hard; I didn't want to mess it up now because I felt intimidated and way out of my league.

The secretary directed me into a conference room where a group of men were seated at a long table. I recognized Fencl but not the others who were introduced to me. Fred Corleto was seated at the head of the table, with Frank Rizzo on his right. Fencl opened the discussion, asking me to explain my problem.

Nervously I laid out the whole story: the letters I had sent to O'Donnell; our amazement at finding out that O'Donnell had tricked us by supporting the halfway house even after he agreed to look into our needs; the decision to demonstrate; and, finally, our request for a meeting with city officials.

I don't know how long I talked or exactly what I said, but I was encouraged that they let me speak uninterrupted, except for an occasional question. When I had concluded my monologue,

Corleto attempted to say something, only to be interrupted by Rizzo.

"Mr. Goode, I'm Frank Rizzo," he said rising to his feet. I looked up to see what must have been the biggest human being I had ever seen in my life. I could only imagine that this is what Goliath looked like to David.

Rizzo was a big, beefy man whose presence made him appear larger than he really was. As he spoke, he pointed a forceful finger in my face to punctuate each word. His deep, booming voice sounded like the wrath of God. I would not want to get into a fight with this man, I thought.

"I want you to know, if you don't want that facility in your neighborhood, you won't have it there!" Rizzo said. "I'm sure Mr. Corleto will take care of it by seeing that a letter is directed to the right officials in the recreation department."

I was riveted to my seat, intimidated by the power of Rizzo's words as well as his command of the room. Doesn't he work for Fred Corleto? I wondered. Why doesn't he let Corleto speak?

As Rizzo continued to speak, I answered my own question. This man is going to be the next mayor, I thought, and Corleto knows it.

When Corleto did speak, he confirmed everything Rizzo had directed. I left the meeting elated and awed by the political process. The issue that had consumed us for months had been settled in a couple of hours.

Our victory earned our league an upbeat "You *Can* Fight City Hall" story on KYW-TV with reporter Andrea Mitchell. When I called a victory meeting of the Paschall Community Betterment League to discuss our next move, two hundred people showed up to cheer and applaud, jubilant that we had fought City Hall and won.

"You should run for state representative," someone shouted from the back of the room. "You're better than that bum O'Donnell!"

I smiled.

"As much as I appreciate that thought, I couldn't win anything in this district," I said. "The politicians outnumber us twenty to one. Besides, it's more fun fighting City Hall and Harrisburg than joining them—at least for now."

CHAPTER EIGHT

Called to Harrisburg

While serving as head of PCCA I thought about other careers I wanted to pursue. Government service headed the list. The first opportunity was presented to me by the Delaware River Port Authority.

I was sitting in my office at PCCA when the phone rang. It was Richard Gilmore, a top-ranking official at Girard Bank. Richard had recently served as chief financial officer for the school district of Philadelphia. He was Gov. Milton Shapp's appointee to the Delaware River Port Authority.

"Wilson," Dick said. "I want to make you aware of an opportunity that fits you perfectly. I am over here as a member of the Delaware River Port Authority, and the job of the deputy director for development is open. I would be very interested in talking to you, or whoever I should talk to, about putting you in this slot."

I asked a few questions, including what the job entailed.

Dick explained that the job involved overseeing bridge construction and governmental operations. "But I think they may be splitting the job," he added.

Despite his uncertainty, I was very much interested in the

position. The bridge construction aspect seemed to be a perfect fit for me.

Later that week I traveled over to Camden to be interviewed. My first interview was with a man from the personnel office. He obviously was not interested in me working there.

"Who told you about the job?" he asked.

"Richard Gilmore," I responded. "He's one of your commissioners."

"I know who he is," he snapped. "Are you some type of political referral?"

"No, I'm a Dick Gilmore referral."

He didn't say anything else, but his facial expression and body language told me that I was not his first choice for this job. Nonetheless, I moved to the next round of interviews, which included a meeting with Executive Director Gen. (Ret.) William W. Watkin, Jr.

That interview went well, and I felt more comfortable than I had in the earlier meeting. Several weeks passed before I was offered the job. Dick was right. They did split the job in half, and the position I was offered was vice president of government and community relations. I saw the job as a "spook that sat by the door" position that would have given me little authority to do anything substantial for the agency. So I turned it down.

Some people were shocked that I'd turn down a vice presidency. My response to them was that I wanted to be treated as if I had a brain. I'd spent eight years overseeing major housing construction projects from start to finish. I wasn't about to throw that experience away on what was essentially a public relations job. The story in the newspaper quoted me as saying I was not interested in "half a job." That summed up my feelings.

Declining the port authority position, I was prepared to remain at PCCA for another five years or so when, out of the blue, I received a call from Terry Dellmuth in the governor's office.

"How would you like to be appointed to the Public Utility Commission?" he asked, barely containing his excitement.

I thought for a moment before replying.

"Terry, I'm happy where I am."

"The governor wants to see you," Terry said, ignoring my

response. "He wants you to come over to his house in Merion to talk with him about the appointment."

"Let me think about it over the weekend."

The next day, Saturday, I ran into Judge Lawrence Prattis at a funeral, and I told him about the governor's offer.

"I'm not sure if I'll do it or not," I said. He looked at me as if I were crazy.

"Wilson, this is one of the most significant appointments a person can have, and you're not sure? Look, what you need to do is go home *now*, get on the phone, call the governor, and tell him you are interested and want to come up and interview. If you're appointed and confirmed to the PUC, that will be a real barrier-breaking opportunity for blacks."

Larry was so animated that his excitement was infectious. I went home and immediately called the governor, who invited me over to his home on that Sunday at 3:00 P.M. On the phone, he really sounded interested.

Sunday morning I went to church and said a special prayer.

"Lord, you know me. You know my every thought. I don't know whether this is the right decision or not, but you know, Lord. And if it is, let me make the right decision."

Rev. Samuel L. Taylor, my pastor, preached a strong and uplifting sermon and concluded it by saying, "Try God. Try God. If you try him, take him as your friend, then everything will be all right."

I left church spiritually uplifted and full of confidence. I had faith that everything would work out. At 2:00 P.M., I was headed toward Merion, a few miles away, to the governor's home.

I was excited and bubbling over with anticipation. I was also nervous, the kind of nervousness that comes from facing one of the most important days of your life.

Arriving at the governor's home, I was met by two pleasant state troopers. I was half an hour early, and the troopers joked about that because the governor was notorious for his tardiness. For twenty minutes the troopers and I sat talking. Not too long afterwards, the governor sent for me. He was ten minutes early.

I went into his office and took my seat. The governor was a man of small stature with a big, pleasant smile. We settled down to talk.

"Tell me about this organization that you *now* run," he said. "Do you like that better than your work in North Philadelphia?"

Ignoring the latter part of his statement, I explained my role with PCCA, my accomplishments, and my philosophy. Shapp seemed to approve of what I was saying.

"The PUC is an embarrassment to me," Shapp said. "I am told that you might help restore some sanity to that body. I need someone in there who can work out difficult problems without a big fuss. I need someone who can disagree without being disagreeable.

"I'm on my way out of office now, but I don't want to leave this burden for another governor."

He was very sincere, and I could tell that he was motivated by an honest instinct to do the right thing. This was not political. This was good government.

We talked for about an hour, and during that time he gave me no indication of what he would do. But before I left, he asked me to come to Harrisburg that coming Tuesday.

That Tuesday, February 17, 1978, I arrived at the governor's office in Harrisburg for my appointment. This was my first time there. Again I was early for my appointment, by about half an hour. I walked into a huge reception area directed by a receptionist.

"Good morning," I said. "I am Wilson Goode. I have an appointment with the governor."

"Yes, Mr. Goode. The governor is expecting you," she said pleasantly. "But you're early, aren't you?"

"Yes, I am. I was anxious."

We both laughed.

"Have a seat. The governor will be with you soon."

When Shapp and I met again, he was even more congenial. During the course of the interview a curious thing kept happening. The governor kept saying how good it was to see me again and made several other vague references to my outstanding work in North Philadelphia. I became really puzzled when he talked about working with me when his company was located at Broad and Lehigh. Shrugging it off, I assumed he'd confused some of my work with PCCA with some other activities. I knew I'd never worked with him before. In fact, I'd never even heard of Milton Shapp until he ran for governor.

The puzzle remained unsolved until a year later, when my cousin James C. Goode saw me at a family gathering and told me about his work with Shapp.

"That explains it!" I exclaimed, as I laughingly told my cousin about the interview.

We both laughed and concluded that the governor had us confused and had probably appointed the wrong Goode.

"You know all blacks look alike," we joked, "or at least all Goodes."

From that time on, each time I saw James I thanked him for my appointment to the PUC.

"Are you interested?" Shapp finally asked after we had chatted awhile.

My discussion with Judge Prattis had convinced me to go for it. "Yes, I am," I said preparing to launch into a series of questions.

"Good! I'm going to appoint you," Shapp said happily. Before I could gain my composure, Shapp led me into a conference room to meet the press and announce the appointment.

"I want you to meet my nominee to the Public Utility Commission," Shapp said. "He has done an outstanding job in Philadelphia, and I am sure he will do an outstanding job here."

The media appeared to be shocked. They had not expected this, and they certainly had not expected me. Reporters immediately threw a barrage of questions at me.

"Do you know anything about regulatory issues?"

"What qualifies you for this job?"

"How do you feel about utility rate increases?"

"Who's your sponsor?"

Finally, I got a word in.

"Ladies and gentlemen, I was just appointed a minute ago,"

I said as pleasantly as possible. "Give me two minutes and I might be able to give you better answers to your questions. But I promise I will work hard and I will be a good representative of the PUC."

With that simple announcement it didn't take long for me to realize I had graduated to the big leagues of politics. This was Main Street. I had arrived, or so I thought.

The PUC was a plum assignment. The commission regulated all the utilities across the commonwealth, and I was the first black to be appointed commissioner. The agency only had a handful of blacks to begin with. At PCCA I had managed an annual budget that never went much above $160,000. Now I would be responsible for $7 billion![1]

The questioning continued for a brief period of time, but instinctively I knew I was in a different league with the media. I had faced the press as a community activist, but this was the political world. All of their questions had a hard edge to them as they proceeded to attack, not ask questions.

That day also taught me that as a politician, I had to guard against my every move in public, no matter how innocent. Earlier that day, as I waited for the governor in the reception area, I absentmindedly bit a hangnail on my pinkie finger. Unknown to me, a news photographer snapped the picture. The next day the Harrisburg newspaper ran that photo with the announcement of my appointment.

I don't know if the decision to run the photo was a slap at me or at Shapp. He was in his eighth year as governor and was a lame duck. The media had battered him unmercifully in recent months. The photo might have been an attempt to make me look like a buffoon or an attempt to slam him by saying, "Look at the guy Shapp has appointed to the PUC."

I returned home to Philadelphia to find the media already giving me little chance of being confirmed by the state senate, basically because I didn't have the support of the Rizzo machine.

Rizzo's point man was Marty Weinberg, chair of the Democratic party. Weinberg had been city solicitor under Rizzo and was now a very influential inside player. Weinberg sent me word through Sen. Francis Lynch that he was opposed to my nomination and would use his power and influence to block the confirmation. He had his own nominee for the job. But I had faith that with hard work I could win confirmation.

I approached the confirmation process much like I approach all serious matters in my life. I was determined to succeed, and I planned to give it everything I had. If I lost the confirmation vote, it would not be because I had not given it a good try.

I made appointments with all of the senators, gave them copies of my résumé, and offered to discuss any aspect of my record when we met. Most of the senators were supportive, but not Francis Lynch. During our meeting he made no secret of his intentions and the reason behind them.

"Senator Lynch, I need your support," I said. "You've heard my presentation. Do you have any questions?"

"Nope."

"Can I count on you for your support?"

"Nope. The boys downtown—you know, the chief—aren't supporting you."

"I know that, but how about you?"

Lynch flatly told me that he would do whatever he was told and, at this point, Marty Weinberg opposed my nomination. Therefore, he did too.

"Those are my instructions. I take orders."

"Thank you, Senator," I said. "And there is nothing I can say to change your mind?"

"Nope."

"Thank you, Senator."

I stood up and left the room.

I had also gotten feedback that Arlen Specter, then a practicing attorney, opposed me. Specter's law firm had represented Centennial Bank, which had gone out of business. Centennial had made a loan to Caldwell Builders, the contractor for Mount Carmel Gardens, one of my PCCA contracts.

It was later reported to me that Specter had given the details of that project to Sen. Richard Tilghman. Tipped off that Tilghman was going to question me about the project at my confirmation hearing, I was ready for him.

I could barely wait to finish my opening statement. After the statement, each senator took turns asking me questions. Sen. Franklin Curry chaired the panel. Finally Tilghman's turn came.

"Mr. Goode, tell me about this Centennial Bank and Mount Carmel Gardens job," he said. "I have in my possession information that suggests that you caused this bank to go out of business." He pointed to a thick stack of papers in front of him.

As he spoke, I fidgeted inwardly like a little boy with a room full of toys awaiting him. I couldn't wait until he was finished. I was ready.

"Chair Curry, Senator Tilghman," I began, "I did represent Mount Carmel Gardens. It was my responsibility to represent Mount Carmel Gardens. I did that and I think I did it well.

Mount Carmel Gardens had been my favorite project, and the pastor, Rev. Albert F. Campbell, my favorite nonprofit leader. He was a special leader: honest, sincere, committed, God fearing, articulate, and competent. He was obviously respected by all those on the board. I made special efforts to do the job right because they were special people.

"We finished the project on time and within budget. I did not represent either Caldwell Builders or Centennial Bank. It was up to their representative to protect them, to do for them what I did for Mount Carmel."

I finished my statement brimming with pride and confidence. The issue never came up again.

During the confirmation process I also got the support of the three black senators—Paul McKinney, Freeman Hankins, and Herb Arlene. They were proud to have a black finally nominated by the governor for this important position.

The second turning point in my favor was that the current chair of the PUC, Louis Carter, Esq., became a big booster of mine. Carter liked me personally, but he also approved of my philosophy about good government.

During the confirmation process, while the governor and his staff worked on getting me confirmed, I was given a desk in the governor's office. It was a long, tedious process. Minutes seemed like hours. One day felt like a week.

After nearly three weeks of hard, and what I perceived to be successful, work, Terry Dellmuth told me that my nomination was at a stalemate because everyone was trying to bargain for something from the governor. My confirmation was the bargaining chip. Dellmuth was noncommittal about how things might turn out. Later David Brown, the governor's chief of staff, came in and confirmed what Terry had already told me. My confirmation was not moving. I waited, and waited, and waited.

Both Terry and David went to great lengths to assure me that the stalemate was not a reflection on me.

"You've done a good job, Wilson, but this place isn't run by a merit system," Terry said. "Sometimes you're lucky and you get the confirmation through quickly. Herb Denenberg and Phil Kaloder never did get confirmed. So don't take this thing personally."

I didn't. I knew the tactics they were using, and I didn't want to be bartered with. A few days later I had a frank discussion with the governor.

"I really appreciate your confidence in me, Mr. Governor," I said, "but I'm prepared to either be confirmed by the end of this week or to withdraw my name. I'm not going to be hung up in this process for two more months. I've talked to the senators, I've talked to you; I've talked to the media. Now it's time to make a decision.

"If you're unable to get confirmation, no hard feelings."

That was 2:00 P.M., Tuesday afternoon. The governor asked me to spend the night to see what he could do. I told him that I had an agency to run back in Philadelphia. I was going home on a late train.

"And I don't intend to return unless there is some real positive movement," I said. "It is probably better for me and better for you if I return home and write you a letter withdrawing my name.

"It's unfair of me to leave my agency, PCCA, in limbo any longer. They have been very kind to me. I can't take advantage of that kindness."

Governor Shapp looked worried, real worried. He had worked hard to get me confirmed, and now he saw his gains slipping away. I felt bad about that, but could not stick it out any longer.

"Look, Wilson, sit tight," said Shapp. "Let's give this thing one more try." Then he left the room.

While I was willing to give up, deep down inside I still believed I would be confirmed. I could accept returning to Phila-

delphia and running PCCA for the next five years, but I had the
faith that that wouldn't happen.

An hour later Terry came into the room and announced,
"They're voting on your nomination. Come on, let's listen to the
box [speaker]."

I followed Terry. My heart was racing a mile a minute, and I
was bursting with anticipation. For nearly a month I had worked
for this moment. Now it was here. The voting started.

"One, in favor. Two, three, four, five, six." By the time the
count reached twenty-six, I was giddy with excitement.

"Thirty-one, thirty-two."

"It might be unanimous," David Brown said. "It might be
forty-eight to zero."

"Thirty-nine, forty, forty-one."

"Wouldn't that be something," Terry added, gleefully.

"Forty-two, forty-three, forty-four, forty-five, forty-six, forty-
seven. Forty-eight! The ayes are forty-eight. The nays are zero!"

The room erupted into applause and cheers of joy and proud
exclamations.

"We did it! We did it! Can you believe this?"

I don't know what Shapp did, but it worked. I was commissioner of the Public Utility Commission.

After the vote, the governor sent for me.

"Congratulations, Wilson," Shapp said. "I want you back
here tomorrow at 10:00 A.M. for the swearing-in ceremony."

I called my brother Alvestus from my office to tell him the
good news. Al agreed to drive Mama, Velma, and me to Harrisburg for the ceremony.

"No, you drive Mom," I decided. "Velma and I will take the
train. The train is reliable and will get me there without getting
a flat tire."

"So now that you're a big shot you're too good to ride with
me," Al chided. "I'll beat that train to Harrisburg. You just watch."

We both laughed, not knowing his words were prophetic.

That night I arrived home around 10:00 P.M. to discover I had
run out of clean shirts. The only clean shirt left was a pink silk.
Refusing to panic, I decided to wear the pink shirt to Harrisburg
but to get there early enough to buy a white one.

The next day Velma and I caught an early train, and all went according to plan when halfway to Harrisburg the train slowed down to a crawl. Nervously I watched the clock—9:50 . . . 10:00 . . . 10:20. By the time we reached Harrisburg, it was so late all we could do was catch a cab and make a mad dash to the governor's office.

When I walked into the conference room, everyone was waiting—the governor, my family, the media. I was so embarrassed!

No one said a word about me being late or asked why I was wearing a pink shirt. Lou Carter, the commission chair, proceeded with the swearing-in ceremony as if nothing were amiss. But the opportunity was too good for Carter to pass up.

"I was told that Wilson Goode was going to be a positive influence on this body," he said to the audience at the conclusion of the formal ceremony. "I was told he would bring creative and new ideas to the commission. Looking at him today, all I can say is you have to respect any man who has enough guts to come to a formal event like this in a pink silk shirt."

That broke the ice, and we all had a good laugh. I was now the first black PUC commissioner, pink shirt and all.

After my appointment to the PUC, I resigned from all community boards and political positions such as the Black Political Forum. I didn't want to be on any board that would even hint at a conflict of interest. Chair of the deacon board in my church was the only position I retained. I felt it was important for me to keep my connections to my church. God's grace had brought me this far and had never left me alone. I was not about to leave him.

My work with the PUC was demanding. As with my venture into housing development with PCCA, I was again in an on-the-job learning situation. I had to prove my competency from the beginning.

A driver took me to Harrisburg daily, a four-hour round-trip commute. Every morning I arose at 5:00 A.M. By 5:30 I was in my car headed for the Lord & Taylor parking lot to meet my driver who took me to Harrisburg. The entire time I was in the car I read. Then I read an additional four hours during the day to help

prepare myself for each public session. As I read case after case,
I became so involved in the issues that the time flew. The trip
seemed to take minutes rather than hours. Often Kathryn Streeter
Lewis, my staff attorney (now the administrative judge of orphan
court), traveled with me. Our plan was to meet at the parking lot
at 5:50 A.M. sharp. We normally arrived in Harrisburg around 7:30
A.M., which enabled us to beat almost all the other staff people.

The staff would marvel at how day after day I made the trip
in such a timely fashion. Over the two years I was at the PUC I
had two drivers, Bob Sampson and Gus Rylander. Occasionally
they would arrive at the parking lot late only to find we had
already left. Since I always had the car, it only took a few train
rides to Harrisburg for them to get to the parking lot on time.

Each week the PUC reviewed cases and made decisions affecting the rates of telephone, gas, electric, water, and taxi cab
companies. Sometimes we mediated as many as eighty cases a
week, deciding on issues ranging from licensing the operation of
a bus company to increasing rates for water companies. I hired
good staff people to work with me and also kept my nose to the
grindstone.

During the early months with the commission, I worked hard
to be a positive influence. The commission had a reputation for
public bickering, and there were several occasions when, in the
heat of a discussion, members threw objects at one another. The
blame for this sometimes juvenile behavior rested on Lou Carter,
the chair.

Some people considered Carter to be overly legalistic and
detail oriented. Other members found his argumentative style to
be offensive. A few months after I arrived at PUC, rumors began
to circulate that the governor wanted to replace Lou Carter as
chair. At the time the rumors started I had no idea I was being
considered as his replacement. I was the newest member of the
commission and probably the most unlikely to be made chair. My
feeling was that the governor would tap Helen O'Bannon, a
commission member from Pittsburgh. But shortly after the rumors started, David Brown, the governor's chief of staff, asked to
see me.

"Wilson, we want to replace Lou Carter," David said. "Some
of us think that you would be a logical choice to replace him."

I was astonished.

"David, how can that be done?" I asked. "I thought the chair could only be removed for cause."

"That may not be as hard as it looks. The real problem is that we can't replace somebody with nobody. Are you interested?"

"David, I would be very concerned about getting involved in a long legal fight. Besides, Lou Carter and I get along fine. We sometimes ride back and forth together to Philadelphia. I would be very concerned if he thought I was trying to take his seat from him."

"Well, Wilson, think about it. We will talk again about this."

I knew he meant that. They were determined, but deep down inside I didn't feel I had been on the commission long enough to accept that role. It was June, and I had served on the commission about ninety days. If I allowed myself to be pushed into the position of chair before I was ready and had gained the confidence of the other members, I would not be successful.

The other problem I had was my relationship with Lou Carter. I had come to really like the guy. I enjoyed his company and he had been a big supporter of mine during the confirmation process. I couldn't allow personal ambition to destroy our relationship. I sent word to David Brown that the timing was not right for me. After a few more months, we could assess it again.

The summer passed without any further mention of the issue, but right after Labor Day, the rumors started again. The news media was speculating that the governor would definitely replace Carter. The only question now was when, and with whom?

By now Helen O'Bannon had become an aggressive candidate for the post. She was lobbying hard and had picked up some support. Frankly, I was perfectly willing to let her become the chair because I didn't want to ruin my relationship with Lou. Because I respected him, it was important to me that Lou Carter not think I was trying to take his job.

For some unknown reason the governor was not comfortable with O'Bannon. He wanted me, and told me so very directly.

After weeks of meetings and discussions with David Brown and other staff members, I agreed to serve as commission chair if they could get Lou to step down without a long legal hassle. They assured me that Lou Carter understood that he had to resign whether I replaced him or not. He preferred me to Helen O'Bannon. I left the matter in their hands.

By the second week in October 1978, the rumors were more persistent. The media declared the change in leadership to be imminent. On Friday the thirteenth, I was to attend a briefing session and tour of Bell Laboratories in New Jersey. I awoke that morning feeling good and lucky, even though it was Friday the thirteenth. By this time I had resolved my uncertainties. I was excited that I might actually become the first black chair of the PUC.

I met the Bell executives at Sixteenth and Arch Streets for our drive to central New Jersey. On the way, I kept thinking about the position of PUC chair. When will the governor act? Will he be able to pull it off? I asked myself. Had I been a little too resistant? Had Helen O'Bannon gotten enough political support after all to change the governor's mind?

As we headed for Bell Laboratories, I paid little attention to the preliminary briefing I was getting in the car. I couldn't concentrate, but after we arrived at the site, I got caught up in one briefing after the other. We were in a session, and at 10:00 A.M. I was interrupted by a telephone call.

"Mr. Commissioner, Governor Shapp is trying to reach you. Will you take the call?"

"Yes, I will," I said.

"Do you need privacy?"

"Yes, that would be fine."

"Okay. There's a private office right next to you," the receptionist said. "I'll redirect the call there. When it rings, just pick up."

I nervously walked toward the office feeling that this Friday the thirteenth was really a lucky day after all.

"Good morning, Governor. It's nice to hear from you," I said.

"Congratulations, Mr. Chairman," Shapp responded. "I have just announced your appointment as chair."

"Thank you, Governor. I promise to do a good job for you. I will give it everything I've got."

"I know that. Good luck and if I can help, don't hesitate to call."

In my excitement I forgot to ask about Lou Carter, but felt if the governor had wanted to tell me what had happened, he would have done so.

I returned to my meeting feeling ten feet tall.

"You are now looking at the new chair of the PUC," I blurted out excitedly. "I walked in here earlier as a member of the PUC and I'll walk out as chair. You are my good luck charm."

Following the briefing, we drove back to Philadelphia and I found it interesting that the Bell executives treated me with a great deal more respect and deference than they had earlier in the day. The media coverage following my appointment as chair also was very positive.

That Sunday I went to the First Baptist Church of Paschall to thank God for his grace. As I sat on the front pew, Rev. Taylor beamed as he spoke.

"We are all very proud of our chairman," he said. "Now the whole state knows what we know. They made him chair of the whole thing in the state. What do you call that, Deacon Goode? Oh, yes—chair of the Public Utility Commission. Let's all stand and give him a big round of applause."

As this salute went on, I couldn't help but think how far I had come since March 1954 when my mother, brothers James Henry, Earn Lee, Ed Louis, and I had walked down the aisle of this church and my mother had declared before the congregation, "We are all joining this church. All my boys. We are all joining."

God had been with me through many things since then; my faith in him was reaffirmed once again. I never once doubted that he would crown my good works with success.

When I arrived at work on Monday, the commission staff were there to cheer me. They clearly liked the way I operated and thought I was making distinct improvements to the commission. Criticism, however, was right around the corner.

The first unpopular decision I made was to return about $500,000 of our budget to the state budget office. We didn't need the money, so I gave it back. My office went crazy.

"Mr. Chairman, are you nuts? We don't give money back to the state. You spend what you have and next year you ask for more."

"Not me," I said. "You spend what you need to do the job

and you give the surplus back. That's my philosophy, and that's the way I operate."

My decision was based upon my belief that you give the taxpayer as much bang for the buck as possible.

My second unpopular decision was to refuse to send representatives to the National Association of Regulatory Utility Commissions (NARUC) convention in Las Vegas. I didn't feel Las Vegas was a proper environment for public officials to meet and spend public money. We went to subsequent conventions, but not to that one. I had long felt that places like Las Vegas were inappropriate for conferences for public officials. The image was wrong both because of the appearance of luxury and the gambling. I couldn't do anything about it until now. But now that I held the executive power to decide, I did.

All the same, things generally moved along smoothly. Six months into my term, we began the company review process for the energy companies that supplied our utilities. On March 28, 1979, General Public Utilities (GPU) was scheduled to explain its plans for its plant on Three Mile Island. We had set aside three hours, 8:00 A.M. until 11:00 A.M., for the presentation.

The GPU representatives brought in slides, charts—the works—to explain their expansion plans and rate requirements for the next five years, among other issues.

Around 8:30 A.M., a secretary came into the meeting to get one of the officials for an urgent call. He returned about ten minutes later and proceeded with his part of the presentation.

"We're having a little problem on Three Mile Island," he said casually, "but the worst has been taken care of."

They continued their presentation.

After the GPU members left, Glenn Kennedy, my chief staff person, walked into my office.

"Did they brief you on what went on over there at Three Mile Island?" he asked.

"No. They said the worst of the problem was over," I replied nonchalantly. "Why?"

Glenn's mouth fell open.

"You don't know?"

"Know what?"

"They have a meltdown. We may have to evacuate all the people on Three Mile Island."

"You can't be serious!"

"I am. It's all over television."

I was so angry I could barely talk to the governor's emergency preparedness unit, which handles disasters. We had been meeting with the operators of that facility all morning long and they never told us about the accident. They didn't have the honesty or the decency to say, "Look, we have to cancel this meeting. The whole future of GPU just changed five minutes ago." As a result, their entire presentation was a sham.

The conduct of the top officials at GPU was shameful. But their conduct with us would characterize their dealings for weeks to come. They were in a state of denial about the accident. It appeared as if they believed it had never happened. Fortunately for GPU, the accident resulted in a shake-up of many of those top officials, and rightly so.

For days after the accident I felt betrayed by the GPU officers who had deceived us in the meeting. Why couldn't they just be honest? Why didn't they just come clean with us and ask for our help? That would have been far more productive for all of us.

The responsibility for dealing with the accident fell to the Nuclear Regulatory Commission. PUC's role was to determine how the accident would affect the customers who got electrical service from GPU. But I saw a larger issue that needed to be dealt with—community fear.

People would want to know how the accident affected them financially, but they would also want to air their feelings about health concerns, property values, and safety to their community. I set up hearings in the area surrounding the plant to let the residents know that their government cared about their feelings following this tragedy. They needed someone to talk with. As chair of the PUC, I wanted to make sure the public didn't see us as bureaucrats sitting in some ivory tower in Harrisburg. We were public servants who cared about our constituents.

Against the advice of the commission members, I went to speak to the people. None of the other commissioners would join me. I was trying to make the PUC too community oriented, they charged, when the PUC was a judicial body, like the Supreme Court.

"Can you see the Supreme Court going out and talking to the people?" one member asked.

I confessed that I could. I felt it was my role as a public servant to be responsive to the people I served. I knew that my view of the way government ought to relate to people was far different from that of most government officials. Earlier I had held some town meetings around the state and found them to be productive, informative, and greatly appreciated by the people who wanted to see their public officials up close.

The public meetings were heart-wrenching. Most were held in small, typically average towns where people had lived their entire lives. They'd been born there, gone to school there, fallen in love and married there. They were raising their children in what they viewed as the security of small-town life. Now that security had been shaken, threatened. Money wasn't plentiful here, but that wasn't what these people valued most. They had stayed for the peace and haven of security that small-town life afforded their children. Now that peace and security were gone.

At a meeting in one of these little towns, a woman stepped up to the microphone and looked me straight in the eye. The expression on her face was a mixture of fear and anger. Her voice shook as she spoke.

"Who's going to take care of my baby?" she shouted passionately, pointing to her bulging stomach. "This baby in my womb is going to be born defective because of the neglect of these operators. Who's going to tell this child that what happened to it was because of the irresponsible behavior of these people?"

Tears streamed down her face as she spoke. I choked back the lump in my throat.

A man approached the microphone next. His voice was steady and quiet, but no less angry.

"I've lived here all my life, some fifty years, but we're moving as soon as I can find a house," he said. "This plant is unsafe. It was irresponsible to let that accident happen. I cannot put my family at risk. I just cannot do it."

From town to town, the same concerns were repeated over and over again.

The hearings continued for several weeks and provided some catharsis for the residents. By the time we began dealing with the rate-relief issue following the accident, the public had received a thorough education in how the utility commission worked, what we could and could not do, and what financial impact the accident would have on consumers.

My goal for the rate-making process was to have no one better off or worse off as a result of the accident at Three Mile Island. I knew that those ratepayers in the community adjacent to the plant would have their health and legal concerns adjudicated through another process. But our job was to construct a rate decision that was fair to all ratepayers, even customers of other utilities. No one should benefit from the accident, but no one should be harmed, either. This was a delicate balancing act. We needed true equity. Once our philosophy was clearly defined, we were able to write the right decision.

The decision we wrote on rate relief was hailed by the media as the fairest they'd ever seen. But what pleased me most about it was that the residents agreed.

CHAPTER NINE

Managing Director

In 1979, Charlie Bowser, a local black attorney, was for the second time a candidate for mayor. He had run on the Philadelphia Party label in 1975 and come in second to Frank Rizzo. The Republican nominee placed third. His chances of winning were considered nonexistent at first, but Charlie put together a great campaign that pitted the neighborhoods against the downtown establishment and energized black voters in a way they had never been energized before. Everyone was amazed that a relatively unknown black candidate could do so well, beating a major party candidate.

Frank Rizzo, who had gone on to become mayor for two terms, was now out of the running. He had tried and failed to mobilize white citizens to "vote white" and revise the city's home-rule charter prohibiting a mayor to hold office more than two consecutive terms. Unwittingly, he also had strengthened black voter unity during his last term in office by making several decisions that antagonized blacks. His support of police brutality against Philadelphia's black citizens eventually led to a federal investigation of the police force. His ouster of Sam Evans, a black elder statesman, from the Bicentennial Commission served to further fan the hostilities of black voters as well as white liberals.

The primary campaign accelerated, driven by a crusade-like fervor. Charlie steadily gained momentum, and the public-opinion polls showed a close race. In fact, some of the polls showed Charlie winning if the three white candidates stayed in the race. But Bill Green was too smart for that. The other two white candidates, former controller William Klenk and former director of commerce and city representative Albert Gaudiosi, dropped out of the race before they damaged Green's chances of winning. Bill Green got what he wanted, a one-on-one contest against Bowser.

Nonetheless, the election was still a close one. Green won 53 percent of the votes to Bowser's 44 percent. Charlie won every black ward in the city as well as two predominantly white wards.

After the primary, Charlie held a series of Saturday meetings to discuss how black leaders could capitalize on his strong finish in the primary. During this time the Republican candidate, David Marston, announced that if elected, he would name a black person to the city's second most powerful office, managing director. Simultaneously, rumblings emerged from Lucien Blackwell's camp that the black city council member would run as an independent candidate for mayor in the fall.

Blackwell believed he could tap into the emotions of the primary campaign and win enough votes in a three-way race to capture the election. Marston and Green would divide the white vote, he surmised, and he could cash in on the black vote and win. But the black vote was anything but unified, as the events of the summer would prove.

That summer a group of black leaders led by Sam Evans, C. Delores Tucker, and Mary Mason pushed for the appointment of a black managing director in exchange for an endorsement of Green. Lucien Blackwell was reported to have been a part of these meetings as well. Being in Harrisburg most of the time, I was out of the loop of local politics and didn't know about these private meetings until much later. In August, however, Green called to ask me to meet with him.

"I just want to sit down and chat with you," he said.

I didn't think much of it at the time. The Three Mile Island community hearings had just concluded, and I thought Green wanted to get my perspective on some political issues. Steve Avinger, a former PUC staff member who was now a staff person for Green, set up the meeting. I arranged to meet them at my old PCCA offices at 1601 Walnut Street. Shirley B. Hamilton, the acting director of PCCA, was more than happy to accommodate us.

I arrived at the office half an hour early and waited for Bill and Steve. When they arrived, we exchanged pleasantries before getting down to business.

"How do you like running for mayor?" I asked.

"It's great!" Bill responded. "I've always wanted to be mayor and now it looks like I have a good chance. I thought I'd win in 1971, but Hardy Williams's campaign hurt me."

As he spoke, I wondered whether he knew what my role had been in the Williams campaign. I was one of the few black leaders who hadn't supported Green. What if he confronts me on this issue? I thought. What if he asks me why I supported Hardy Williams? But he didn't ask, and I was relieved.

I had spearheaded Hardy's campaign, and many of our planning sessions took place right here in this office. It was now Bill's turn to ask me some questions.

"Tell me something about the Public Utility Commission and what you do," he said.

I explained my role with PUC in detail. I emphasized my management philosophy, that I believed in giving clear direction and involving the entire organization in the decision-making process. I also explained that I based my philosophy about government spending on zero-based, performance-based budgeting.

"An organization must manage by objectives," I said, then gave an example.

"Right after I became chair of PUC, I reduced the budget because we were spending below our allocation. My staff tried unsuccessfully to convince me to spend all of the money and to ask for more next year. I didn't see the logic of that. I turned money back to the state and told them we wouldn't be needing that money this year."

I noticed that Green seemed to be enjoying the story.

"After I had done this, my staff had what they called a 'here are the facts of life' conference with me. 'Mr. Chairman,' they informed me, 'in this organization we spend all of the money we get, and then we ask for more next year. That's the way the game is played. When you give back money, they reduce your budget.' "

"What did you do?" Green asked.

"I told them that's not the way I play the game. I believe in honest budgeting. I will take my chances with an honest budget. My staff looked at me in amazement as if to say, 'How stupid can you be?' and walked out. But I have never had a problem with getting my budgets passed by the governor or state leadership."

"That's wonderful!" Green exclaimed.

We also talked about the Three Mile Island rate case that had just ended.

"Sounds like you're having fun," Green said.

I readily agreed. "I'm having a ball! This job is the best of all possible worlds. I get to play judge without being a lawyer. I get to manage a major state agency, and I travel all around the state with my town meetings. It's a great job!"

"But not as good as being mayor," Green said, laughing.

We both laughed, said goodnight, and left. I later learned that this little chat was probably a preliminary meeting to assess whether I should become Green's managing director. The first hint I got of the seriousness of the meeting came by way of a news story that appeared after Labor Day.

I was at home reading the Sunday paper when the item caught my eye: a headline with photos of me and Dick Doran, a Green confidant, named us as leading candidates for top posts in the Green administration. The story indicated that I would be selected managing director. I was shocked and embarrassed.

How can they run a story like this without consulting me? I wondered.

I knew the story would probably affect my role as chair of PUC. Earlier that year long-time PUC member Helen O'Bannon had left unexpectedly to become secretary of welfare for the new governor, Dick Thornburgh. The former chair, Lou Carter, had also left with little warning. I cringed thinking about the questions I might get following this story. My colleagues had to be concerned. My departure would leave only two people out of what had begun as a five-member commission. Very little work could get done with only two members. Commission bylaws required a majority vote on issues, so the two members would have to agree before anything would pass. It could take months to find new candidates for these PUC posts and to get them confirmed. My colleagues would now suspect that I, too, was about to leave the PUC, and I wasn't even sure the story linking me to the Green cabinet was true.

My meeting with Green had lasted maybe an hour. Could he have possibly assessed my suitability to become managing director in that brief period of time? I doubted the veracity of the article, but even as I doubted it, the thought of becoming Philadelphia's first African American managing director excited me tremendously.

Unsure of what to do to clarify the story, I did nothing. That no one called me about it either made me doubt its credibility even more. It wasn't until weeks later that I learned the story had been planted to send out two messages—one to the black community, the other to me. The messages were that if elected, Bill Green would appoint a black person to the city's second-highest office. That carrot was a teaser to put black voters on the alert that Green had matched Marston's offer and they should vote for him. The other message was to prompt me to start considering whether I would accept the position if offered.

For many years I had harbored a secret interest in becoming managing director, confessing to confidants that I thought the managing director job would be even more exciting than being mayor.

The article appeared in September. I didn't hear anything else and got antsy. Shortly before the November election, I called Dick Doran to ask what was going on. Was Green really interested in me? When would he talk with me about the position? Doran didn't offer much assurance. He said he wasn't sure what Green would do but that I should keep my options open.

I was excited about being considered, but I was ambivalent about accepting the managing director position even if it were offered. One day I would think how wonderful it would be, only to be riddled with doubts the next day. It was far safer to stay with PUC, I concluded.

Being managing director would be a tremendous burden and

responsibility. As chair of PUC, I headed a commission for the
Commonwealth of Pennsylvania, had statewide visibility, and
had another eight years of appointment remaining. The last time
I'd had that much job security was in the army. PUC gave me
status and security, since I couldn't be removed from my job or
the position of chair without cause. My family had sacrificed
much for me as I'd built up my career. I felt I owed them something by holding on to some security. Why should I consider
jumping into this political quicksand?

I knew the managing director position was politically sensitive. From the moment I learned I was being considered for the
post, I sensed there would be some real problems with this job.
For one, I would be breaking racial barriers. My performance
would be heavily scrutinized by the media and the public.

One day during this time, Hillel Levinson, the managing
director under Frank Rizzo, came to Harrisburg to visit me.

"I understand you're thinking about not accepting this job,"
he said.

"That's true," I admitted.

"Well, let me tell you. It's the best job you could ever have,"
he said. Levinson then proceeded to tell me how challenging and
intellectually stimulating his career as managing director had
been. I listened, fascinated. I knew Hillel only by reputation. He'd
also heard some things about me. We'd met at public gatherings
a few times but weren't friends. I couldn't think of any political
motivation for him to encourage me to take this job, so I accepted
his visit as a gesture of good will from someone who wanted to
share information and give his viewpoint.

I got the feeling that Levinson would have preferred to have
me in the slot rather than some of the other people whose names
were being bandied about at the time.

Green won the election that fall, decisively beating Marston
and Blackwell.

About three weeks after the election, I finally received the
telephone call from Bill Green asking me to come for an interview. By this time I had made up my mind to accept the job if it
was offered—I had become convinced that the advantages far
outweighed any risks. The interview was a good one; I was
comfortable and confident. Evidently I gave Green the answers

he needed to remove any doubts he had about me.

Not too long afterwards, Green held a press conference to publicly announce my appointment along with several others. As I expected, my appointment unleashed a flurry of media attention as reporters bombarded me with questions. The questioning grew so intense that Green eventually interrupted.

"We have four appointments here today, not just one," Green told the media. He said it pleasantly, but something in his voice suggested he didn't like the attention I was getting. Unfortunately there was more to come.

The other three appointments were: Richard "Dick" Doran, director of commerce and city representative; Edward DeSeve, finance director; and Alan Davis, city solicitor. The four of us worked well together and formed an outstanding cabinet for Mayor Green.

Earl Stout, president of District Council 33 of the blue-collar workers union, responded to my appointment by threatening a citywide strike. He publicly declared that I was anti-union. Privately he told friends he was disgruntled because Green had promised him that Orville "Pat" Jones would be named managing director. Now Green had reneged. For some reason Earl Stout felt he had the power to veto my appointment.

On inauguration day 1980, Stout did attempt a work stoppage but got little cooperation from the workers. John Dykes and George Wroten, the leaders of the sanitation union, visited me at my home the day before the wildcat strike to assure me I had nothing to worry about, despite Stout's actions.

"Mr. Goode, we want you to know that Mr. Stout is not speaking for the majority of our union in opposing your appointment," Dykes explained. "We're here to tell you that we support you and want to work with you."

Relieved, I thanked them and said I was pleased to hear that. "I don't know where Mr. Stout got this stuff about me being anti-union."

Wroten clarified the issue.

"Don't believe what you hear. Earl knows you're not anti-union. What he really means is he can't control you. He thinks he has a better chance of working with Pat Jones."

"But Mr. Stout should know that I am becoming managing

director and that he's starting off on the wrong foot with me."

Dykes suggested that Stout and I should meet, "since you have to work together. Just pick up the phone and call him. He will be shocked."

I followed Dykes's advice and called Stout a few days later. "Mr. Stout, this is Wilson Goode, the new managing director."

"I know who you are," he said gruffly. "What can I do for you?"

"I think it would be good if we got together to discuss our differences," I suggested.

"We don't have any differences. That man lied to me," he said referring to Bill Green. "I needed to teach him a lesson."

Stout and I met at the John F. Kennedy Memorial Hospital one morning that week.

"So, you're the new man, huh?" he asked, looking me over. "Yes, I am."

Stout then launched into the vilest string of profanity imaginable, describing himself in very colorful terms. After a few minutes of this, I interrupted and reminded him that I was a Baptist deacon and unused to all of this profanity.

"So we have a Sunday school teacher here, huh?" he said derisively. But the conversation and the language took on a less harsh tone. From that day on, Earl Stout and I understood how different our communication styles were.

Philadelphia's political climate had undergone a radical transformation in the previous decade. Voter registration drives increased the number of black voters by six points to 38 percent. In some elections the rate of voter turnout in predominantly black wards was as high as 63 percent.

Biracial coalitions and reformers were dominant forces in city politics. No longer regarded as an anomaly, black and liberal white voters were now taken seriously and had often become pivotal in deciding the outcome of close elections.

Consequently, there was a movement in the Green administration to strengthen the biracial coalition by appointing blacks and other minorities to key positions. I made black appointments to at least three of the ten commission spots, as well as two of the five agencies.

Another one of the major thrusts was to reform several city departments. Our job was to clean house and turn government around. We started with the Philadelphia Police Department. The police reform team was made up of Morton Solomon, Donald Gravatt, and Bill Devlin.

Police corruption and brutality were legendary, and several officers had been convicted of accepting bribes as well as stealing drugs for resale. In 1980 the force was also a citadel of white authority in a city whose black population exceeded 39 percent. Only 17 percent of the police department was black. Of that 17 percent only a handful of blacks held positions with any real power or authority.

Mayor Green wanted to set a tone from the top that police brutality would no longer be tolerated in Philadelphia. The first step we took to deliver this message was to enact a "deadly force policy" that restricted the use of police weapons in making arrests or quelling disturbances. The policy also set limits on how police could use their night sticks. The limits worked. Solomon carried out the policy with outstanding precision and fired any officer who misused his authority.

That first month we also laid off seven hundred police officers and two hundred firefighters. The uproar that resulted was immediate. Police and firefighter unions launched public protests with members picketing outside City Hall. Still we didn't budge. The reformers were on a mission.

When Green took office, the city faced a $167-million deficit and a declining bond rating. The mayor's goal was to streamline city government and eliminate some of the waste that resulted from years of political patronage and mismanagement.

As managing director, I had control over ten service departments, including sanitation and police. To his credit, Green didn't try to restrict my actions but gave me the freedom to run my department as I saw fit. At the same time, it became very clear that I was not one of the "good ole boys" in the mayor's inner circle — Dick Doran, Alan Davis, and Ed Deseve were part of that group. Instead, Mayor Green and I had a cordial, if somewhat distant, relationship. I found him to be a little distrustful of people, including me. He often quoted an old adage he had learned from his father: "Never write a letter and never throw one away."

I knew this was more than just a saying to him. He took those words to heart.

Green was a careful, methodical man who was very suspicious of other people's motives for doing things. Because he craved success, he tried to be a team player. His ambition was to be perceived as a reformer, following in the footsteps of earlier reform mayors such as Joseph Clark and Richardson Dilworth.

The cuts in the police and fire departments were the first of many I directed to get a runaway budget under control. Not too long after the layoffs, I asked for a full accounting of the city's leased vehicles. The Public Property Department had controlled the fleet cars for the past decade. To my amazement they didn't know how many cars were in the fleet or who was driving them. The more questions I asked, the more questions were generated and left unanswered. After a week of playing cat-and-mouse games with memos and telephone calls to Charles Dougherty, the operations director for the managing director's office, I asked to meet with him and his staff to get some answers.

"Mr. Dougherty, I asked you these questions a week ago," I said as we sat at the conference table. "I trust you've had plenty of time to do some research. How many cars do we have in the city fleet?"

I could tell he was uncomfortable.

"My records indicate we have about ten thousand," responded one person. Another estimate was seven thousand. Someone else said eight thousand. I got numbers all over the place, and nobody knew whose figures were correct. Frustrated, I decided there was only one way I would find out how many cars the city leased and where they were.

"I want all the cars brought in," I told Dougherty. "Arrange it."

The entire recall was organized by the Public Property Department and took several days. We parked the cars at Veterans Stadium. The visual statement made by turning the stadium into a city parking lot was more powerful than any figures I could have presented. Some people were astounded to find the city leased so many vehicles. Some employees were livid at having their transportation disrupted.

Some city employees whose jobs didn't require a car had

been using fleet cars at taxpayers' expense for years! They never returned the cars except for servicing or to get another car after wear and tear had broken down the one they had. Similar abuses had occurred with credit cards that were issued to employees. Again, no one knew how many credit cards had been distributed or who had them.

After the car audit was completed, we initiated a new distribution process. We reissued some of the cars, put others up for auction, and took several away from employees who were never entitled to cars to begin with. Many of the cars remaining in the fleet were then replaced with smaller, more gas-efficient Plymouth Horizons.

Angry employees wanted to know, What was I trying to prove? Who did I think I was? The loudest complaints came from police and fire department officials who wanted to keep the luxury cars at their disposal, no questions asked. Now not only were some of them forced to use their own cars or take public transportation, but officials with city vehicles complained that the new cars were too cramped to ride in comfortably. It didn't matter that I used the same car. They were used to luxury.

Not all the complaints involved bruised egos. John White, Sr., one of the founders of the Black Political Forum, now worked for me in the managing director's office. John had what I considered a practical problem with the new compact cars. He literally couldn't fit into them.

Over the years, John had let himself get terribly out of shape. He stood about six feet four inches tall and was very heavy. He presented his problem simply and forcefully.

"Mr. Goode, I want to cooperate with you. I think what you are doing is marvelous," he said. "But I'm afraid this body will not fit into that little car."

Looking at John, I knew he was right.

"John, maybe we can remove the front seat. You can sit in the back and drive from there," I teased. We both had a good laugh. I assigned a station wagon to him and John lived happily ever after with his new wheels.

Another area that I streamlined was the function of operations manager. As managing director, I was responsible for the day-to-day operations of the city, but I couldn't do much without going through the office of the operations manager. This person served as the supervisor of all civil service staff in the managing director's office. All my instructions to staff had to go through him. The whole process of working with the operations manager was unnecessarily cumbersome and bureaucratic. It made it impossible for me to function.

Determined to change the process, I began reading the city charter and the personnel manual to find a loophole. My answer came one Sunday morning as I pored over the personnel manual for what seemed like the hundredth time. I learned that the operations manager position had been created by the previous managing director and was an appointed position that I had the authority to abolish.

So I eliminated the position as well as an assistant's post. After reassigning the two employees to the next highest civil service slots, I now had the freedom to run my own shop my own way.

The streamlining eventually paid off. By the end of the first fiscal year of the Green administration, the city reported a $37-million surplus.

Despite the grumbling, some people thought the reforms were exciting. For too long, Philadelphia city government had lacked accountability. The Green administration was seeking accountability for the citizens of Philadelphia. Former managing directors had acted largely as brokers for the patronage positions the mayor handed out. It didn't much matter if the persons taking patronage jobs were qualified. Nor did many politicians seem to care how an inept bureaucracy would affect city services. If a favor was owed, the managing director made sure it was paid.

But Bill Green was a different kind of mayor from Frank Rizzo. While Rizzo constantly sought ways to repay favors by hiring patronage employees regardless of their suitability for the position, Green wanted a professional operation. He had nothing against patronage employees; he just wanted qualified people to do the job. I shared that view.

My vision of good government was one where quality management ruled. Carrying out my job, I constantly sought ways to downsize offices or to restructure departments to make them more efficient. Again I made new enemies as I demanded efficiency and department accountability. Employees who were unable to function as topnotch administrators in their jobs were subsequently fired.

I ruled by common-sense management in a bureaucracy that I felt was not used to setting objectives, meeting goals, and improving on its successes. As I saw it, city governments usually operated on a combined system of selective bloating and voodoo economics. Each year departments got bigger and bigger, demanding more and more money to meet needs that were never satisfied. Budgets were either nonexistent or based on some esoteric notion of spending to achieve the results you wanted. If you met your goal within the allocated budget, fine. If not, you asked for more money for the coming year. Few people, however, had been asked to justify their spending habits or to seek ways to control them.

I challenged all of that. I demanded to know how much city services cost and why. "How much does it cost to pick up a ton of trash?" I would ask. "Why? How much should it cost?"

That first year in government was a real eyeopener for me as employees struggled to buck the reforms. I didn't realize just how entrenched the lifelong habits of city bureaucracy were and how difficult it could be to get even the simplest of things done.

A group that constantly pointed out city inefficiencies was the Tenant Action Group (TAG). This tenant advocacy group fought to have landlords make repairs to keep their houses up to code. When a landlord refused to repair a broken furnace or leaky plumbing, TAG brought the issue to Licenses and Inspection (L & I), asking them to make the repairs and bill the landlords. This was L & I's job.

Unfortunately L & I was sometimes as bad as, or worse than, the landlords. TAG was constantly demonstrating in my office about Licenses and Inspection issues. Belinda Mayo and Eva Gladstein were the leaders. They would bring dozens of mothers and crying children into my office for a sit-in to complain that they had no heat or hot water. Almost all of their concerns were legitimate. I would promise to get the problem fixed within the next few days. Then I would turn the issue over to the department of Licenses and Inspections. I was always embarrassed when L & I failed to get the work done. This happened over and over again for nearly a year until we got the problem squared away. The L & I bureaucracy was very resistant. They had been accustomed to doing things their own way. It took a whole year, but I finally prevailed in seeing that L & I responded to tenants' concerns appropriately.

As managing director I was required to respond to all fires above three alarms, water-main breaks, and other disasters. The job sometimes kept me hopping twenty-four hours a day, seven days a week as I got calls announcing, "Mr. Director, this is the fire board. We have a four-alarm fire."

This had become routine and my response was always the same.

"Thank you, I'm on my way. Tell the commissioner I'll be there in a few minutes."

I would then jump into my Plymouth Horizon, turn on my siren and flashing lights, and head for the fire.

I remember getting a call at 3:00 A.M. one winter morning. It must have been fifteen degrees below zero. Tired and cold, I jumped into my clothes and set off in my Horizon, sliding down Woodland Avenue. Riding on the city streets, I felt every bump, hole, and uneven surface in that car before hitting the Schuylkill Expressway at sixty-five miles per hour. Cars and trucks pulled out of the way as my flashing lights and whirring siren alerted them that an emergency vehicle was coming. I can just imagine their surprise when my little Plymouth Horizon scooted by.

Making my way onto Lincoln Drive, I navigated the tight curves the best I could. The car skidded as I turned onto Harvey Street, but somehow I managed to keep it under control. I turned onto Wayne Avenue and then Washington Lane. The sirens were at a deafening pitch now, and I could see the flashing lights at the fire scene. It was a church.

Fire commissioner Joe Rizzo — Frank Rizzo's brother — was already at the scene.

"Director, this is a bad one," he said solemnly. "Not much we can save here. We got here as soon as we could, but everything was involved when the first engine arrived. We are doing our best."

"Thanks for your effort," I said.

"This is Rev. Lafayette Gooding," Rizzo said, directing me to a man standing on the sidelines. "He's the pastor of this church. Rev. Gooding, this is the managing director, Wilson Goode."

"Rev. Gooding, I am sorry to meet you under these circumstances," I told him. "Is there anything we can do to help?"

"No, not right now," he said, shaking his head sadly. "This is a shock. This is our fifth fire, Mr. Goode. Please pray that God will see us through all of this."

"I'll pray, Reverend," I said.

The fire out, we could see that the church was destroyed. With as many fires as I saw, I knew I would never get used to the feeling of loss.

I managed to get home, shower, shave, and dress to make a 7:00 A.M. staff meeting at my office.

Every morning I met with a different group of staff people to get a weekly update on their department. I believed my role was to be the mayor's eyes and ears in city government and on the street. I wanted to feel the pulse of the city, but I couldn't do that from my office on the sixteenth floor of the municipal services building. So besides meeting regularly with staff, I went out to where the people and the problems were.

August 28, 1980, was one such day of reaching out to the people. I remember it for two reasons: My mother celebrated her seventy-seventh birthday, and a police officer shot and killed a young black man named William Green.

Rumors spread like wildfire.

"His hands were tied behind his back when he was shot."

"The police shot him for no reason at all."

A call alerted me that a large crowd was gathering at the Twenty-second Police District headquarters at Seventeenth and Montgomery Streets. Irate citizens were demanding justice.

I arrived on the scene to find an uncontrolled situation. Young black men were hurling rocks and bottles at the police station as a mob shouted and jeered outside. Believing I could disperse the crowd, I walked west toward Seventeenth Street, speaking through a hand-held loudspeaker.

"I want all of you to disperse. We will have an investigation," I shouted. "We will work this out."

Before I knew it, a hail of bottles and bricks were raining in my direction. One grazed my shoulder. The others fell short, shattering thousands of glass fragments around my feet. I hastily retreated into the station house to regroup and call Mayor Green, who was out of town.

"Mr. Mayor, this is Wilson Goode," I said. "We have a real serious problem here at Seventeenth and Montgomery. There's been a police shooting. Things are getting out of control and—"

I was cut short by his words.

"Wilson, I have a very important dinner engagement. I can't be running back to Philadelphia each time there is a problem. Keep me posted."

"Yes, Mr. Mayor. I will handle it and keep you posted."

Hanging up the phone, I wondered why he had been so abrupt with me. I didn't like to bother him at his summer home in Longport, N.J., but this seemed important enough.

Hesitantly I went back outside to try to calm things down. I had identified the ringleaders. Calling them aside, I asked them to call off the confrontation before someone got hurt. We argued back and forth several minutes.

"Look, I'm black, man, like you," I said. "I know what your concerns are. We will deal with this problem in the appropriate manner."

After some very difficult negotiations, the crowd was calmed down. Two neighborhood activists, Jean Hobson, leader of a group called Mothers Concerned, and Edwina Baker Robinson, helped disperse the crowd and restore the peace. Mayor Green returned late the next day.

The shooting and rioting were now national news, and the media clamored to interview Mayor Green about the incident. He never once asked me to brief him about the near riot or to be available for a media session. I must confess my ego was bruised and my respect for Mayor Green somewhat diminished. Things were never quite the same after that. I always questioned his real passion for the job and for solving problems.

After the shooting, we spent three tense days monitoring the volatile situation in that community. I prayed daily for heavy rains, believing that rain would keep rioters and looters at bay, since people didn't protest much in the rain. Some rain did fall the second night, and it helped cool things off.

It was weeks before a sense of calm returned to the city with the help of community leaders like Father Paul Washington. The police officer who did the shooting was arrested and charged. Several months passed before the case went to trial. When it did, the officer was acquitted. Fortunately it was winter. Very few people riot in cold weather.

While serving as managing director, I learned that my basic nature was that of an advocate or defender of the underdog. One of my most enduring battles was for the rights of the homeless.

In 1982, I advocated for the rights of the homeless for decent shelter, food, and clothing. As I sat in my office one night, with temperatures outside below freezing, the lessons of compassion that I'd learned at home and in church returned to prick my conscience. I answered my phone to find Health Commissioner Stuart Shapiro calling for advice.

"Mr. Director, we really must do something about the homeless tonight," he said. "I suggest we use a firehouse or a police station. It's bitterly cold."

As Dr. Shapiro talked, my mind drifted back to an incident that occurred in Seaboard, North Carolina, when I was thirteen.

A hobo came to our farm seeking a handout. He was a dirty, ragged, tired-looking old man, and when he knocked on the door, we didn't let him in the house. But Mother fixed him some soup and biscuits, which he ate hungrily while sitting on the porch. He gobbled that food down as if he hadn't eaten in weeks. Humbled by the sight of the starving man, we gave him more.

As the man drank down his last bit of soup, I remembered something. Running to my room, I rummaged around until I found the dollar in change I'd been saving for my next trip to the movies. I returned to the porch only to find the man walking down the road.

"Wait!" I yelled, running after him. "Mister, I have something for you."

He stopped. As I ran up to him, our eyes met and I immediately felt pity for the pain and sorrow those dark eyes contained. I took his calloused, wrinkled hand and placed the change in it.

"Boy, I can't take all of your money," he said. "Take it back."

"No, it's yours," I told him, backing away.

Then I turned and ran home as fast as I could as the old man continued his slow trek down the road. Back home, Mother asked me what I had given the old man.

"He dropped something and I took it to him," I fibbed.

As I relived this memory, I heard Dr. Shapiro's voice in the background talking about the cold and the homeless. I knew I would work extra-long hours that night in search of warm shelters for the homeless.

Two public programs that I was especially proud of created closer ties between the neighborhoods and City Hall. The first was a Saturday cleanup caravan called the Clean Team; the second was the town meeting.

Clean Team members were representatives from various city departments. Every Saturday morning, we visited various neighborhoods around the city.

"Good morning. We are here to help you clean your street," we would announce.

The statement always produced a chuckle from some people. Looking at these stiff bureaucrats in suits, brooms in hand, few citizens took us seriously until we had proven ourselves.

"Mr. Goode, you know you aren't going to clean any streets with that suit and tie on," one woman challenged.

"Watch me," I said. "Give me that broom."

As I swept my way down the street, a group of neighbors broke out in applause. I walked back to the first woman and asked, "How am I doing?"

"Fine," she said approvingly. "We're sure glad to see you act like you know how to use that broom. Come back here next Saturday and you can do the whole block!" After a while we stopped wearing our business clothes—for practical reasons. My family started coming along, too.

Each week the team hit six to eight streets in the city. The program went on for nine months, between March and November. Block captains directed the activities. Over time, I came to develop a close relationship with these neighborhood block captains. They responded to me like a native son, inviting me to their front porches for a chat or refreshments. Through them I learned more about what was going on in the neighborhoods than any formal survey could have told me. The block captains were like family, and I valued their views.

Town meetings were launched to discuss budget issues and help inform citizens of how city government works. We held evening meetings in each police district. My job was to explain where the budget money came from and where it went.

"I want to discuss each city department with you," I would explain to the group gathered. "I want you to know what the departments do and what it costs you to receive a unit of service. This year, for example, it costs you $40 to have a ton of trash removed from your neighborhood. It costs $45 to fill a pothole. I'm working to find out how to cut such costs." The only problem was I couldn't find any other cities around the country who were doing performance-based budgeting.

My office held information meetings all over the city. An old mobile library was converted into an office to travel with the Saturday motorcades. After eighteen months of holding successful community meetings, I learned from close friends that the mayor disapproved.

"What did I do?" I asked innocently.

"Come on, Wilson. You're everywhere. You can't turn on television without seeing your face at some community gathering. The mayor is jealous of all this attention you're getting. He thinks you're acting too much like a mayor. The word is he's going to clip your wings. His advisers are already telling him to watch out for you, that you're running against him."

Although I'd heard this comment more than once, I chose not to pay too much attention to it. Mayor Green had to know that I wasn't a threat to him. I was just trying to do my job. Not too long after this conversation, though, my mobile office was suddenly taken away from me and my name removed from the door. It was replaced with "Mayor William J. Green III." My friends were right; my wings had been clipped.

I first became aware of the back-to-nature group called
MOVE in 1976 while I was still involved in housing development.
As far as I was concerned, the group was just another eccentric
organization making newspaper headlines. My first contact with
them came that winter.

I'd gone to Powelton Village to discuss assisting a community
group with some housing issues involving Drexel University.
Powelton Village was a racially and culturally diverse residential
neighborhood located near Drexel University and the University
of Pennsylvania. The neighborhood was home to college students, professors, community activists, and countercultural people who were considered at worst antiauthority and at best eccentric. In many ways MOVE members and their sympathizers fit
right in.

The day was cold and snowy. At the meeting a young white
man who was a self-described MOVE sympathizer tried to domi-
nate the five-hour conversation. Nothing the man said made an
ounce of sense to me. He would string a number of run-on
sentences together and then burst into a long diatribe on society.
Every conceivable profane word punctuated his statements. No
one could control him or get him to be quiet. If he represented
MOVE's sympathizers, I thought, I'm afraid to imagine what the
real members are like.

Later on when my Public Utility Commission job took me to
Harrisburg daily, I was rarely in town when MOVE members
demonstrated. Therefore, my early knowledge of MOVE came
largely from what I read in the news. There was plenty to read.

*Founded in the early seventies, MOVE drew most of its fol-
lowers from the radical white students and underprivileged
black residents of the Powelton Village neighborhood. Occasionally outsiders were drawn to the group and became members.
Delbert Orr, a minister of information with the Black Panther*

*Party in Chicago, was one such person. He joined MOVE follow-
ing a visit to Philadelphia.*[1]

*The group's spiritual prophet and founder was a semiliterate
handyman named Vincent Leaphart who took the name "John
Africa." Along with a white social worker named Donald
Glassey, Africa developed a document containing the teachings
of John Africa, which became the philosophical basis for MOVE's
rejection of most modern technology*[2].

*John Africa's break with modern society was both erratic
and eccentric. A soft-spoken man who fancied himself a writer,
Africa was usually seen walking his pack of dogs in the Powelton
Village neighborhood. Some people considered him a dreamer;
others called him paranoid. In homage to him, all MOVE members took the surname Africa and adopted his back-to-nature
habits which shunned modern life.*[3]

*Members rejected time, listed their age as one, and shunned
soap and bathing. Childbirths were natural, with the mothers
licking their babies clean and biting the umbilical cord with
their teeth. Their daily diet consisted of raw food, mainly fruits
and vegetables, but sometimes raw chicken as well.*[4]

*MOVE's home was a rambling, three-story, red-brick struc-
ture at 307 North Thirty-third Street purchased by Glassey. The
house used no electricity or gas. Piles of firewood lay in the front
yard along with old trash barrels that were used as cookstoves.
A corner of the yard was strewn with layers of eggshells, banana
and orange peels, corn cobs, human and animal excrement,
and other garbage to "return to the earth what we got from it."*[5]

*Dogs, squirrels, and rats were among the menagerie allowed
to wander free. While their surroundings were no Eden, MOVE
members saw their lifestyle as a wholesome environment, unpol-
luted by modern technology and artificial substances.*

*Yet MOVE members were no purists. Dressed in their uni-
form of heavy sweatshirts, blue jeans, parkas, work boots, and
dreadlocks (long, twisted locks of natural hair), members traveled around the city in an old, yellow school bus to hold demonstrations. They also owned several cars, a telephone, and a
typewriter.*[6] *Adults who already had been tainted by cooked food
were allowed to eat cooked chicken. The children weren't so
lucky.*

Throughout the early seventies, the group appeared to be basically harmless, if not the most sanitary and socially accept- able people to be around. The origin of their name, MOVE, was unknown. MOVE members held regular demonstrations to ex- press their beliefs in natural law, seeking, for example, to have zoo animals returned to their natural habitats. Their protests against the school board and the zoo were legendary. They were persistent, disruptive, and offensive; profanity and disorderly conduct were used as weapons of psychological warfare. Be- tween October 1974 and April 1975, approximately forty MOVE members were arrested 150 times for misdemeanors. They racked up $210,000 in bail requirements and $15,000 in fines. [7] *For MOVE, acting out in court was a form of social protest.*

For years regarded as a nuisance to the Philadelphia Police Department and criminal justice system, sometime in the late seventies the nuisance became a menace.

In the spring of 1977, several members appeared at their West Philadelphia house brandishing weapons and wearing military fatigues. The group was also accused of hiding weapons and materials to make bombs. Arrest warrants were authorized but not served. Frank Rizzo, the mayor at the time, had been elected through a law-and-order movement that his supporters understood as a pledge to keep blacks and criminals in line. For several months, negotiators within Rizzo's administration met with MOVE members to try to get them to stop the numerous health and other code violations. The negotiations broke down on August 8, 1978, and the city sought to evict MOVE members from their home at Powelton Village.

More than three hundred police officers entered the neigh- borhood in the early morning under cover of darkness. When MOVE members failed to allow police access to the home and retreated to a basement fortress, police used a crane as a batter- ing ram to destroy the house and high-pressure hoses to flood the basement.

Suddenly, shots rang out. A brief gun battle ensued. When it was over, Officer James Ramp, only two months away from retirement, lay dead. Fifteen other people were injured, three seriously. The MOVE house was razed to the ground.

The next day, Philadelphia Inquirer *headlines screamed,*

"MOVE Routed in Gunfight; Officer Killed, House Leveled." Philadelphia residents were also treated to a graphic scene of police brutality played on television and newspapers in sordid detail.

Wearing jeans and no shirt, a defenseless Delbert Orr Africa was beaten repeatedly by police officers as newspaper and TV cameras recorded the story. In one series of newspaper photos, Africa stands with his head bowed, his arms stretched out like a thief being crucified. An officer has a shotgun trained at Africa's head while another policeman hits him flush in the face with a police helmet. He falls, sprawled among the debris of the MOVE house. An officer grabs him by the hair and drags him to the sidewalk, where other officers wait to deliver kicks and punches as Africa tries to cover his face. He is later handcuffed and led away.

Commenting on the incident, Mayor Rizzo declared, "The only way we're going to end them [problems with MOVE] is to get the death penalty back in, and I'll pull the switch myself."[8] Rizzo also criticized the news media for showing scenes of police brutality.

"I'm going to repeat one more time for you. Every week in your goddam newspaper, every weekend, they have headlines in your paper about policemen did this, did that, murder, murder, murder," Rizzo told an Inquirer *reporter. "Not one of them has been convicted. You convict them in your newspaper. That's what's wrong with this city. You are destroying it. The people you represent are destroying it."[9]*

Nine MOVE members were convicted of Officer Ramp's death and sentenced to thirty to a hundred years in prison. Loyal to their MOVE brothers and sisters, various MOVE members launched crusades to have the case reopened for investigation. That's how I met MOVE member Gerald Ford Africa. Stating that no conclusive evidence had ever been provided to prove the fatal shots that killed Officer Ramp had come from MOVE guns, Gerald Africa wanted the case reopened.

In the eyes of the Philadelphia police, MOVE was a violent, militant group whose antipolice and antiestablishment tactics had led to the death of one of their own. They wanted no mercy. For nearly four years after the jailings, MOVE was less visible.

The media coverage painted MOVE as an evil, radical group that was both violent and destructive. Therefore, I was taken aback when soon after my appointment as managing director, my executive assistant, Shirley Hamilton, called to say that Gerald Ford Africa wanted to meet with me.

"I don't think you should meet with him," she advised.

"Set the meeting up," I said. "If I don't meet with him, he's going to start bothering the mayor. The mayor doesn't need that. That's why I'm here."

The meeting was set up. Later that week I stood looking at a tall, robust man, his serious, unsmiling face framed by a veil of long dreadlocks. No matter where I moved, his eyes followed me, never resting to look elsewhere.

"Mr. Africa, I'm Wilson Goode. It's good to see you."

"Cut the formal stuff out," he said solemnly. "I'm here on serious business. My brothers and sisters are in jail, and I want you to get them out. Plus I want you"—he emphasized the *you*—"to give us a new house since you tore down our house."

Before I could catch my breath, the agenda was placed before me. He was articulate and direct. His eyes were brooding, penetrating.

"I can't get your brothers and sisters out of jail," I said. "That's not within my jurisdiction."

"You're the number-two man, aren't you? Are you just a show nigger or can you really do something?"

"I'm a lot more than show," I said, "but I don't have the power either to get your sisters or brothers out of jail, or to replace your house. That's out of my jurisdiction."

He was unmoved.

"Let me restate my position, Mr. Goode. I am here to ask you to release my brothers and sisters from jail. They are there illegally. They had a kangaroo court. The police tore our house down. That's wrong. You know it's wrong. All we want is justice."

I was persuaded by the sincerity of his cause. I knew he believed what he was saying. As this articulate, proud black man looked me in the eyes, something inside me said that this was the beginning of a long, difficult relationship with this organization. From the very beginning, the conversation was a no-win situation. My feelings stirred uneasily as I failed to shake the nagging thought that this would not be the last time I'd encounter MOVE.

I was not managing director in 1978 when the MOVE house was razed. Nor did I have all the facts about the whole situation. But I could see that Gerald Ford Africa was determined to pursue his cause. He would not rest until he got what he wanted. And I knew I couldn't give him what he wanted. Already we were at a stalemate.

I told him District Attorney Ed Rendell could help.

"As district attorney, Ed Rendell has the authority to reopen these cases. You have to talk to Ed Rendell," I said.

"He won't see me," Africa responded. "I have been trying, but he won't see me."

Later I called Rendell and told him of my visit with Gerald Ford Africa.

"Ed, I can't solve this problem, but you can," I said.

He sighed. "Wilson, the issue is closed. The trial is over."

He never did discuss with me whether he would see Gerald Ford Africa, but Africa finally got his meeting with Rendell. Later Rendell told me that, by coincidence, he and Africa had met on the street. Rendell told him the case would not be reopened.

CHAPTER TEN

Running for the Prize

After I became the city's first black managing director, few people doubted that I could become Philadelphia's first black mayor. The only question was, Would I run in 1983—immediately following my term as managing director—or in 1987?

My dilemma was that Bill Green, my boss, was planning to run for reelection. My term as managing director had been so successful that some people thought I should run against Green. Among the most vocal proponents of this idea was the Guardian Civic League, the city's organization of black police officers.

In January of 1982, the league decided to boycott Green's Martin Luther King, Jr., celebration. They charged Green with reneging on a campaign promise to push affirmative action policies on the force and help black police officers move up the administrative ranks in the city's police department. Two of the officers—Harold James and John Green—came to me privately to feel out my loyalty to Green and let me know what was happening.

The league was fighting for affirmative action, having been dissatisfied both with the low number of black police officers and the number who had ascended to positions of authority. I met occasionally with John Green, who is now a sheriff, and Harold James, now a state representative, to discuss the status of minority hiring in the police department. We had just finished such a meeting and were sitting back savoring our lunch.

"You have to run for mayor next year," John suddenly announced.

The statement was so far removed from what we'd been talking about that for a moment I thought he was kidding. A second look at his face told me he wasn't.

"Come on, I work for Bill Green," I said trying to lighten the mood. "He's probably going to run again."

"Doesn't matter, Wilson. You have to run. We need you."

"We who?" I asked, feigning innocence.

"Black folks . . . liberal groups," he said, "anybody, really, who wants to end this police state in Philadelphia and the unjust treatment that so many people have endured for years. The city must be reformed."

We had had similar conversations before. This was the first time, though, that the suggestion of my running for mayor had had a timeline and purpose attached to it. Before I could recover from the shock of his suggestion that I challenge Green for the mayor's seat, John hit me right between the eyes with another remark.

"You know the breakfast the mayor is holding to celebrate the King holiday next week?"

"Yes."

"We don't want you to attend it."

I chuckled. It was bad enough that the Guardian Civic League was planning to boycott the breakfast. Surely John Green knew that for me to boycott that breakfast in support of the league would be a public criticism of Green.

"I can't do that," I protested. "I work for Green. My job would be on the line."

"Wilson, don't give me that. You can do anything you want, including run for mayor of this city. There are a lot of people out there who are ready to support you. But you've got to decide if you want to be mayor or give in to party politics."

I left the meeting that day with my head spinning. I had thought only casually of running for mayor, but I also felt that I owed my loyalty to Bill Green. He had given me the chance to become managing director. Didn't I owe him something?

All that week I grappled with my feelings, flip-flopping between my loyalty to Green and whether I should run for mayor. What would Bill Green say if I refused to attend the breakfast? Would he feel betrayed? humiliated? On the other hand, was there a coalition ready to support my candidacy for mayor in 1983? Was I about to throw away a golden opportunity to make history and achieve something that I really wanted?

The date of the breakfast crept up on me like a thief in the night, and still I didn't know what I would do. Experience soon taught me that when you hesitate too long in making a decision, fate will help make it for you. Late that afternoon I got a call from a reporter with the *Philadelphia Inquirer.* They were doing a story on the league's boycott and criticism of Green's position on affirmative action.

"Mr. Goode, what are your feelings?" the reporter asked. "Do you agree with Bill Green's position on affirmative action?"

I hesitated before answering. I'd thought about this for the past week. Now that someone wanted to know what I thought, I still wasn't sure what my response would be.

"No, I do not agree with Mayor Green's stance on affirmative action," I said. "I think there is a need for a more aggressive affirmative action policy within the police department."

"Then do you support the Guardian Civic League's boycott of the breakfast?"

I took a deep breath.

"I support the people who feel their rights are not being properly dealt with," I said. "If they want to step back and not attend the breakfast, then I support that."

Before she asked, I knew what the final question would be. "Will you attend the breakfast?"

"I don't know."

The story hit the newspaper the next day. I was immediately summoned to Green's office. Word was that he was livid over this article. When I entered his office, he appeared to be relatively calm. But there was something that changed about Bill Green's face when he was angry. Looking at his face I sensed he was angry even though it wasn't obvious.

"Wilson, what is this story in the morning paper?" he asked. "I didn't expect this from you. I expect your support."

The way he emphasized the word *you* immediately humbled me. After we finished chatting, I concluded that I should attend the breakfast.

I don't know if the story did it or what, but something had pacified the league and my other supporters. So while I chose to attend the breakfast, that in no way diminished the support I continued to get from people who were trying to draft me to run in the '83 election.

Henry Nicholas, head of the hospital workers union, and Robert Sugarman, an attorney and longtime friend since the Hardy Williams campaigns, organized a "Draft Wilson Goode for Mayor" campaign that spring.

Frankly I was flattered by the attention and the public vote of confidence. I felt I could handle the mayor's job. That others thought so too and were willing to state it publicly seemed amazing. Logic told me I should squash the movement in deference to Green, but I didn't want to offend the organizers. Also, I consider myself to be relatively modest, but even the most modest people have egos that like to be stroked and flattered. I was immensely flattered that some people thought that I, this sharecroppers' son, should be the next mayor of Philadelphia.

I had decided I would not run against Green. My sense of loyalty and integrity was preventing me from pursuing my personal desire. After all, Green had given me an unparalleled opportunity to serve as the first African American managing director. I felt I owed him something for that. He could have picked anyone to serve in that post, but he chose me. I still didn't know how or why I had come to his attention. But I was grateful that I had and that he had shown such confidence in me.

Toward the end of the summer, I was told to stop sitting on the fence. "Either resign and announce that you're running for mayor or announce that you are not going to run."

They were right. I had let the draft movement run too long. It was unfair to Bill Green. This wasn't the way to express my gratitude to him. A number of reliable sources confided that Green's advisers were urging him to fire me. They said that Green was reluctant to do so because he feared the negative fallout. He didn't want to make me a martyr, I was told.

I decided not to run. Deep down inside, I knew I had made that decision a long time before and had allowed the draft movement to go on too long. Immediately after Labor Day I notified the committee that I would not allow myself to be considered as a candidate if Bill Green was running. They did not like my decision but they accepted it.

After the decision, I settled back into my job as managing director, free from the distractions of the "Draft Goode for Mayor" committee. Mentally I put together a three-year plan for my life: I would finish out my term as managing director and perhaps serve two years or so into Green's second term.

Nothing significant happened for the next two months. But to my surprise, on Monday, November 1, 1982, Mayor Green asked to see me at the Garden Restaurant. I thought I was going to be fired. I just knew his advisers had finally convinced him to cut me loose.

When I walked into the Garden Restaurant, my anxiety jumped another level when I saw Howard Gittis, James Gillin, and William Batoff seated with Green. These were the three people who were supposedly trying to get me fired. I sat down at the table, my face a mask of solemnity.

"Hi, Mr. Mayor. How are you?" I asked, masking my fear.

"I'm fine, Wilson," Green replied. "You know these folks, don't you?"

"Yes, Mr. Mayor, I do. Gentlemen, how are you doing this evening?" I asked. They seemed to speak at once.

"Fine, thank you."

"Very well."

"Good, thanks."

Afterwards they fell silent. I noticed they looked unhappy. Green launched right into the reason for the meeting.

"Wilson, I want to tell you that I am not running for reelection," Green said.

For a moment I was stunned, unable to comprehend what he had said.

"What did you say, Mr. Mayor?" I asked.

He repeated it slowly, emphasizing the word *not*.

The words hit hard, catching me off guard. I was shocked

and totally unprepared. My mouth dropped open and I sat stunned, disoriented. I guess someone expected me to speak, but I didn't know what to say.

"Do you want to talk about it?" Green asked.

"Yes," I said quietly. We went back to his office to talk.

For the next two hours we talked about Green's decision not to run, his reasons, and what this meant for me.

"What are you going to do?" he asked.

My answer was immediate.

"Mr. Mayor, I plan to run for mayor," I said. Green was, as usual, methodical and thoughtful. He questioned me extensively about whether or not I could put together a winning organization. But when he finished, my mind was even more settled. I was going to run for mayor. And I would do it with or without Green's support.

I went home and woke Velma to tell her what had just happened.

"This is it," I said, concluding my story. "If I am ever going to go for it, this is my chance to do so."

Velma and I were so excited that neither of us slept much that night. The next morning I arose bright and early to go to my office, even though it was a legal holiday. Once there, I contacted the people in the "Draft Goode for Mayor" movement and asked them to spread the word. I was resigning to run for mayor.

The next day—Wednesday, November 3, 1982—I walked over to the mayor's office and handed him my letter of resignation as managing director. Less than forty-eight hours had passed since Green had told me he would not seek a second term.

That done, I left to attend a press conference I had called to announce my resignation. Walking to the small conference room of the managing director's office, my whole body was charged with energy. In my years as managing director I'd never held a major press conference, and I was excited.

I walked into the conference room to face dozens of cameras and reporters. It was hot! My staff had packed as many media people into the small room as they could. It was filled to over-flowing. The room lacked ventilation, and the hot lights and close bodies made it even more oppressive.

I didn't mind. Facing the cameras and reporters, I spoke

clearly and calmly. I knew I was embarking on one of the greatest adventures of my life.

"I will leave my job as managing director on November 30, 1982," I said. "I do so to provide an orderly transition and to remove any appearance of politicking from this very important and significant office.

"I take this action because within the past several months, and increasingly in recent days, there has been much speculation regarding my future in government. It has, in fact, caused some distractions from my role as managing director.

"I believe that it is important for the job that I now occupy to remain free from all politics. At this point I'm only taking one important step, and that is to remove myself from my office so I can have a clear head to think about my future."

While I did not say it, the media and everyone else knew I was running for mayor. My resignation as managing director was only preliminary to the main event. I knew I was going to run for mayor, but I needed time to think about how I would run for office, organize a campaign, raise money, and complete an orderly transition from my current office.

It didn't make much sense to announce my candidacy for mayor before all my ducks were lined up. After answering a few questions, I left the press conference, happy.

My resignation letter to Mayor Green was sincere. In it I wrote, "I want to thank you for the freedom you have afforded me in pursuing my management duties and responsibilities. Equally appreciated is the opportunity of having been a cabinet member of one of the most effective administrations in the history of Philadelphia municipal government."

Green responded with a handwritten note that he shared with the press. In part it said, "The energy and devotion you brought to your duties are well known by all and appreciated by me."

In the period between November 3 and November 30, I was careful to keep political issues separate from government issues as I wound up my term as managing director. It was hard. Often I felt as if I were walking a tightrope. The momentum that was building for my still-unannounced campaign didn't help.

Following my resignation as managing director, numerous

columns and editorials began appearing about me. The articles were favorable and added fuel to the excitement that was already building.

The day after the press conference, Acel Moore, columnist and associate editor with the *Philadelphia Inquirer,* wrote:

> Goode decided to resign from office and apparently has made up his mind to make the run for mayor. He has been under tremendous pressure since this summer from individuals and groups who initiated a draft-Goode movement and who wanted him to resign and an-nounce his intention to run for mayor in next spring's primary.
>
> Goode resisted the pressure and stuck by a decision and a prom-ise that he would not be a candidate if his boss, the mayor, was going to seek re-election.
>
> Goode is a man of strong moral character and conviction. He is also a man with proven administrative and management skills. His dedication to his job has been the trademark of his tenure as manag-ing director.[1]

The media stories continued to build. I began granting some interviews. On November 7, in an interview with Roger Cohn of the *Inquirer,* I candidly discussed my views.

> I think this administration [Green] has demonstrated that govern-ment can work effectively. . . . We're not where we want to be in government, but we're a heck of a long way from where we were three years ago. And I think that with a lot more of what we've been doing in the last three years being continued in the future, this city can become a model for the country.[2]

Various stories ran throughout the month. On November 30, my last day as managing director, Carolyn Acker of the *Daily News* summed up my tenure in the managing director's office this way.

> On a Thursday evening in September, city Managing Director W. Wilson Goode took his traveling civic class to the 17th Police District in South Philadelphia.
>
> The slide show is a cram course in the city's budget process, a presentation of pie charts and figures that lures a surprising number of listeners. On this occasion, 320 residents turned out to learn more about their corner of Philadelphia.
>
> During the past year, Goode told them, the city cleaned and sealed 471 vacant buildings in their district; collected 29,837 tons of rubbish; cleaned 1,989 storm sewer inlets; put out 632 fires; resur-

faced 45,720 square yards of streets; and made 216 repairs to recreation facilities.

He told them how many houses were inspected, demolished, rehabilitated and given away; how many traffic lights were replaced and repaired; how many alleys and streets were cleaned or repaired; and how many emergencies and false alarms were answered.

And he told them how much it cost for each job.

This was the first year a managing director had been able to assemble numbers like that, according to past and present members of that office, thanks to a system that measures city services like widgets from a factory.

That system, and others like it, are among the first accomplishments Goode cites in looking back over his three years as managing director, which end today.[3]

I was amazed at the detail Acker presented in recapping my three-year career and getting public officials to comment. The article was like a newspaper version of "W. Wilson Goode, This Is Your Life." It even included a photo of me from my high school yearbook. Through Acker, the public learned that I began work at 7:00 A.M. and usually concluded late at night three to four times a week. She wrote:

His enormous capacity for work is awesome . . . to public officials who routinely work weekends and evenings themselves.

He has found friends in labor, where he bargained two one-year wage freezes, and he has propelled himself into politics largely by making government—in the person of himself—accessible to average citizens at countless community meetings across Philadelphia.[4]

In summary, Acker and the people she interviewed affirmed my vision of good government. I was thrilled as they lauded me for transforming the managing director's job into a public service that reached out to the people of Philadelphia. An especially heartening statement concluded:

Goode brought a standard of fair play to the delivery of routine city services, according to interviews with several of the 10 commissioners he supervised.

The object was to render equitable services to the citizens of Philadelphia in an honest, coherent way, and there was never any suggestion to do anything other than what was fair, equitable and managerially sound.[5]

On December 6, 1982, I officially announced my candidacy for mayor of Philadelphia. The Philadelphia Centre Hotel at Seventeenth Street and JFK Boulevard was the staging ground. Four hundred people packed into a room reserved for three hundred to cheer the announcement. Walking into that room full of cheering people, with Velma at my side, I could feel an enormous surge of energy surrounding us.

By God, you really are running for mayor, I thought to myself. The impact of this moment was almost more than I could handle. Who would have ever thought, in all those years of praying and hoping to be somebody famous, I would find myself running for mayor of the nation's fourth-largest city?

Slowly I made my way to the podium, stopping to shake hands, receive a hug, or accept a kiss. Finally I stood before the crowd. My heart full and my throat tight with emotion, I said, "I am here this morning to announce that I am a candidate for the office of mayor of the city of Philadelphia."

The crowd roared its approval. The room resounded with the noise of cheering, clapping, foot-stomping people. Tears welled up in my eyes and I couldn't speak. When the cheering died down, I continued.

"I am a problem solver," I said. "I offer to the people of our city, to all who will work with Philadelphians all over the city, someone who is committed to confronting and solving the problems we face."

Upon tossing my hat in the ring, new supporters emerged to join the campaign. A business coalition began forming with the chief executive officers of some of the biggest firms in the nation. They included Henry Wendt of SmithKline Beckman; Roger Hillas of Provident Bank; M. Todd Cooke of PSFS; George Bartol of Hunt Manufacturing; William Fishman of ARA Services; and Harold Sorgenti of Arco Chemical Company.

Also on board were John and Otto Haas of Rohm and Haas Company; Irv Cross and Ollie Johnson, former professional athletes; and Kenneth Gamble of International Records.

My announcement for mayor came with a lot of blind faith. I didn't have a job, a political coalition, campaign manager, or anything other than my ambition and faith. Deep inside, I believed I could win. But even if I was wrong, I knew I had to try. I knew I had to be bold enough to take this stand.

For months leading up to the announcement, something

inside of me kept nudging me to run! run! run! I had prayed about this inner voice, and nothing told me to delay. Earlier that summer I had also talked with my family, asking them what I should do if the opportunity to run for mayor presented itself. Everyone agreed that I should run—except my youngest daughter, Natasha.

Natasha, born in 1971, had always been a daddy's girl. She was an unexpected gift to us, as we had planned to only have two children. Natasha was fond of playing with me, spending time with me. Until she was about six, she used to like to lie on my stomach to take a nap. Natasha never expressed the reason she didn't want me to run for mayor. I think it was because she thought she would be losing her daddy to all those people in the city. She was never comfortable in the spotlight. In 1983, when a reporter tried to photograph her, she put a big campaign hat in front of her face. The newspaper ran the photo on the front page.

Only after I made the announcement did I fully realize the enormity of the step I had taken. I had nothing to work with—no structure, no strategy. Nothing! Nothing, that is, except my faith and belief that God would see me through this campaign.

As has been the case with most of my challenges, my faith began to release miracles. A man named Peter Clark called me and said, "Look, I'm between jobs. I can drive your car and be your assistant if you want the help."

"Yes!" I said.

Peter was a godsend, and I readily accepted his offer. Clark's wife, Tama Myers-Clark, worked in the solicitor's office and we were friends. I knew her as my staff attorney on prison matters. She was an excellent lawyer, and we had great rapport.

Tama was also a graduate of Morgan State, my alma mater. Her father had taught economics at Morgan during the years I attended. Naturally I felt a special kinship to her and welcomed her husband's help.

During that first month my campaign team consisted of me—Wilson Goode the candidate—and Peter Clark—driver, alter ego, and analyst. Peter's LTD was our campaign car. Together we drove all over the city attending meetings and coffee klatches to develop a base of support and raise money. I don't know if blanketing the city with our presence was the best strategy, but it was the only strategy we had. Just as in college, Velma again became the major breadwinner of the family, although I helped out by working part-time as a housing consultant for a law firm.

As the campaign progressed, Tama became interested in running for judge. Peter was a little embarrassed to ask me to support his wife, so he approached the subject gingerly.

"Wilson, you know Tama may be interested in running for judge," he said.

"When?" I asked.

"She's interested in the primary coming up."

"Tama's a fine attorney and would make a fine judge," I said.

"Do you plan to have a ticket?" he asked, almost sheepishly.

"I don't know. It's really too early to tell."

"If you do, Tama would like to be a part of it."

"It would be my pleasure to have her run with me, if I decide to have a ticket," I responded. He sighed with relief.

Tama Myers-Clark ran on my ticket and was elected to the Court of Common Pleas. Peter ran her campaign and kept his fingers in my campaign as an adviser.

As Clark became more involved in his wife's campaign, I had to move rapidly to get a campaign staff together and to raise some money.

I had interviewed many people to run my campaign before finally settling on Steve Murphy. Steve was white and a political outsider. I thought both traits to be important because I didn't want anyone from inside any of the city's political organizations running my campaign. All of the city's potential campaign managers were aligned with some politician and would have set their own agendas.

Greg Naylor was my registration coordinator. His strategies became the key to getting the votes I needed to win. Greg's office registered new voters and checked to ensure that those already registered were still eligible to vote. Our drive registered over one hundred thousand new voters. According to our records we also had 100 percent of all eligible black voters on the rolls.

In the first six weeks, I raised about fifty thousand dollars. I used the bulk of those funds to conduct a poll which revealed I could beat my Democratic opponent, Frank Rizzo, by 58 to 28 percent. I used the results of that poll as leverage to raise more money. May 17, the date of the primary, was only five months away.

The business leaders were quick to respond. They represented the financial core of the city and were looking for new energy. Philadelphia had been dying a slow financial death for years. High crime and high taxes had driven many former city businesses elsewhere and contributed to the loss of 150,000 jobs in fifteen years. An average of 10,000 jobs had left the city annually.

My goal was to infuse a new spirit of cooperation into the city and build on the momentum of good government that Mayor Green had started. Rooting out police corruption and brutality was a major issue of my campaign, as were building a cable television system, building a convention center, and addressing the issue of graffiti.

A campaign strategy that worked remarkably well was the "truth squads" I organized to attend Frank Rizzo's rallies. Their job was to set the record straight about Rizzo's achievements in office and prevent him from rewriting history. For example, if Rizzo maintained that he had created 50,000 jobs while in office, the group would provide the figures showing that it was actually a loss of 10,000 jobs annually. Like any smooth politician, Rizzo wanted to write his own history. The squads, however, would do the editing.

The squads weren't hecklers but sophisticated community and business leaders who were well respected. They attended Rizzo's press conferences and public appearances. Afterwards, equipped with flow charts and data to support their statements, they held their own press conferences to set the record straight. Everything was done in an orderly manner.

My biggest base of support, however, came from the black churches. Those many years of working with church and community groups through PCCA, as well as work in my own denomination, had created a widespread base of support that spanned most of Philadelphia. The Baptist Ministers Conference and the Black Clergy of Philadelphia represented some four hun-

dred thousand black Philadelphians. Their endorsement set in
motion a momentum that continued to grow throughout the
campaign.

One of the greatest resources the churches provided was
church coordinators who did two things: registered voters and
raised money for my campaign. One person worked out of my
campaign office to network with the churches.

To this day, I believe the effort by the churches represented
one of the most dynamic political coalitions ever developed by
the black church in Philadelphia. I had grown up in the church,
and these good citizens knew me as a Christian brother and
leader. As chair of the Public Utility Commission, and later managing director, I had spoken in many of the churches around
town to maintain our close kinship.

The churches viewed me as a native son. I was one of their
own whom God was lifting up to help fulfill their dreams, values,
hopes, and aspirations. Their support flowed toward me naturally and sincerely. They were God's gift to my campaign.

As chair of my deacon board for the previous eight years and
a church deacon for about sixteen years, I had handled nearly
every financial, administrative, spiritual, and management problem that could occur in a church. The variety of issues and people
I had dealt with over the years was invaluable training for a
position like mayor.

Members of the congregations knew I was no pseudo-reli-
gious Christian coming to church to capture a few votes. If anything, my participation in church leadership had helped prepare
me to become managing director. To many church members
throughout Philadelphia, my candidacy for mayor was not an
indication of the greatness of Wilson Goode but a witness to the
power of God.

As I visited the churches, the introduction by the minister
became almost a cliché.

"We all know Wilson Goode" was the standard phrase, and
it was true. Church life was the foundation of my upbringing. The
church family was as important to me as my childhood family,
my wife, and my children. The church had helped stabilize and
strengthen me and had given me the inner security I needed
when discouraging circumstances told me to give up. Who

knows where I would be in life today if Muriel Lemon hadn't encouraged me to apply to college?

When I spoke in the churches, I reminded them of my tenure as chair of the Public Utility Commission, as well as my role as managing director of the city.

"But the real leadership position that qualifies me to be mayor of Philadelphia has been my tenure as chair of my church's deacon board," I would say. "Anyone who can survive as chair of the deacon board in the black church, anyone who can run the deacon board and be the chief layperson in the church, can certainly run this city's government.

"Nothing can be more difficult than trying to manage the day-to-day affairs of a church as chair of the deacon board."

The analogy never failed to elicit a round of resounding amens as it brought the point home in a way they could identify with.

My church background also enabled me to get into the pulpits of churches that had never opened their doors to politicians. Sometimes we worked out schedules that allowed me to speak in five or six churches each Sunday. Ministers adjusted the time they gave to their sermons to let me speak; some even cut their sermons short to let me have my say. Can you imagine a Baptist preacher postponing a sermon or cutting it short to give the pulpit to a politician? With God all things are possible!

The tremendous support of the churches was not an affirmation of my political savvy but another example of God pouring out his blessings upon me. I had lived for the Lord most of my life through my involvement in the church and my attempt to uphold God's values in the community. Now he was giving back to me tenfold what I had given to him.

I felt a strong kinship with the churches. I didn't want to disappoint them by shifting my fundamental Christian values in political office. It was important to me that I would remain the kind of Christian in public office that I was in the community. I didn't care if I wasn't viewed as a good politician by the public. I wanted to be a good Christian, a good public servant, and an honorable man who happened to be mayor.

Most of the people who later became involved in my campaign were people recruited out of the churches. A group of black women organized "Women for Goode." Emma Chappell and Ruth Wells were the leaders and organizers of events involving women all over the city.

Their coalition included young, old, rich, and poor women. Some of the women commented that they had waited a long time to see their "son" run for mayor. They were going to see that he was victorious.

The group's trademark was a T-shirt that read "I am a Goode woman." The shirts sold like hotcakes and rapidly became collectors' items. Whenever we saw someone wearing one of the T-shirts, Velma jokingly reminded me that she was the only real "Goode woman" in my life. I thought about getting her a shirt that read "I am the real Goode woman," but I don't believe she would have approved.

For the most part, everyone who helped in the campaign fund raising followed the rules. They brought in personal checks or money orders; no cash contributions over one hundred dollars. This was the law. And even if it had not been the law, it was good management practice. But there was one notable exception. After an evening fund-raising event, Mary Mason, WHAT radio personality, brought in ten thousand dollars in cash in a paper bag. The money was given to Shirley Hamilton, who was now campaign administrator. She initially took the money, not knowing what else to do. She called me. I asked her to return the money immediately and to let Mary Mason know that we did not accept cash over one hundred dollars in this campaign. She was concerned about giving back all that money, but I persisted. The money was returned. Mason subsequently gave two five-thousand-dollar checks to the campaign. I don't know where the ten thousand dollars in cash came from.

Not long after her contributions, Mason started talking to me about the Commission on Human Relations. She wanted to chair the commission. I didn't want her to chair it; she was the wrong person for that job. I told her that I was committed to making Rev. James S. Allen the chair. She was unhappy with me and Rev. Allen.

I was worried by her judgment. If she would bring me ten thousand dollars in cash, could she have good, sound judgment? Where did she get the money and why did she use cash? She did not set the kind of example I wanted for chair of the Commission on Human Relations. Further, rumors existed that Mason was also very close to Frank Rizzo. Was this money some kind of trick to set me up? I just didn't know. What I did know was that accepting ten thousand dollars in cash was wrong.

The turning point in the campaign came following my first debate with Rizzo. Rizzo was a hardball player, a machine politician who had used patronage and favors to gain enormous control and power. Rizzo's folks had asked for the debate and most people thought he would wipe his feet on me as if I were a doormat. Understandably that first debate drew lots of attention from people eager to see what would happen.

Because my demeanor is so low-key, some people had questioned whether or not I had media presence. Others wondered if I was too bureaucratic. Could I articulate the issues in ordinary language? Still other people worried about my stuttering.

The debate was not only a forum for the issues but also my coming-out party, so to speak, to allow people to see how well I functioned under pressure.

The minute before the debate started was the longest period of my life. I was scared to death and unsure of myself. It seemed like I was waiting an eternity for things to get underway. Once it started, though, I settled back into a calm and peace that was beyond my imagination. I felt comfortable and very much at ease. This attitude came through in my presentation. After sailing through that debate without a problem, I was confident that I would win the primary.

As the campaign gained momentum, it dawned on me just what I was doing. By God, I could win this thing; I *would* win this thing, I thought. This was not just a campaign for the sake of having a campaign. I was not running against Frank Rizzo just to see what would happen. I was running to become mayor of Philadelphia — and the odds were looking good that I would be elected.

As my dream came within reach, I felt humbled. I remembered that little son of sharecroppers, working in the fields of North Carolina, barely able to speak from stuttering. Now I stood on the threshold of defeating a political legend, Frank Rizzo, in this primary election. This little sharecroppers' son might just become the first African American mayor in Philadelphia's history. Ain't God good?

Reflecting on the road I had traveled, my mind went back to that conversion experience on that mourner's bench when I was twelve years old. How scared I had been! I thought about Rev. Byrd saying, "If you put your trust in God, then all things are possible. God will open doors for you that no man can shut."

I had lived and worked in good faith all my life. Now it appeared I could accomplish a goal that was only a pipe dream just a few years before. The very thought of God's providence and goodness humbled me. I was thankful and determined to keep on trusting in this God who had opened so many doors for his children.

Throughout the many stages of the civil rights movement, hundreds of people had given their lives for the right to vote, for the right to a better way of life. I thought of them now, and how in this big city of Philadelphia thousands of black people were helping register thousands of other black people to elect a black man—me—as the first African American mayor of this city.

The night before the primary election, someone put up Frank Rizzo posters directly across the street from my home. I lived in the Fortieth Ward, a district that had given the majority vote to George Wallace during his bid for president. Rizzo was strong here, and the subdivision where I lived had a large number of Rizzo supporters.

Election day dawned sunny and beautiful. When I went to vote, the poll workers were very cordial. Television cameras milled around everywhere. Velma and I voted and flashed the "V for victory" sign before we left. It felt great knowing that I was voting for myself.

I learned that lines and lines of black people had been gathering in black districts all across the city since 7:00 A.M. that morning. They stood thirty, forty, fifty people deep. It was as if some mysterious floodgate had opened, pouring out this huge mass of black humanity.

They were young and old, male and female, with one common goal that day—to vote for the candidate of their choice. I had announced my candidacy on December 6, 1982. Now on May 17, 1983, the voters had their chance to respond.

The black turnout for that primary was totally unprecedented in the city's history. Frank Rizzo was defeated by nearly sixty thousand votes! I got 98 percent of the black vote and about 22 percent of the white vote, which was highly unusual.

My opponents for the fall election would be John Egan and Tom Leonard. Egan was a businessman and the endorsed candidate of the Republican party. I knew that in the fall election, many white voters who had voted for Rizzo would support the Republican candidate, and there were more white voters in the city than black. Therefore, the general election would be riskier. Tom Leonard, however, provided a plus, running as an independent. Leonard would be an option for white Democrats who did not want to vote for either a Republican or a black Democrat.

Charles Dougherty had been a candidate for the Republican nomination for mayor. He lost. It was expected that naturally he would support his party's nominee, John Egan. But Dougherty had always been a maverick, and ambitious.

After the primary, he had a series of meetings with me. He was trying to decide what to do. He had a *quid pro quo* for his endorsement. He wanted to be city representative and director of commerce. I explained to Charlie that the best I could do would be to keep an open mind, but I could not promise him anything. Even though I never promised him anything, Dougherty decided to endorse me over John Egan. Frankly, I was surprised.

After the election, Charlie came knocking again. This time he wanted to know what I was going to do for him. I was really not interested in doing anything for Charlie. He had violated my basic principle of good government. He seemed to think that he could earn an appointment with an endorsement. He could not. He was unhappy and remains unhappy even today.

Frank Rizzo endorsed me. Rizzo was then a Democrat and a good party man. His endorsement came to promote unity within the Democratic party. But I also knew he hoped his endorsement would buy him influence with me and help keep his brother in office as fire commissioner. My long-standing problems with Frank Rizzo began when I refused to accept both his advice and his brother in my administration.

The fall election was largely anticlimactic. By early afternoon the exit polls showed clearly that I had won. By 6:00 P.M. it was definite. The only thing remaining was to see the margin I had won by.

Throughout the day I thanked God for his blessings and this great victory he had given me. The final polls indicated I'd won by 123,000 votes.

At 12:30 that evening my family and I entered Convention Hall to face a crowd of wall-to-wall people. I was moved beyond belief as I felt a wellspring of emotions flood my soul and rise up in my throat. It was one of the most emotional moments of my life. Without thinking, this reserved, low-key public servant walked onto the platform, threw his fist in the air, and leaped for joy! It was the most incredible moment of my life. Nothing had happened to me before, nor has happened since, to equal the exultation and joy of that moment.

I looked at that room full of people and thought about the long road we had come. God, this is it! I said to myself. We have done it!

The noise was deafening as the crowd chanted "Goode! Goode! Goode! Goode!" repeating my name over and over again in a joyful litany. I just stood there watching, drinking in the scene. Then, walking to the microphone, I shouted the phrase that had become my slogan during the campaign, "Will you help me?"

Dr. Bernard Watson, head of the William Penn Foundation, had coined the phrase for me in my first campaign speech. I wanted to get people involved in working with me. So in every speech I had intoned, "I want to build a better Philadelphia. Will you help me? I want to change housing conditions in this city. Will you help me? I want to put unemployed people back to work. Will you help me? I want to wipe out corruption in this city. Will you help me? I want to give children a chance to be all they can be. Will you help me? I want to change educational priorities. Will you help me? I want to change the landscape of our neighborhoods. Will you help me? I want to build a trash-to-steam plant and do what is needed to improve the quality of life in this city. Will you help me?"

I would build and build on the speech until it crescendoed to a fever pitch and people stood on their feet shouting "Yes! Yes! Yes! I will help you!"

As the crowd heard my familiar battle cry, the room erupted with thunderous shouts of "Yes! Yes! Yes!" The emotion was so high I actually kept pinching myself to see if I was awake or dreaming.

Is this you, Wilson Goode? I asked myself, laughing. Are you awake or are you dreaming? It's hard to believe this is happening to you.

Following the rally, my family and I went back to the Belle-vue-Stratford Hotel to spend the night. Natasha was hungry and wanted a cheeseburger. Try as we might, we couldn't get her a cheeseburger through room service. The kitchen was closed.

Frustrated, my little daughter looked at me and said, "You mean you are going to be mayor and you can't get me a cheeseburger?"

I laughed to myself. Just elected mayor and already my administration was in trouble.

Early Highlights

Eight years old in
Seaboard, N.C.

Velma at seventeen,
six months after
we met.

Our wedding—
August 20, 1960.

ROTC ball as newlyweds—
the night we had to
sleep in a car!

April 1962, Fort Carson, Colo., promotion
to First Lieutenant.

Holding Muriel, five,
and Wilson Jr., two.

Velma speaking at the
dedication of the 72nd
Street playground. To
her right is Hardy
Williams, who was
then campaigning for
state representative.

A 1969 visit with my sister Mary
in the Watts area of Los Angeles
(l. to r.: Mamie, me, Velma, Mother,
Dad, Mary, Wilson Jr., Muriel).

Philadelphia, 1958—my
grandmother, Babe Goode,
with Dad and Mom.

Accompanying the Paschall youth
group on a field trip to Harrisburg
in 1972. Bernard Lee, my Island Ave.
picketing partner, is the one
with the big smile.

All decked out for Mom and Dad's fiftieth wedding anniversary celebration in 1975.

Walking with proud developer Alice Lipscomb through Lipscomb Square at 12th and Bainbridge.

With my PUC colleagues in 1978 (l. to r.: Michael Johnson, Helen O'Bannon, Lou Carter, Robert Bloom).

August 1983, a visit to my birthplace after beating Rizzo in the primary.

Velma and I pose with Wilson Jr., Natasha, and Muriel after I was sworn in as managing director, January 4, 1980.

Working with volunteers in the 1981 campaign to clean up Philadelphia.

Another "Clean Team" brigade. That's me behind Malcolm Poindexter.

Talking with Commissioner Joseph Rizzo in front of the new Fire Department headquarters building.

Campaigning

Eileen C. Ryan

Right at home
campaigning in one
of Philadelphia's
black churches
in 1983.

Buying lunch
at the
20th Anniversary
March on
Washington,
with Velma,
Marian Tasco,
and Bill Gray,
August 28, 1983.

A 1983 campaign
stop at 9th and
Washington.

Visiting with leaders
at the Holocaust
Museum during the
1983 campaign.

Mayor Bill Green presents
me with a "large"
campaign contribution.

On the campaign trail
with Tama Myers-Clark
(2nd one to my right).

Receiving Ed Rendell's
endorsement in 1983.

Being interviewed with Frank Rizzo
after our first public debate.

Watching election
returns with friends
and supporters.

First Term

My family shares
the excitement
of my swearing-in
ceremony (l. to r.:
James, Alvestus,
me, Mamie,
Earn Lee, Mary,
Mama).

My first cabinet (standing l. to r.: Leo Brooks,
David Brenner, Dianne Semingson; seated:
Barbara Mather, Julia Robinson, Dick Gilmore).

Mount Zion Baptist Church in
Seaboard, N.C., after they
rebuilt the original wooden church.

A "photo op" in Washington, D.C., presenting
Philadelphia's 1984 agenda for the city (l. to r.: me,
the late Sen. John Heinz, Rep. William Gray,
Rep. Thomas Foglietta, Sen. Joseph Biden).

The Osage Avenue Disaster

The front of the MOVE house before the confrontation.

An aerial view of the bunker.

The police stake out team in position.

The fire rages.

Sifting through the remains.

Police personnel
surveying the scene.

Amid tear gas, the helicopter
approaches to drop the explosives.

The water cannon
trying to dislodge the
MOVE bunker.

Rev. James S. Allen leads area clergy
in prayer for the community.

The devastation left by the massive fire.

Happier Moments

Opening the Airport
High Speed Line.

Honoring Arthur Ashe
on the "first birthday"
of his Youth Tennis
Center in Philadelphia.

Velma and I in 1984,
with Sixers great
"Dr. J" and family.

Helping Bobby
Williams (next to the
baby) in his campaign
for district attorney.

Sam Evans greets Velma at the dedication of a bust of my likeness. Looking on are Thacher Longstreth, Joe Coleman, and myself.

A family photo with Michael Jackson at the Live Aid concert in 1985.

Walking with children through the Richard Allen Housing Development.

Muriel's graduation from Temple Law School. I received an honorary doctorate.

Warming up for a benefit game—
the mayor's team vs. city council.
I made a three-point shot!

With Ricardo Muti, former
conductor of the
Philadelphia Orchestra.

1987: Vice President and Mrs. Bush visit
Philadelphia for the celebration of the
200th anniversary of the Constitution.
They're greeted by Pennsylvania governor,
Robert Casey, "We the People 200" chair,
Willard Rouse, and myself.

The July 4, 1987, balloon race
highlights the city's new skyline with
Liberty Place One in the background.

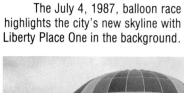

Second Term

City council members and my family look on as I'm sworn in for a second term on January 4, 1988.

My family poses after the inaugural ceremony.

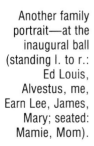

Another family portrait—at the inaugural ball (standing l. to r.: Ed Louis, Alvestus, me, Earn Lee, James, Mary; seated: Mamie, Mom).

Velma and I share a smile with Bishop Desmond Tutu in front of the Liberty Bell in 1988.

The Press—my constant companion.

With Philadelphia comedian Grand Marshal David Brenner at the 1988 Thanksgiving Day Parade and Parade Host Peter Scolari.

The NAACP's Benjamin Hooks is honored at the annual luncheon of the Philadelphia Martin Luther King, Jr. Center. C. Delores Tucker and Waverly Easley of the Center join Governor Casey and me to present the award.

Q.B.D. Harris

July 4, 1990. Muriel, Wilson Jr., Velma, and I stand with former president Jimmy Carter after I presented him with the Liberty Medal.

Delivering a budget message, March 28, 1990. Behind me is council president Joe Coleman. I'm flanked by city council members Thacher Longstreth, John Street, Augusta Clark, Anna Verna, and Lucien Blackwell.

Velma and I, with Temple University president Peter Liacouras and Temple's most famous alumnus, Bill Cosby, at a scholarship fund drive in 1989.

Presenting Liberty Medals to President Oscar Arias of Costa Rica and Dr. Rony Brauman of Doctors Without Borders.

With Commissioner Willie Williams, incoming president of the National Organization of Black Law Enforcement Executives (NOBLE).

My staff in 1991 (standing l. to r.: Karen Warrington, Cathy Weiss, Clarena Tolson, Chris Cashman, Ed Schwartz, Shirley Hamilton, Bill Hankowsky, Tim Spencer; seated: Betsy Reveal, David Pingree, me, Charisse Lillie, Gerri Walker).

New
Directions

Professor Wilson Goode
by the water wheel
on the Eastern College
campus in St. Davids, Pa.

CHAPTER ELEVEN

Meet Mayor Goode

The Philadelphia I inherited as the city's first African American mayor was on the verge of collapse, slowly hemorrhaging to death from high inflation, a declining population, and an anemic revenue base created by the exodus of thousands of jobs.

As I had pointed out during my campaign, for fifteen years prior to my election in 1983, more than 10,000 jobs flowed out of the city annually, for a total of about 150,000 jobs. I wanted to infuse a new spirit into the city, revitalize the business sector, and make Philadelphia a place where people would be proud to live and work. City government had started to move in that direction under Mayor Bill Green. But I knew if the damage done during the terms of Frank Rizzo and his predecessor, James H. J. Tate, was to be undone, I had many years of hard work ahead of me.

My top priority was to restore jobs to the city, to put people to work. I also wanted to get long-stalled projects back on track. Some projects like the Center City commuter tunnel and the Airport High Speed Line were essentially finished, but bureaucratic red tape and disputes between SEPTA, the regional transportation authority, and the city's Public Property Department had stalled completion for months. Other important projects such as building a new convention center and constructing the new Vine Street Expressway were in the early stages of planning. Plans to construct ramps for I-95 to allow riders to get off in Center City had been stalled for nearly fifteen years by neighborhood opposition.

Likewise with cable television. The problem wasn't finding adequate vendors—Mayor Rizzo had done that but left office without making a final selection—but one of political consensus. Mayor Green had wanted to appoint one vendor to provide the service. The city council wanted four vendors, one for each quadrant of the city, so as to allow a minority firm to participate in one of the areas.

Trash disposal problems had also plagued the city for a decade. We desperately needed a trash-to-steam plant and a landfill. But that too had been bogged down by a city council who had refused to approve any package submitted by Mayor Green. Frank Rizzo had also failed to take advantage of an opportunity to build a trash-to-steam plant with Philadelphia Electric in the late 1970s.

In the eighteen years they had served Philadelphia, neither Mayor James Tate nor Frank Rizzo proved to be progressive or aggressive in resolving these issues. Instead, they operated as ward politicians, using government as a political tool to reward their friends and punish their enemies. Cities around the country had built convention centers and trash-to-steam plants and had installed cable television services. New highways and expressways had also made these cities more competitive. But not Philadelphia.

Rizzo, in particular, had been an impediment to progress. He maintained control by appealing to the fears of the white ethnic communities that voted for him. Whatever the white ethnic neighborhoods wanted, Rizzo wanted. Whatever they were against, he was against. Rizzo appealed strongly to people who wanted to preserve the status quo of their individual neighborhoods. And if that status quo meant keeping out minorities, voting down mental-health centers and housing for the poor, or rerouting an expressway, Rizzo supported it, even if the action was detrimental to the city as a whole.

Consequently, Philadelphia had stagnated in its provincialism and was probably fifteen years behind the times. That had to change.

Bill Green had run for mayor in 1979 on a reform platform, pledging to return stability to the city and to streamline a cumbersome, ineffective bureaucracy. His vision for Philadelphia was cut short, however, when he decided not to run again in 1983.

I was grateful to Mayor Green for bringing me into city government. I also shared his vision. Therefore, in my role as mayor, I felt I could build on many of the programs started by Green. Like me, he had sincerely wanted to reform government, to do things a better way. But he hadn't had time to see it through.

My campaign pledge had been "I'm going to create jobs. I'm going to bring jobs back to Philadelphia. I'm going to stop the bleeding." Therefore, my first duty as mayor was to appoint a commerce director who could reach that goal. I chose David Brenner, former chair of the Chamber of Commerce.

I appointed David just one week after my election in 1983. Six weeks before I took the oath of office, I was off and running, trying to set a tone, to create a climate that would improve the city's business environment.

David was a retired partner in a prestigious accounting firm that was well respected throughout the business community. If anyone could help stanch the flow of jobs out of the city, he could.

I told David that I wanted him to concentrate only on job development, business expansion, and business retention. He was not to worry about the other functions traditionally expected of the commerce director, such as mayoral spokesman and public relations expert.

Traditionally, the commerce director doubled as city representative. The city representative was the chief spokesperson for the mayor and was also in charge of planning all ceremonies and special events. I knew that if David had to focus on planning daily ceremonies and special events, as well as stand in for the mayor, he wouldn't be effective in focusing on economic and commercial issues. Therefore, I split off the public relations functions and appointed Dianne Semingson, an Arco executive, to be city representative. Now David could concentrate on commerce and jobs.

"David, by the end of the year I want you to have brought one business back into the city," I told him. "If you can have a net gain of one business by the end of 1984, then you will have been successful as commerce director."

Immediately David started assembling the best staff he could find. Charles Pizzi, now president of the Chamber of Commerce, and Joseph James, now commerce director for the city of Chicago, were recruited as deputy directors. David's strategy was to find people who were used to working with businesses and who understood the dynamics and pulse of the business world.

His focus was so successful that in December, even before I took office, we had negotiated a deal to bring Gould Electronics back to Philadelphia. Gould was a large electronics firm that had established part of its business in Philadelphia and the remainder in the suburbs. Through our efforts, Gould executives agreed to consolidate their operation in Philadelphia.

Encouraged by the success with Gould, in January I established the Economic Roundtable, a coalition of business leaders who could act as spokespersons for the business community. Out of their input came the idea to survey all thirty-seven thousand businesses in the city to assess their needs and concerns. Why did some want to leave? What were the concerns of the businesses that were willing to stay?

The survey revealed that, like most Philadelphia citizens, business owners were seriously affected by quality-of-life issues: police protection, crime, cleanliness, and deterioration of streets and roadways. The wage tax—or city income tax—was also an important factor. To make up for a close to 5 percent wage tax charged employees, Philadelphia-based employers said they had to pay employees almost 5 percent more than the suburban businesses to remain competitive. The businesses themselves were also encumbered by a series of three or four business taxes they had to pay. From the outset I wanted to demonstrate success. I put forth a business-tax reform package in Harrisburg and within my first six months in office, succeeded in getting it passed, giving me my first legislative victory. A business privilege tax also served to streamline a very cumbersome business-tax process.

For twenty-five years, the quality of life in various parts of Philadelphia had been steadily declining, especially the north-central sectors inhabited largely by blacks, Hispanics, and some poor whites. In the late fifties and early sixties, urban renewal had revamped some areas of the city, but for the most part, Philadelphia's redevelopment was a crazy quilt of activity with little rhyme or reason to it.

Our Economic Roundtable was my attempt to get those businesses who were most affected by the city to share their visions, hopes, and dreams for the city. We included small and medium-sized businesses as well as large corporations in these meetings, attracting a wide cross section of the multiethnic business community.

I made it clear to the business leaders that their well-being was a high priority. I wanted business development to work, so I needed two-way communication with them.

"The indicator of whether or not we are successful in responding to you during my first term in office will be measured by our response to your complaints," I told them. "If any complaint you had was not responded to by the commerce section, then we didn't perform our job. But if during my time as mayor, I don't get any phone calls from you complaining that you're dissatisfied with my commerce department because no one addressed your complaint, then I will know we did our job."

I am proud to say that in the four years of my first administration no business leader ever called me to complain about poor service from the commerce department.

Despite the success of getting the business efforts moving, there were rumblings from the black community that I was spending too much effort on downtown projects and not enough on theirs. This wasn't true, of course, but it appeared that way because the downtown projects were high profile and attracted media attention. At the same time that we were revitalizing Center City, we were also completing work on two new neighborhood shopping centers in North Philadelphia and revitalizing two existing neighborhood shopping strips in West Philadelphia. But they didn't get the publicity.

At the same time I strongly believed that the central business district and the city's economic infrastructure were the lifelines of the city. They made up the heart that pumped life into the body of the city. If the heart was weak, the city was weak. But if the heart—the central business district—became stronger, the rest of the city, including the black community, would benefit. So, despite opposition, I persevered, ultimately launching a business renaissance that would create a new skyline and downtown services district that became the pride of Philadelphia.

Early in my administration I learned that working with the city council was not going to be easy. The council president, Joseph E. Coleman, was a pleasant, stately man who always said the acceptable thing, and I believed he was sincere in his efforts. But Joseph Coleman was a weak leader. He allowed David Cohen to call the shots, and he seldom challenged John Street and Lucien Blackwell. In fact, the three of them set more of the tone for city council than did the president. Therefore, I was trapped by being required to follow protocol by working with a weak president and the de facto leaders of council—Cohen, Street, and Blackwell.

As I settled into my new role as mayor, I became even more aware of the dynamics of political deal making and rivalry. Without the support of the council, a mayor was unable to implement his agenda. Take Bill Green's struggle with the council and the trash-to-steam plant issue.

Mayor Green had wanted to build a trash-to-steam plant in South Philadelphia and buy a landfill in Chester County to dispose of the city's ash. All had moved well in his planning. He had selected the builders for the plant, identified landfill space, and entered into an agreement with the landfill operator. The only roadblock to the process was the city council.

Try as he might, Green could not get the city council to approve most of his projects, especially after he had publicly declared the council to be "the worst in the free world." Following that statement, various council members had pledged to never again approve anything Green proposed.

In my efforts to complete many of the projects that Green had begun, I approached the mayor's role with a conciliatory attitude, feeling I could accomplish the most if I didn't care who got the credit.

The second week of January 1984, I met with council president Joe Coleman and council member David Cohen to discuss whether they would approve the landfill in Chester County and the trash-to-steam plant.

It immediately became clear that both projects were so deeply associated with Bill Green that even a new mayor couldn't reduce the hostility that the council felt about them. Despite my arguments that the city needed this facility and that it would save money, Cohen stonewalled by discussing potential zoning battles, environmental issues, and expansion problems. Lucien Blackwell was more direct.

"I'm not approving anything for Bill Green," he declared. "I'm not approving anything for Bill Green's law firm or Bill Green's friends. Don't bring this thing back here anymore, because I'm not going to approve it no matter how many times you bring it back to me."

I was amazed at the determination of these politicians not to let Bill Green get credit for anything, even when he was powerless and out of office. While I had made every effort not to develop the same acrimonious adversarial relationships in my dealings with the council, they resisted my willingness to compromise and work together. The project was still too close to Green.

Realizing that all I was doing was beating my head against a wall, I tried another approach. It became clear to me that David Cohen would look at the need for a trash-to-steam plant only if he had the chance to chair a committee on the issue and present some alternatives.

"All right, take four to six months to study the problem," I told David, "then come back to me with some alternatives."

Four months turned into six. Six months dragged into seven, eight, nine. Finally, after a year of missteps and mishaps from the committee, I went back to the original plan, which I had shelved for a year.

Frankly, to have given David Cohen all that time was a mistake. I should have confronted the council early in the process. I should have stood firm and taken my case to the people;

perhaps I could have been successful. But Bill Green was not far wrong when he described the council as "the worst in the free world." I doubt that too many other legislative bodies have ever had representatives as parochial in their views as that Philadelphia City Council. And I can't imagine any body with two officials who could match David Cohen and John Street in their outrageous behavior on issues.

So from the very beginning, city council was a challenge. If you fought them openly, they wouldn't cooperate. If you expressed a desire to work with them, they would drag their feet until they got what they wanted. David Cohen remained an obstructionist on the trash-to-steam issue to the bitter end. He, more than any other individual, is responsible for the city spending tens of millions of dollars for trash disposal.

There was also tremendous community opposition to the steam plant by South Philadelphia residents who complained, "We don't want you dumping anything else down here. We already have refineries, the stadiums, and the arena. We have enough smoke and toxic chemicals from industries down here already. Put it someplace else."

The trash-to-steam plant was to be built on the grounds of the naval shipyard. I believe the community's resistance to that decision later came back to haunt us when the shipyard was slated for closure. The steam plant might have kept it alive.

Early on, we also lost our option to buy the landfill, which was bought by Chester County. The irony of this is that within two years after Chester County purchased the landfill, the city of Philadelphia was contracting with Chester County to take our trash. That landfill could have been ours. But because of political infighting and the short-sightedness of David Cohen, the loss has cost the city tens of millions of dollars. Ironically, the press played this as my inability to get council to approve the landfill, while previously they had blamed not Mayor Green, but council, for the project's failure.

While the overall war with the city council was endless, I did win some battles. Among the first was the fight to legalize the use of kerosene space heaters.

The kerosene heaters were a big public issue, especially among poor people who used the heaters as a form of inexpensive heat. It was illegal to use the heaters, and Joe Rizzo, the fire commissioner under Bill Green, had opposed their legalization because they were regarded as a safety hazard. Improperly used, the heaters *were* unsafe. But they were also vital to poor people as a means of inexpensive heat.

I worked with the fire department to formulate an ordinance for the legalization of kerosene heaters, as well as a citywide educational program on their proper use. I felt that if people understood the dangers and how to prevent them, we could eliminate some of the hazards.

After the legalization was approved and the education plan put into effect, we had fewer fires and deaths from kerosene heaters. My rationale for the legalization was that poor people were going to use the heaters whether or not they were legal. By making them legal we at least had a system within the law that we could use to help people remain safe.

While concentrating on the big picture, I also had to concentrate on the nuts and bolts of the government. I started with the nerve center of the government—the city telephone operator's room. In my first week in the telephone operator's chair, I fielded calls from the public to determine how long it took to answer calls. I visited the mayor's complaint office, toured sanitation yards, and on occasion even picked up trash. By the end of the first week, I was energized by this hands-on approach and saw it working as a morale booster. So I kept the pace up, trying to lift morale and improve the system as I sought to be a visible leader.

Despite all of these good efforts and results in the field, the struggle with city council went on.

Bill Green had left office with the cable TV issue unresolved. He had tried desperately to work out his differences with council, but they were deadlocked over having one vendor or four.

I analyzed the problem and decided that I could either spend years fighting with the council over cable television franchises or I could get the cable TV system built. I chose the latter.

Many people get hung up on processes and procedures and forget about the goal. I knew that city council would never give up on the four franchise areas. I also knew that I couldn't just sign off on that idea without asking council to provide me with some mechanism for accountability. As long as we failed to move on the issue, the people of Philadelphia would be without cable television.

Reviewing the law and several proposals, I concluded that the granting of the franchises could be a legislative matter rather than an executive one. I presented my proposal to council and essentially offered a compromise that allowed them to name four cable franchisers to city contracts—with my approval. It worked! Today 98 percent of Philadelphia is wired for cable.

Another challenge Philadelphia had faced for two decades was the graffiti that had scarred new buildings and turned otherwise beautiful houses and schools into eyesores. I had made a major campaign pledge to clean up the graffiti. Organizing the Philadelphia Anti-Graffiti Network, I appointed a twenty-five-year-old neighborhood leader, Timothy Spencer, from the Mantua section of the city to accomplish for the city what he had done in his neighborhood. Spencer had reduced graffiti in a significant way. His first step was to invite the wall writers to come in and, in a sign of unity to the cause, turn in their spray cans and take a pledge not to vandalize the walls again. Instead they would become wall artists, working on specific projects. The media and public were skeptical, but it worked.

Today, graffiti has been reduced significantly throughout the city. Young men and women who once wrote on walls as graffiti vandals now proudly demonstrate their talent in the beautiful wall murals they have painted throughout the city. More than one thousand murals have been created, and the program has been recognized as a model by the U.S. Conference of Mayors and the Ford Foundation.

At the same time, I established the Mayor's Literacy Commission, making it the only such commission of a mayor's office in the country. Dr. Marciene Mattleman, a professor at Temple, was appointed executive director. She took the program and almost overnight turned it into a national model.

Helping people to read and write was a real passion of mine. All my life I had watched my father struggle with illiteracy. Dad could not read, write, or count. Even the simplest words and documents were as complex as Greek to him. For a long time I had thought Dad's problem to be unique. I later learned that about four hundred thousand adults in Philadelphia shared his pain.

When I began my advocacy-for-literacy campaign, only twenty literacy centers were operational citywide, and only a few of them had computer capabilities. Before I left office, 560 literacy centers were operational and 120 had computers.

Challenge after challenge came my way that first year. Relishing my role as mayor, I dealt with them openly and directly. Perhaps one of the most important was the proposal of developer Willard "Bill" Rouse to erect a building that exceeded the height of the hat on the William Penn statue. For most of its existence, Philadelphia had been characterized by a staid traditionalism that most people had been reluctant to challenge or change. That became very clear to me with the development of Liberty Place.

When Willard Rouse came to me with the concept for Liberty One and Two, he offered the key that would usher Philadelphia into the twenty-first century—a high-tech, downtown business complex that would create jobs; give Center City a new, sophisticated look; and be the catalyst to help create an exciting skyline to replace an otherwise quaint but boring one. First, however, we had to get past William Penn's hat.

For more years than anyone can remember, a "gentleman's agreement" among developers and city officials had stated that no building could be taller than William Penn's hat. It was believed that the huge statue memorializing the city's founder should remain the center of activity and the focal point of Philadelphia.

For me, William Penn's hat was symbolic of what was wrong with this city. As long as we were unwilling to build above William Penn's hat, we would never see beyond William Penn's hat and would remain bogged down in a tradition that had no bearing on the needs of the present or the future.

True, we would remain the home of the Liberty Bell and the city where the Constitution of the United States was written. But we would die a slow death in the process.

I was excited by Rouse's proposal, but my thirty years in Philadelphia had taught me that tradition and custom die hard here. People were very sentimental about the history of their city.

As Rouse's proposal became public, my mail ran a thousand to one against the project. The primary supporters were architects and builders. Boxes and boxes of postcards came, and my telephone was constantly ringing. People stopped me on the streets or confronted me at community meetings to plead, "Don't let them destroy our city."

As the city's first African American mayor, I had a special concern. Should I be the one that was blamed for messing up a cultural tradition? Would all these people look at me and say, "Look, we elected a black mayor, and the first thing he does is go and turn the city over to developers"? But my dream for this city pushed away all of those negative thoughts. I knew that opportunities for real change were few. I also knew that I had not been elected to preside over the status quo but to change things — to change the direction of the city. This was my opportunity. I had to take full advantage of it. I went to work. But I needed support.

Hoping to inspire all the members of my planning commission, I took them for a meeting on the observation deck of the William Penn statue. Looking at the view over the city, I turned to them and said, "I want you to see that if you drive anywhere in the city to the southwest or west, there is no clear view to William Penn. Therefore building west and southwest of William Penn will make no difference at all. William Penn will be no more obscured than it is now." I already had support from Graham Finney, the chair of the commission. The others supported it after their visit.

The second advantage I pushed was that the new shops at Liberty Place would help energize the city and bring in revenue. However, some people still opposed the development of the business complex I envisioned. Edmund Bacon, the father of the downtown redevelopment area in the 1950s and 1960s, remained vehemently opposed to the building of Liberty Place. I believe that as Liberty Place One and Two evolved, Bacon saw that his vision for Center City, which had guided earlier redevelopment, was being replaced by a new one. Ed Bacon is one of this country's best visionary planners. I greatly respected that his vision had transformed Philadelphia once. Now it was time to transform the city again.

After much public debate, Rouse's plans received my approval. Approval from the planning commission and city council followed. Because there had never been a law passed setting the height limits, no formal requirement was actually needed, but I wanted everyone on record.

There are times when you make difficult decisions based on pure instinct—on your gut feeling. It feels right. Something inside of you tells you that it's the right thing to do. And leaders must have the vision to look beyond what is to what can be. Leaders can't always take the popular position and must sometimes go against the prevailing public opinion. It would have been easy for me to be just another politician and follow the majority. But my decision was for the future of Philadelphia. My gut told me I was right.

Consequently, we now have a dynamic skyline that comprises Liberty Place One, Liberty Place Two, the Mellon Center, the Blue Cross Building, Commerce Square One, and Commerce Square Two. We also have the Bell Atlantic Building and Logan Two. As a result of this development, some $5 billion has been invested in the downtown area and 50,000 new jobs were created during this economic explosion. Unfortunately, the recession of 1991 and 1992 has all but wiped out those gains, but without the earlier growth, things would be a lot worse.

I had warned Bill Rouse that we couldn't just "drop" these buildings downtown. We needed a downtown plan. The Planning Commission, led by Graham Finney, had the task of developing a Center City plan for rezoning the downtown area, and setting height limits and building standards.

The plan was developed, accepted, and is now the guiding document for downtown development. One of the major recommendations set forth in the plan was that a special services district would be created where businesses would pay a special tax for their own street cleaning and other services.

Philadelphia now has a downtown area that is far safer, cleaner, and more beautiful than anything this city has experienced in a long time. Over the past eight years, the downtown area has undergone a miraculous transformation.

As we concentrated on the physical side of Philadelphia, I

was equally concerned about the human side. I wanted to change the face of government.

For the most part, Philadelphia's city government had been run by a white male club, with few women and few minorities participating. That had to change. To my cabinet I appointed three women, three men, three blacks, and three whites. Many of the appointments were barrier-breaking ones; this was the first time women and minorities had been appointed to these offices. I put Richard Gilmore in finance; Barbara Mather in law; Dianne Semingson as city representative. Ángel Ortiz in records was the first Hispanic to hold a commissioner-level position, and Angela Dowd-Burton was the first woman to head procurement.

Business contracts to minorities and women had been practically nonexistent over the 302-year history of the city. We now had a "set-aside law" that allowed city government to reserve a percentage of the contracts for minority and women vendors. It was my job to implement it — to make sure that blacks, women, and minorities got their fair share of the contracts. The law called for 15 percent of the contracts to go to minorities and 10 percent to women. We met those goals, and by the time I left office, more than $500 million of business had been awarded to women and minorities.

Under my leadership a strong human-services program also emerged with the creation of the Office of the Homeless, the AIDS Activities Coordinating Office, the Mayor's Commission on Sexual Minorities, and the Mayor's Commission on People with Disabilities. In my advocacy for human rights I made it clear that gays and lesbians would not be discriminated against in my administration. I proclaimed "Gay Pride Month" and marched in the Gay and Lesbian Day Parade to show my solidarity with all people.

Some colleagues, like former councilman Frances Rafferty, asked why I would "help those faggots when they brought us AIDS." I reminded him that AIDS is a disease that strikes all people, even the ones exercising their right to be different. Some religious people also wrote and challenged my support of the rights of homosexuals. "How can you call yourself a Christian? What you are doing is against the teachings in the Bible. How dare you call yourself a Christian?"

My response was always the same: "I don't just call myself a Christian; I *am* a Christian." I believe that Christ would have shown the same compassion for all of his children.

My strongest stand, however, was for the children. Fights had abounded for years over the amount of money needed to run the city's human-services program for children. The state always short-changed us, giving fewer dollars each year. I opted to pay the difference for children but had to cut back other services to do so.

In support of children, I also appointed strong child advocates to the school board and supported tax increases for the school districts because I saw good education as the key to ending poverty.

While many of these programs fell under the banner of social services, they all were designed to improve the quality of life for Philadelphians.

So as I sought more private investment downtown, I also sought to increase public investment to benefit children, women, families, and those most at risk. The mayor's office would be a strong advocate for all of those persons at risk in our society.

But as important as downtown was to me, North Central Philadelphia was also critical. When I moved to Philadelphia in 1954, North Philadelphia was nicknamed "The Jungle." The area continued to be neglected by the city's mayors, and tens of thousands of people had moved out. In more recent years, Mayors Tate and Rizzo had encouraged a deliberate policy of disinvestment and demolition in the area. Their attitude was to let it die a slow death, that investment there was a waste of money.

I changed that policy and that attitude. I directed the city planning commission to develop a North Philadelphia Plan; my administration's policy would be to promote reinvestment, revitalization, reconstruction, and renewal.

The plan was developed and released. With it we began to change the mind-set of an area. North Philadelphia was on its way back as new housing units, new shopping centers, new churches, and new streets and roadways emerged from the ashes of the area. A new spirit of hope was born. Since then, $100 million has been invested in the process to bring North Philadelphia back to life.

As we proceeded with the human services and neighbor-hood improvements, we also kept our eyes on other physical developments. The airport was expanding, and we planned for a new international terminal.

Things moved very well for me during my first year in office. After about ten months of negotiation, the commuter tunnel finally opened. I invited Frank Rizzo, who had initiated the proj-ect during his tenure, back to help cut the ribbon. This $350-million construction job had been a boon to the construction industry, creating thousands of jobs. Now it would pay off for all of Philadelphia, improving the transportation for thousands of workers and shoppers. It was a great moment for Philadelphia.

But no sooner had we opened the service when a routine inspection of the Ninth Street Bridge in North Philadelphia found the bridge to be unsafe. The bridge was encased in a building that housed the R. W. Brown Boys and Girls Club. Everyone pan-icked.

I called an emergency meeting and asked what could be done to get the bridge fixed. Bureaucrats from public property and SEPTA told me it would take nine to ten months to complete the process of planning, design, and construction. I challenged the conventional wisdom in the room.

"We have an emergency," I said. "Let's deal with it that way."

After much discussion, I prevailed. We found a contractor, issued an emergency contract, and directed around-the-clock work. I visited the site twice each day for the three weeks it took to complete the project. If I had not been aggressive in bypassing traditional approaches to solving problems, this project would have dragged on for nine to twelve months and rendered a $350-million project inaccessible.

But I quickly learned that in city government, one crisis fol-lows another. I had just finished overseeing the bridge project and was on my last morning of inspections. I was happy—I felt victorious. As I walked away from the site, a WCAU radio re-porter, Al Novak, walked up to me and stuck a microphone in my face. I just knew he wanted to talk about the bridge.

"Do you have any comment on the Eagles moving to Phoe-nix?" he asked.

My mouth fell open in surprise.

Leonard Tose, owner of the Philadelphia Eagles football team, was a businessman who had grown up poor and had made good in the trucking business. Despite the money he had made, Tose was never accepted by the Philadelphia business and social establishment. So when he ran into financial problems with the Eagles, it was no surprise that the banking establishment would not help him. Tose needed money, and he had found it in Phoenix. Suddenly I had another political problem.

To allow the Eagles to leave Philadelphia would be like losing a beloved family member. The team had always been here. It was as much a symbol of pride among Philadelphians as it was a source of income for the people who worked at the stadium. I knew we had to keep the Eagles here, whatever the cost.

I sat down with Tose and told him point-blank, "Look, no one is going to loan you the money you need. We want the Eagles to stay here in the city, and we're prepared to sit down with you and work out an agreement on the stadium that will enable you to have a better cash flow."

What Tose wanted was for the city to build "skyboxes" for the Eagles. The skyboxes, which are executive box seats with price tags of fifty thousand dollars and up, would cost about $2 million to construct. During the first ten years, the Eagles would get the major part of the revenue. The second ten years, most of the revenue would be the city's.

After much negotiation, we developed a contract that renegotiated revenue sharing with Tose and extended the Eagles's stay in Philadelphia until the year 2011. We also gave Tose a better deal on the parking and concession stands.

The Philadelphia media unfairly and prematurely criticized me. They blasted me in headlines implying giveaways to Tose. They never read the fine print. They never took the time to understand the whole deal. They would later eat their words.

The public was outraged by our agreement to build the skyboxes—that is, until someone offered to buy them from us for twice the amount we invested. After that we got very little criticism.

After we arranged the deal with Tose, we renegotiated a mutually satisfactory agreement with the Phillies baseball team as well.

I ended 1984 with a wide variety of successes: renegotiating the contracts for both the Eagles and the Phillies to stay in Philadelphia, the rebuilding of the bridge in record time, the remodeling of the airport, and starting the process of getting the city wired for cable television. I had chaired the Pennsylvania delegation to the Democratic National Convention in San Francisco. I had even been interviewed as a possible vice-presidential running mate by Democratic nominee, Walter Mondale.

I entered 1985 exhilarated, prepared for another successful year. The only shadow I could see looming in the distance was the problem with MOVE. In meetings with neighbors the year before, I had tried to answer some of their concerns. Now it was becoming clearer and clearer that a serious confrontation was brewing between MOVE and their neighbors. Something had to be done soon to avoid a violent clash.

CHAPTER TWELVE

Fireball!

I started 1985 full of optimism. I had had a terrific first year in office and had neatly laid out my agenda for the year. I thought that if I could get the same teamwork and cooperation in 1985 that I'd had in 1984, then many major issues could be settled as we worked on the projects started in my first year. Thus far, my vision of turning around this city was working.

Just as I started to put all the wheels in motion, Leo Brooks, my managing director, called to inform me that the MOVE issue was surfacing again. I had not heard any reports since August of 1984, and had hoped, despite my fear, that the problem had subsided. Not so, Leo told me. As I talked to Leo, I recalled the meetings I had had the previous year with MOVE neighbors on Osage Avenue in West Philadelphia.

I had first met with the neighbors on Memorial Day 1984, and then again that July Fourth. Fewer than a dozen people attended the meeting led by Clifford Bond, a resident and the son-in-law of one of the Osage homeowners. Bond had opened the meeting with a passionate speech:

"We are here because these MOVE people have turned our neighborhood into a living hell!" he said. "They have blocked off the rear driveway. They are running up and down on our roofs, and they have threatened people on the block. But the worst part of it all is that our children are being negatively affected by MOVE. As *our* mayor, we want you to protect us and to protect our children."

"What do you want me to do?" I asked.

"We want our neighborhood back!" someone yelled. "We want our block back. We want these people off our block."

"I can't just go in there and move people out because you don't like them."

"We are taxpayers!" another neighbor exclaimed. "We deserve protection. We shouldn't have to put up with this. What would you do if they were next door to you?"

"I don't know," I admitted. "Probably the same thing you are doing. But we just can't go in and arrest them."

"You are just like all the other politicians," someone at the other end of the table yelled. "Talk, talk, talk, and you do nothing!"

I could hear the mounting frustration in their voices and feel the tension building in the room. I felt as if I were sitting on a powder keg. Any wrong move might cause it to explode.

"I do care," I said, projecting calmness. "I care very much. Let's talk about some things we can do to help you out."

"We want that alley cleaned up, and we want the obstruction removed!"

"Okay, we will take care of that."

"We want some help for our children. They need counseling," a woman said tearfully.

"I will arrange that through the West Philadelphia Mental Health Consortium," I assured her. "They have programs for children. I'm sure we can take care of that."

"We need to get the kids out of this environment so they can play, so they can study."

"We will work out a plan," I said.

At the conclusion of the meeting, I could tell no one was really satisfied, but at least they seemed willing to give me a chance.

It was clear that MOVE was creating an intolerable environment for these families. The question now was, How could I fairly and peacefully resolve the problem and prevent bloodshed?

I did not feel that neighbors' rights exceeded those of MOVE members. All had rights. My job was to find the balance.

In a nation that respects people's rights to free speech and expression, MOVE members had a right to live their lives their way. They even had the right to use profanity over a loudspeaker system, even if it interrupted the calm of neighbors and meant children were confronted daily with words like Mother F——, Son-of-a-B——, and every other profane term they could utter.

I have always had strong feelings about freedom. To deny freedom to people because you don't like their lifestyle is to deny equal protection under the law. We simply could not go into the MOVE house and arrest people because neighbors had complained about their lifestyle. I made this point very clear to the neighbors.

I had no more discussions with neighbors about the MOVE house for nearly a year. Nor were there any reports about MOVE from commissioners, cabinet officers, or the police. The only significant event occurred on August 8, 1984, the sixth anniversary of the 1978 MOVE shootout with police in Powelton Village that had left a police officer dead and nine MOVE members in prison. The police had mobilized in anticipation of trouble, ready to carry out (I later learned at the MOVE hearings) an evacuation plan developed by Sgt. Herbert Kirk on orders from Greg Sambor, the police commissioner. The plan had called for the use of explosives, tear gas, and high-pressure water hoses to flush MOVE members out of the house and force them into a quick surrender. No problems occurred that day, however.

The summer passed fairly peacefully, as did the fall and winter, although I learned at the MOVE hearings that in October police had confirmed neighbors' reports that MOVE members were building a "wooden shack" on the roof.

By early spring of 1985, Leo Brooks, had received police intelligence information that suggested MOVE's activities were about to become more aggressive and could result in violence. Brooks briefed council president Joe Coleman, the elected officials who represented the Osage Avenue area, and me on the situation.

By the end of April, neighbors had become more and more

agitated as MOVE behavior took a more hostile turn. On April 25, more than thirty neighbors met at the Cobbs Creek Community Center to complain of harassment and threats by MOVE members. A few days later, on April 29, spectators and police surveillance officers listened as MOVE members speaking over loudspeakers threatened to kill the mayor and the police.[1]

The activities of the neighbors now were front-page news. Editorial writers were urging that I do something about the problem. Elected officials also started calling me. Later that week, councilman Lucien Blackwell met with me several times to say, "You have to do something."

Blackwell had no suggestions about how it should be handled, but the political heat was being turned up on him, too. The neighborhood was in Blackwell's district, and constituents told him they were expecting him to make the tough decisions.

My overriding concern was the potential for a violent outbreak between the neighbors and MOVE. I did not feel that we could arrest MOVE members without just cause, but I wanted to explore alternatives with some of the leaders in government. I wanted to assess our options.

I assembled all of the key participants in a room: Ed Rendell, the district attorney; the police commissioner, Gregore Sambor; the managing director, Leo Brooks; and council member Lucien Blackwell.

No sooner had we started the meeting than Rendell produced a memo he had sent me back in July of 1984 detailing the fact that some MOVE members had outstanding warrants for parole violations and assault. It became clear that Rendell was uncomfortable. He kept drawing attention to the memo's date, in spite of the fact that he hadn't followed up on it with me in the nine months since he'd sent it.

Looking back, I regret that we didn't act on the outstanding warrants in July of 1984. Perhaps we could have averted the tragedy to some degree by making arrests before tensions had gotten so high. But after the managing director, the district attorney, the police commissioner, and I had discussed the matter, we decided not to do anything until after August 8, 1984. Then after the non-event of August 8, we were all lulled into a belief that the problem with MOVE had perhaps subsided. In any event, neither the district attorney nor the police commissioner had called to get authorization to proceed with the arrests.

We needed a judge to sign off on the warrants, Rendell said, but he felt that would be no problem. We concluded that before we explored any other alternatives, we had to arrest those with outstanding warrants.

I was ready to act — not because of pressure from the neighbors or the media but because I now realized we had legitimate grounds for action. Up to this point I had not been certain the city had legal cause to intervene in the lives of these MOVE members.

Although I was now confident of our legal footing, I did not see this as a solution to the problem with the neighbors. Even after the arrests, most of the MOVE members would still be in the house. I was very clear with all involved: This was not an eviction, but the serving of warrants. Before we concluded the meeting, every person had a task, and we agreed to meet again the next day to go over the details.

When we met the next day, Rendell provided more details on the procedures for obtaining arrest warrants. Next, Greg Sambor was asked to present his plan for serving the warrants. At this time Leo Brooks leaned over to me and whispered, "We shouldn't discuss this stuff in front of Ed Rendell and his people. You know he talks too much."

I was hesitant. Leo persisted.

"His place is a sieve. It goes straight from him to the media. Let's wait."

Leo convinced me to stop Sambor from giving a full report. I interrupted Sambor and told him we would talk later. This decision later came back to haunt me. During the MOVE investigation, Rendell testified that he believed the meeting ended abruptly because I didn't want to know the details. Of course he was wrong in that assessment. In fact, on two occasions after that, I received a detailed briefing from the police commissioner.

Throughout the meeting, I kept trying to shake an eerie feeling that nothing good would come out of this. I wanted to avoid any confrontation, but somehow I felt that the next meeting between MOVE and the police would be more deadly than the first.

∽

The plan was to have officers serve search and arrest warrants at 6221 Osage Avenue early on Monday, May 13, 1985, just three days away.

I was sixteen months into my first term as mayor and, frankly, I had reservations about my police commissioner, Gregore Sambor. If I had followed my deepest gut instincts, I probably would have fired Sambor a year before.

Prior to becoming police commissioner, Sambor had been the training officer at the police academy. My initial impression of Sambor was of a man who was an intellectual and extremely capable of getting things done. Maybe his military training compelled me to see him that way. I saw him as someone who could professionalize the police department and improve training and morale as well as community relations.

As the months passed, another picture emerged as Sambor's behavior took some strange twists. The uniform came first. Police commissioners had always worn civilian clothes instead of a police uniform. Sambor changed that, adopting a Philadelphia police uniform with four stars emblazoned on bars across his shoulders, like a four-star general.

At first I thought it was an interesting thing to do. I figured he was identifying with the troops and trying to get the officers to view the department as a quasi-military operation. But the more I saw Sambor in that uniform, the more I was reminded of a general commanding his army.

It was also becoming increasingly clear that Sambor didn't respect me. Early in my term I'd heard rumors about him making jokes at parties about my stuttering or complaining to friends about taking orders from two blacks whom he clearly saw as not worthy of being his bosses.

Leo Brooks, as managing director, was my chief assistant and Sambor's supervisor. He was the person I most relied on to carry out the functions of city government. I had come to trust Brooks. This was especially encouraging since he had been appointed through an open recruitment process.

The recruitment process was part of my philosophy about

government reform. I didn't want to load my cabinet with friends and cronies, no matter how competent they were. I wanted an open, competitive process that would allow any qualified person to compete. As a result, only one of my cabinet members was someone I could call a longtime friend; that was Richard G. Gilmore, the finance director. Everyone else was new to me and held no built-in loyalties to me or to my vision. What I counted on from them was professionalism and commitment to good government.

Therefore, I felt blessed when a rapport developed between Leo and me. I don't make friends easily. In Leo, I felt I had found a friend I could trust.

Leo was a retired army major general, and I admired his spit-and-polish professionalism. He was also a respected Christian with deep personal convictions who appeared to always be in control, with a well-thought-out plan or opinion about a situation readily at his disposal. I liked that. But even more importantly, Leo said he could handle Greg Sambor. I especially needed that. I had gone to Leo when the rumors about Sambor ridiculing me surfaced.

"Leo, I'm concerned about Sambor," I confided. "I'm concerned about him walking around with those four stars on his uniform and his apparent lack of judgment. He's developing a real ego problem. What are we going to do about him? I have a strong suspicion he's not the man for this job."

Leo hesitated a moment before answering.

"I have some of the same concerns about him, Mr. Mayor," he said. "But you let me handle him. I'm his supervisor. If you have confidence in me, let me take care of it."

As we talked about Sambor, I remember thinking how fortunate I was to have someone I could trust. Leo exhibited strong traits, and the fact that he had risen to the rank of major general in the army meant a lot to me.

As Leo talked, I remember also thinking, Leo is the managing director. Let him do his job. The charter gives him the authority to run these departments. That's why we have a managing director, to take the weight off of the mayor.

I knew I had to let Leo do his job his way. I could not be both mayor and managing director.

On the Friday before the arrest of MOVE members, Sambor called to ask for an appointment to see me. In my heart I hoped he was coming to tell me the arrests were off, that he wanted more time. I was looking for a way out — any way out. But when Sambor walked into my office, his expression confirmed my worst fears. His face was impassive as he stood facing my desk.

"Mr. Mayor, I want you to know that everything is in place for Monday," he said.

"Have you briefed Leo Brooks?" I asked.

"He's out of town."

"Try to reach him."

"I'll try."

Despite his assurance, his words were not convincing. I knew that I had to reach Leo myself.

"I hope you know the magnitude of what we're getting into here," I said, trying to gauge Sambor's emotions behind the blank expression. "I pray that no lives will be lost and that we'll handle this with a minimum of bloodshed."

Sambor's face remained blank, unreadable, as was often the case.

"Mr. Mayor, you know these MOVE people are violent people; so when you go after them, there's no telling what will happen."

"Maybe this time will be different," I said.

Deep down inside, I felt Sambor was not telling me everything.

"I want to review the plan with you again, Commissioner."

He took a deep breath.

"Okay. Here it is in a nutshell, Mr. Mayor."

"All right. Run it down for me."

He ran down the list, using his hand to make each point.

"Number one, we will do everything possible to pick up the children. That's our number-one priority, to pick up the children.

"Number two, I will personally serve the arrest warrants.

"Number three, we will use water — high-powered water hoses — to try and dislodge the bunker.

"Number four, we will use small devices to put holes in the interior walls to enable us to listen to what's going on inside. And we will also be able to put tear gas into the house, if necessary.

"Number five, we will shoot only at targets that are shooting at us so as not to risk the lives of MOVE members, police officers, and firefighters.

"Number six, I will not use police officers who were part of the August 8, 1978, confrontation against MOVE. We don't want any hotheads out there." I had given these instructions a few days earlier.

"I think you've got it, Mayor," he said. He then turned and left the room with no further comment.

As soon as Sambor left, I tried to reach Leo and learned he was in Virginia attending his daughter's graduation. I reached Leo on Saturday. He was surprised that Sambor was ready to make the arrests so soon.

"I want you to review the plan to arrest MOVE members and tell me if you think it's sound," I told him.

"Mr. Mayor, I'll try to be back as early as possible on Sunday, but that's the day my daughter's graduating," he replied.

We chatted for a few minutes more before I hung up. I was dissatisfied with the conversation.

My apprehension was based on the fact that Leo was not in town and that he had not reviewed Sambor's plans. I knew that once he reviewed them, he would give me his candid views. He did not sugar-coat his views but was direct, plain, and sometimes brutally blunt. I wondered if he would have enough time to review the plan and get back to me. In addition, Leo had confided a few days earlier that he planned to resign as managing director the next month. But I had to put that concern aside; the immediate goal was to get through this situation with MOVE safely.

I had one additional meeting with Sambor in my office on Saturday, May 11. I wanted to make sure that nothing had changed. Again I had him review the plan with me. He very methodically went through each point, again emphasizing each with his hands and fingers. There was no deviation. He detailed to me exactly the same plan that he had on the previous day.

Sunday, May 12, 1985, was a busy day. I was the commencement speaker for Hampton University. Dick Gilmore, my finance director, and his wife, Jackie, were to attend the ceremony with me. Jackie's sister was married to William Harvey, the president

of Hampton. I had chartered a private plane to make the thirty-
minute journey, and we arrived in Virginia in time to have breakfast with the Harveys at the presidential home.

After breakfast I called Sambor and learned he was unavaila-
ble. I was frustrated. On Saturday I had told Sambor I planned to
check with him from Hampton. I could not reach him even
though I had arranged to call at this time. I decided not to try him
again but to wait until Brooks returned.

I proceeded with my commencement speech. These
speeches are often very difficult, but I had made a special effort
in preparing this one. Facing that sea of expectant, young, black
leaders, I gained strength from their innocence and eagerness to
make their mark in the world. I proceeded to tell them:

> You hold the future in your hands. In a few years, those of us
> sitting here facing you will pass the baton on. It will be your turn to
> run with the baton. And you have to run the whole race. Whatever
> you do, don't drop the baton. Generations before you passed it along.
> Hold fast to your dreams.
>
> There are four things I have learned in life: **Put knowledge in
> your head** — learn all you can — and always have a thirst for knowl-
> edge. **Put a ballot in your hands** — use your franchise. Many who
> went before you were beaten, jailed, and some even died for the right
> to vote. You have it, use it. **Put money in your pocket.** Earn your
> way through life. Don't take short cuts. And **put God in your heart**.
> Some will tell you that education and God don't go together. You tell
> them that God will be there with you when all else fails.
>
> So, knowledge in your head, a ballot in your hands, money in
> your pocket, and God in your heart. Go out and do it!

The crowd stood and cheered. I said my good-byes and
headed toward the car after being stopped several times to sign
autographs and have photos taken.

The airplane trip back was quick. The speech had gone well.

"That's the best speech I've heard you give, Mayor. Good
job!" Dick Gilmore said. Jackie nodded her head approvingly.

But for some reason I couldn't enjoy the moment. I had
strong, mixed feelings about what I would face back in Philadelphia. My mind kept focusing on Monday, May 13. I can't explain
the feeling even now, but deep down inside I kept looking,
searching, begging for another answer. For intervention, yes,
divine intervention.

Returning home late that afternoon, I drove around Cobbs Creek Parkway to see what was going on. I was surprised by the masses of barricades and the number of police on the street. It looked like a prelude to war! Suddenly the gravity of what was about to happen fully dawned on me and I was gripped by apprehension and anxiety.

"I don't want this to happen," I said to myself. "There must be someone, anyone, who can figure out a way to make it go away."

Four days earlier I had arranged for Robert Hamilton, Fareed Ahmed, and Charlie "Boo" Burris to act as liaisons to try and get a meeting between Gerald Ford Africa and myself. The three of them had had contact with Africa over the years. The purpose of the meeting was to see whether there was any way to resolve this matter peacefully. Gerald Ford Africa, according to the three, refused to meet.

Arriving at my home on Fifty-ninth Street (we had moved there six months earlier) I went straight to my den to pray.

"Lord, help me to sort this thing out," I prayed. "Help me to find the right solution. Please don't let anyone get hurt."

For a long time I sat there praying, meditating, and hoping for the best. I don't know how long I remained there, but after a period of time Velma called me.

"Wilson, are you all right? I don't hear any noise in there."

"Velma, I'm fine," I answered. "I'll be out in a minute. What's for dinner?"

"Well, you know, it's either fish or chicken. You don't eat anything else."

As I continued to think about the impending situation, I remembered that my initial thought had been to go to the command center before coming home.

The command center was located on the top floor of Walnut Plaza, at Sixty-third and Walnut Streets, three-and-a-half blocks from Osage Avenue. The command center was where all activities would be coordinated during the day.

Then I received some troubling information. Three people who had always provided me with reliable information stopped by my home. They had obtained information alleging that if I went to the MOVE scene, I would "catch a bullet with my name

on it!" It would be made to look like an accident, but they told
me unknown members of my own police force had targeted me
for death if I came near Sixty-second Street and Osage Avenue.

I was outraged! At the same time, I battled my gut instincts
to be at the scene of the action. I feared being killed.

Later, after Brooks had returned to Philadelphia, I was able
to talk with him by phone.

"Have you reviewed Sambor's plan?"

"Yes, I have, Mr. Mayor."

"Well, what do you think, Leo?"

"I think it can work."

"Can it be done safely?"

"Oh, yes. These people are professionals. I have confidence
in them."

"Leo, would you review with me the essential elements of the
plan as you understand them."

Leo presented the same elements that Sambor had given me.
I was satisfied because Brooks was confident that the arrests
could be made in a safe fashion.

As Leo was about to hang up the phone, I mentioned to him
that I had been planning on coming to the command center
along with other elected officials. We would meet there at about
5:00 A.M. Brooks was totally against that. He did not think that it
was wise for me or any of the elected officials to be present at the
command center. He was persuasive.

Let Leo and Sambor do their jobs without looking over their
shoulders, I told myself. You are now the mayor, and there are
other issues to be dealt with. You need to protect yourself.

*Late that Sunday night, close to five hundred police officers
moved into position around the MOVE house. Meanwhile, nine
women and children huddled in the basement garage awaiting
the dawn in anticipation of the battle that finally erupted
around them early on May 13. They were: Rhonda, Ramona,
and Theresa Africa, and the children—Birdie, Tree, Netta,
Tomaso, Phil, and Delicia. The men—Conrad, Frank, Ray-
mond, and MOVE founder, John Africa—remained in other*

*parts of the house. The small band of women and children spent
that day sitting tightly together, frightened and hungry. Tomaso,
the youngest at eight or nine, cried and whimpered. A woman
hugged him to her breast.*

At about 8:00 P.M., the telephone rang. Novella Williams, the
president of the community organization Citizens for Progress
and a longtime Frank Rizzo supporter, had called the city hall
switchboard and they'd patched her through to my home.

"Wilson, call all of it off!" she commanded. Novella lived
about seven blocks from the MOVE house and had surveyed the
scene of the impending battle. "Nothing good will come of it.
You're going to destroy yourself with this, Mayor. You're being
set up. Call it off!"

I could feel my body tense as she spoke.

"Novella, this has gone too far for me to just call it off," I said
quietly. "There has to be some other intervening situation. I can't
call it off."

"Why not?" she demanded. "You're the mayor! Just call it
off."

"There are too many factors involved that I can't explain," I
responded. "I can't just call it off."

Deep down inside, I was unsure of Novella's motives. She
had supported Frank Rizzo against me. Was she now my ally?
What was her motive? Was she trying to set me up?

In any event, things had gone too far. We'd evacuated hundreds of people from Osage Avenue that night, and they had
insisted that the MOVE members be arrested before they came
back. To back down now would be an admission that the police
department wasn't willing to arrest those who had violated the
law. I was in a no-win situation. If I didn't act, I would be viewed
as a weak and indecisive leader by citizens who were already
saying, "What am I paying my taxes for? Why must our kids be
exposed to all of this profanity? If these people have warrants
outstanding against them, then make the arrests. There should be
no double standard."

It was on the issue of double standards that I was especially sensitive. I had not wanted to treat MOVE members differently if they had committed no crime. But, now that we had the arrest warrants, there should be no special treatment either. We should take our time, plan well, and make the arrests.

I was restless that Sunday night. Before I went to bed, I went into my study again, turned on the lights, and fell on my knees to pray.

"God, if it's your will to stop this confrontation, please give me the wisdom to know how," I pleaded.

I don't know how long I prayed, meditated, and daydreamed about the coming dawn.

"Please let them come out. Please don't let there be any bloodshed. Help me to solve this," I prayed. "Give me some way to solve this without bloodshed."

Shortly before 5:00 A.M. Monday morning, at my invitation, elected officials began arriving at my house: Joe Coleman, Hardy Williams, Pete Truman, and Lucien Blackwell. The location of the meeting had been changed to my house after my earlier discussion with Brooks. Throughout the morning we watched the events unfolding on television, and I received calls from the command center with updates. Not much happened, but every now and then bursts of gunfire from the scene two miles away rang outside my window, loud and clear.

Hearing the first burst of gunfire, I was puzzled. Sambor had told me he would fire only at known targets. Where was all of this gunfire coming from? I wondered. I wanted to talk to Leo Brooks.

"Leo, I thought there wasn't going to be any gunfire," I said after reaching him at the command center.

"Mr. Mayor, the gunfire for the most part is coming from the house," he replied. "The police are firing their weapons over the house."

Satisfied, I repeated the conversation to the elected officials present.

As we waited, I silently prayed to myself, "Please, let them come out. Let them come out."

～

Police had sealed off the area at 10:00 P.M. Sunday evening, warning neighbors to be out of their homes or risk arrest. A gas works crew had shut off gas to the MOVE house, and an electric company crew had turned off power to the entire block. Osage Avenue was a darkened ghost town, save for the hundreds of police officers that moved stealthily throughout the area. They included officers from the bomb-disposal unit as well as the stakeout unit, officers trained in the use of high-powered and automatic weapons.

In response to the police activity outside, at midnight MOVE members began vilifying the police over a loudspeaker system.

"Send in the CIA! Send in the FBI!" a man's voice boomed. "Send in the SWAT teams. We have something for you!"

The attempt to arrest MOVE members began at 6:00 A.M. Shots rang out from inside the house as firefighters unleashed high-powered hoses on the wooden bunker on top of the house.

The remainder of the morning, May 13, was uneventful. There was little progress in convincing MOVE members to come out and turn themselves over to the police. Around 9:00 A.M., the other elected officials and I left my home and went to our respective offices. Before they departed, I made sure I had their telephone numbers so I could reach each one of them.

Around noon, a coalition made up of members of the black clergy, Pan Africanists, and community activists came to my office to ask me to call off the arrests. The Rev. Urcille Ifill, president of the black clergy organization, led the group.

"This is a conspiracy against you, Wilson," he said solemnly. "Nothing good can come out of this. Use your influence, your power, to call it off." I searched for other answers with the clergy, throwing out a number of suggestions.

"Why can't the people in the house come out if I promise we won't hurt them?" I asked.

"Why would they trust you?"

He had a point. MOVE and the police had a long adversarial history. MOVE members clearly saw me, in my role of mayor, as being in league with the devil.

"What about letting the black clergy go into the streets to ask MOVE to surrender?" I asked.

They liked the idea. Within minutes we had created a plan for Rev. Ifill and members of the black clergy to go to Osage Avenue to try to talk MOVE members out of the house.

I immediately called Leo Brooks from my office to arrange for Rev. Ifill and his team to come out to the scene. Telephone communications to the site were horrendous! I reached Leo by calling a police radio and leaving a message for him to call me back. A police officer then had to find Leo to relay the message. Afterwards Leo used the telephone to call me back.

When I finally spoke with him, Leo was reluctant to implement the plan. I was determined.

"I want you to do everything possible to avoid bloodshed," I said. "Just do it! I'll be standing by my phone for a progress report."

All three local television stations carried the news live. I had television sets set up in three different rooms. The one in my office was an old set and had the worst reception. The picture was far from clear.

My heart leapt with hopeful anticipation when shortly after 4:00 P.M. Rev. Ifill appeared on the television screen, bull horn in hand. A contingency of black clergy stood behind him.

"This is the black clergy," his voice boomed. "If you're in there and alive, please come out. You will not be harmed."

Over and over again he repeated the message for the next twenty minutes. No response. I was back and forth on the telephone with Leo for updates. Yes, there were people in the house, Leo assured me, and they were alive. Surveillance was picking up movement.

In another call Leo outlined an alternative plan.

"We're going to use a crane to knock the bunker off the house," he said.

"Is that safe?" I asked.

"Yes, it's safe."

"I'll keep you posted," he said before hanging up.

"Good luck," I said. I could feel my heart racing as I continued to pray that this thing would be resolved peacefully.

I don't know how long they spent trying to position the crane before finally deciding it was a fruitless effort. The crane would not allow maximum security for the police. Around 5:00 P.M. Leo called with another alternative.

"We're going to blow the bunker off with explosives," he said.

"Is that safe?" I asked.

"Yes, it's safe," he said wearily.

I recalled being apprehensive about the plan. My main concern was for the police officers who I thought were going to crawl over to the bunker and place some plastic explosives around the bunker to dislodge it.

By 4:00 P.M. that afternoon, Leo Brooks and fire commissioner William Richmond had met with police commissioner Greg Sambor and agreed to let Sambor use explosives to try to dislodge the bunker from the roof. The officers assigned to perform the task were Frank Powell and William Klein.

Powell, forty-one, a seventeen-year veteran of the Philadelphia police force, had worked his way up from beat cop to lieutenant in the juvenile division to commanding officer of the Bomb Disposal Unit of the police academy. As a policeman, he had received fifteen days of training in explosive disposal and related areas by May 13, 1985.[2]

Klein, thirty-eight, a thirteen-year veteran of the force, received his explosive training while serving in the Marine Corps in Vietnam. Using C-4 explosives, he had opened up enemy tunnels, destroying fortifications, caches of weapons, and booby traps.[3] Klein's assignment was to make the bomb. Powell was to drop it from a helicopter onto the roof of the house.

With Leo's words ringing in my ears, I stepped outside of the room to think. The plan was to use explosives to blow the bunker off the roof. This was the first time I had heard the word *explosives*. What kind of explosives? Leo said it was safe. They must know what they're doing, I concluded. "It will take awhile to set up," Leo had said. It was a little after 5:00 P.M.

When I returned to my office, the television screen was playing a scene straight out of a war movie. A helicopter approached the MOVE house as television commentators gave a blow-by-blow description of the action. I watched the scene in horror.

"My God, what are they doing?" I heard myself say. "What on earth are they doing out there? What is that helicopter doing out there? Whose helicopter is it? Get me Leo Brooks on the phone!"

Ironically, as this disaster was happening, contractors were breaking ground for the construction of Liberty Place One, the flagship building that launched the renaissance of the new downtown. Liberty One would signal the rebirth of the city. But first we had to pass through hell.

I was vaguely aware of movement in the room as staff scurried to the telephones. My eyes remained riveted to the television screen as fear rose in my throat, choking me. The helicopter approached slowly, menacingly, delivering death.

Just before the bomb was dropped, the MOVE men joined the women and children in the basement garage where they sat under a wet blanket to escape the oppressive smoke. As the explosion shook the stone house, the children screamed in terror. Within moments, more smoke poured into the garage and the heat inside the house reached a dizzying level.

"The children are coming out!" one of the men, Conrad Africa, yelled. Lifting Tomaso on his back, he began to crawl out of the garage door only to be driven back by a burst of gunfire. "The kids are coming out!" Conrad yelled again, handing Tomaso to Theresa. The crying, frightened children joined the sad chorus.[4]

"We're coming out! We're coming out!" they screamed.

Thick smoke surrounded the area like a smoky veil, obscuring visibility. It was suffocating! The crackling pop of windows shattering punctuated the air like strange firecrackers. Unused ammunition also exploded in the searing heat.

As burning debris fell into the garage, the women and children scurried through a wall of flames toward the fence in the yard. Stumbling, Birdie watched helplessly as Ramona Africa climbed onto the driveway and then helped Tree and Phil to what appeared to be safety. Birdie later said Phil's skin looked like it was melting from the heat.

Ramona extended a hand to help Birdie out of the yard, but the small, tired youngster fell back into the alley. Staggering toward the west end of the alley, Birdie waded in chest-high water. Exhausted, he fainted face down in the water. Watching the scene were police officers James Berghaier, Michael Tursi, and Charles Mellor.

Ramona walked towards the officers, her body scarred and her spirit weary.

"Don't shoot. I've had enough," she called.

Berghaier handed his shotgun to Tursi.

"I'm going to get the kid," he said.

"Watch yourself, this could be a trap," said Tursi.[5]

Shortly after the device was dropped from the helicopter, I saw a fire on the roof near where the bunker was still intact. Because of the poor reception on my television, I thought that the fire was being extinguished. However, when it became apparent to me that it was not being put out, I panicked.

"Put the fire out!" I yelled at the screen. "Put the fire out! Get me Leo Brooks on the phone!" I shouted a third time. "Why can't we reach him?"

I couldn't stand still. As people scurried around me, I paced from room to room, banging on desks and talking to the television screens.

Lynn Fields and Karen Warrington, my press personnel, were in and out of the office answering phones, as was Shirley Hamilton, my chief of staff who occupied the office adjoining mine, and Debbie Goens, my executive secretary. From time to time, Lt. Fred Ragsdale, my chief security officer, also came in to ask if he could help.

The office was a madhouse of activity with people scurrying around grabbing telephones and watching the television screens in horror.

For a moment all of us stood together in silent horror watching as flames rose high above the roof.

"How can anyone be so stupid?" I wondered. "Why won't they put the fire out?"

"Why can't they put the fire out?" I asked no one. "Put the fire out! What's wrong with you people out there? Put the fire out! What's going on with the fire department?"

I was suffocating as I watched the screens. This couldn't be happening. This wasn't supposed to happen.

"This is terrible. Why is this happening?" I groaned. "This is the worst thing that ever could have happened. Get me Leo Brooks on the phone!" I screamed a fourth time.

Finally someone thrust a receiver in my shaking hand and I heard Leo's voice on the other end.

"Leo, put that fire out!"

"I've just given the order," he said, his voice trembling.

"What are they doing out there?"

Leo paused. "I don't know."

I couldn't believe what I was hearing.

"What's the problem?" I asked, my voice rising. "Is there a problem with the water pressure?"

Somehow in the midst of the confusion I heard a television reporter say something about the police dropping a bomb from the helicopter on the house. The words hit me with the impact of an explosion. This was the first time anyone had used the word *bomb*.

I yelled into the phone, "Did the kids get out? Did the kids get out of the house? Did the people get out of the house, Leo?"

For the next hour I received a series of wild reports from the media and the command center. People believed to be MOVE members were seen running west toward the park. People were seen running across the alley to other houses.

With each report my emotions seesawed and my heart raced as I alternated between hope and fear. At times, I was just plain scared for the children and other MOVE members. Then I was scared for the police and the fire department.

It was believed that MOVE had dug tunnels under their house to the park and other homes as an escape route—an underground railroad—in the event of a violent confrontation. None of it was true.

By the time attempts were finally made to control the fire, it had taken on a life of its own. The fire had burned for forty-five minutes before the order was given to fight it. Brooks had ordered Sambor early to do so; Sambor did not carry out the command. Eventually the bunker fell through the burning roof into the house. By then flames had leaped from building to building and across the street, turning Osage Avenue into an urban inferno.

Before it was over, eleven people died in the MOVE fire. Five of the victims were children. Two hundred and fifty people were suddenly homeless, their property and memories gone, destroyed.

That afternoon watching the television screens, I saw everything I had worked for all my life go up in smoke. I had worked my entire professional life to preserve life, to build houses, to build communities. This was totally opposite from everything I ever wanted to happen. Why was it happening? I had tried so hard to prevent a disaster.

Why couldn't they put the fire out? I wondered. This was so tragic, so unnecessary.

When I saw Birdie and Ramona Africa come out from the area around the house, my heart soared. I presumed the others had escaped also. I hoped they had.

When I finally met with Greg Sambor, Leo Brooks, and Bill Richmond, I was so upset I could barely speak.

"Who gave the order to let the bunker burn and not even try to put the fire out?" I demanded to know.

"I gave the order, Mr. Mayor," Sambor said, his face a blank mask.

"Why?"

"I was trying to get them out."

I could barely comprehend what I was hearing.

"How did you lose control of the fire?"

He shrugged. "Ask the fire commissioner about that."

I turned to Bill Richmond.

"Talk to the police commissioner," he responded, throwing the ball back to Sambor.

I couldn't believe it. A tragedy of this magnitude and my police and fire commissioners were playing verbal Ping-Pong over how it had happened. I would later learn that Richmond had given in to Sambor's authority and had allowed the fire to burn unabated for forty-five minutes.

"I don't think you should be talking about this," my attorney said interrupting the debate. "There's bound to be an investigation. Hold this until we've had a chance to advise you, Mr. Mayor."

The conversation ended as abruptly as it had begun. But I never had a chance to finish that conversation with Leo Brooks, Greg Sambor, and Bill Richmond. What took place was a press conference with Greg Sambor, who told the world he had let the fire burn uncontrolled.

People who heard that naturally assumed he was following orders. It was some time later than Sambor made it clear he alone had made the decision to let the fire burn.

And me? I wasn't particularly savvy with the press. Throughout the day I had gone into the mayor's reception room, where a corps of reporters were staked out awaiting periodic updates. Part of the time I half-answered questions, failing to say exactly what I meant. Such as the time I responded that we would get the MOVE members out of the house "by any means necessary." At the time I spoke those words, I had no idea that the police would shoot ten thousand rounds of ammunition into the house, blow the front of the house off with explosives, drop an explosive device from a helicopter, and let the fire burn in order to serve arrest warrants. My words were inappropriately and carelessly spoken. When viewed in the context of what eventually happened, they were damaging indeed. But never in my wildest imagination could I have thought that the police commissioner would undertake such measures.

Of course that statement came back to haunt me. At another point when asked if I would take the same action again, I stupidly answered, "Yes, I would do it again." What I meant was that I would attempt to make the arrests again. But in retrospect the question had actually been, "Would I repeat the horror of May

13?" Of course I would not. This statement, too, continues to torment me.

Clifford Bond, the resident who had first articulated the neighbors' concerns, angrily told the media, "We asked the mayor to give us peace. We didn't expect him to burn down our houses and our neighborhood. That's not what we wanted."

Sambor and Brooks also continued to talk to the media. Brooks even went so far as to say he had briefed me beforehand that the explosive device would be dropped from a helicopter.

Privately I challenged him on that. "Mr. Mayor, I thought I told you," Brooks said. "Now that you mention it, maybe I didn't."

I believe now, as I believed then, that Sambor carefully worded what he said to Brooks so as not to have Brooks veto what Sambor planned to do. I also believe that Brooks carefully worded what he told me. Both Sambor and Brooks knew me well. They knew what I would veto.

They knew that if they had told me they planned to use a helicopter to drop a bomb on the roof of a house occupied by innocent children, I would have said no!

Sambor knew that if he had asked Brooks or me about letting the fire burn, we would have said no so loudly they could have heard us from City Hall.

The fact of the matter is there is nothing I have done in life, no decision I have ever made, that should allow anyone to believe that if I had been given the facts about the bomb and the fire, I would not have vetoed the decisions instantly.

I declare here and now, with God as my judge, that I did not know a helicopter was going to drop a bomb on the MOVE house. Nor did I know anything of Sambor's decision to let the fire burn, defying direct orders from Leo Brooks to put it out.

But even if I can't convince another soul of my intentions, I am satisfied that God knows what happened. And I am perfectly satisfied to let him be my judge, because I know God will be just and compassionate.

Throughout the week following the fire, each time a body was pulled out of the MOVE house, I received a report. With each discovery of a body, a little bit of me died all over again.

I had worked all my life to help people, to build houses, to protect children, to mold their lives to help them become productive citizens. I was now being told that I was responsible for destroying the very things I had worked so hard to preserve. I wanted people to know that I could never intentionally do what they were telling me I had done. I could never take a life; I could never destroy a house. I wished they could know me as I am—my feelings, my intentions, my love for life—not the way the media and my critics were now portraying me.

I played the events over and over in my mind, trying to make some sense of it all. Much too late I realized I was wrong to appoint Sambor and to trust Brooks's confidence in him. Hindsight proved he was the wrong person to handle the situation. I was wrong not to go to the command center despite the death threat. Now it was too late to recover the losses.

Sadly I realized that the police had killed two birds with one stone—MOVE and me.

What about my future as a public servant? If I fired Brooks or Sambor now, it would look as if I were looking for a scapegoat to feed to the media wolves. That wasn't my nature. This had happened on my watch and I had to take the responsibility for the outcome. Many people did not understand what I meant by "taking responsibility for what happened." I did not mean that I approved it. I did not mean that I could have prevented it. I feel responsible to the extent that I misjudged the ability of some of my staff to appropriately handle such a delicate crisis. In the sense that a manager—and a mayor—is accountable for the actions of his or her subordinates, I am willing to take my share of the blame.

And what about God's role in all of this?

I believe that even for those of us who have faith, God sends tragedy into our lives to strengthen us. I never believed that whatever goodness and faithfulness I had would exempt me from dark days. God sends tragedies into the world to remind us of our responsibilities to one another. In the midst of difficulties, more than at any other time, we realize how much we need one another and how much we need God. Over the years I have struggled with the universal question, Why does God allow suffering? Though I have no complete answer, I have come to believe that sometimes in carrying out his plan, God allows people—even innocent people—to suffer.

Although I knew I would never fully understand how this tragedy fit into God's plan, I asked God to give me the strength to seek and find truth. I asked for forgiveness for my failings and comfort for all those who were suffering. I prayed for healing for the people of Philadelphia, that they would still have confidence in my leadership so that I could finish the job God had for me to do.

The only real hope I had of getting through this was that the people who really knew the kind of man I was would know that I couldn't commit murder. They knew I was a decent, hard-working individual who cared about this city. May 13 had encompassed one day of my administration. One terrible event. The people wouldn't judge me on that alone. Or so I hoped.

CHAPTER THIRTEEN

Investigation

Almost immediately after the MOVE tragedy I started thinking about my next step. It was clear to me that an investigation was needed. But by whom? Would the federal government step in? Could I launch a credible investigation of my own city officials and myself? On the other hand, if I turned the investigation over to Ed Rendell, the district attorney, could I be sure he wouldn't use it against me?

Rumor had it that Ed was about to resign to run for governor. Friends suggested to me that he really wanted to run for mayor. If that was true, to allow Ed to conduct an investigation would be political suicide. I would literally be placing my career into the hands of a campaigning politician who could use my problems to gain public support.

As I wrestled with my problems, I got a call from Charlie Bowser suggesting that I appoint a blue-ribbon panel of seven or nine people to investigate the bombing and to clear my name. Charlie had run for mayor in 1975 and 1979. He'd lost both times but was well respected in local politics. The panel should have my full cooperation and complete access to all records, public and confidential. In his opinion, this would be the only way to give credibility to an investigation.

After giving me this advice, he also scolded me by reminding me of a warning he had given me earlier.

"Wilson, I told you some of the people you appointed were going to get you in trouble and embarrass you," he said. "Some of these people don't understand anything about government."

Bowser had been appointed deputy mayor back in 1966. So I knew he had a pretty good idea of what running the city entailed. We continued to talk about the panel, deciding that we would work out the details together before presenting it to anyone else.

Before that could happen, the newspapers found out what we were doing and reported it. The information to the media had to have come from Bowser or someone he told—I told no one. It wasn't long before my phone was ringing off the hook. One of the first people to call was Sam Evans, an eighty-year-old elder statesman. Sam got right to the point.

"Wilson, you would be a fool to appoint a blue-ribbon panel to investigate yourself," he said. "You can't control a panel. It will just open a Pandora's Box and put all this stuff out in the public. Television cameras will be everywhere, and the whole thing will do you more harm than good.

"Your best bet," he said, "is to leave it in the hands of the district attorney. At least in a grand jury investigation all the testimony is secret, and you won't be airing your dirty linen in front of television cameras. Listen to me for once and forget about this blue-ribbon panel."

Of course Sam reminded me that I had never taken his advice before, even though history had proven him to be right about many things he had said. My instincts told me Sam was probably right this time too, but my mind steered me towards the blue-ribbon panel. The panel concept would be more my style. I was a public mayor. I had nothing to hide. I desperately wanted the media and the people of Philadelphia to see that I wasn't trying to hide anything. Let the facts fall where they may.

I wanted to do the right thing in the right way. My political career wasn't as much a factor as my public reputation. I wanted to clear the air and get this situation behind me with people knowing who Wilson Goode really was—a man of faith and integrity who would never harm innocent people.

Oddly, while I was concerned about public perception, for the first two months following the fire my public rating remained very high. Two days after the MOVE tragedy, I was being honored by the Police Athletic League at their annual dinner. As I walked into the room, people leaped to their feet and the room exploded with applause and cheers. The reception was unbelievable. Apparently former mayor Bill Green thought it was undeserved. He said nothing, but I could read by the expression on his face that he thought I had really screwed up.

Often when I went into restaurants or other public places, people gave me standing ovations. There was a tremendous amount of sympathy for the decision I had made and the horrible aftermath. Some people thought I had acted courageously confronting MOVE. Interestingly, Daryl Gates, the police chief of Los Angeles at the time, even wrote me a letter of support praising my actions against MOVE.

I found the response baffling. I was anything but proud of what happened. I should not be cheered for that. While some of the people, like Gates, were applauding the action that we took, I could never be proud that police fired ten thousand rounds of ammunition into a house with innocent people inside. I could never be proud of a police commissioner who would drop a bomb on a roof and then when that did not achieve the desired goal, let a fire burn until it destroyed sixty-one homes and killed eleven people.

I could never be proud of a police department that fired their guns at women and children trying to escape a burning inferno. No, we had done nothing to be cheered for. I was ashamed— ashamed of myself for having presided over such a fiasco, ashamed of my police commissioner and of those officers who fired all of those rounds into the house. I was ashamed of those officers who stood in the rear alley of the MOVE house and who forced innocent children and women to die in that burning hell!

I was ashamed of the silence of police officers who knew what had happened but, because of their "code of silence" to protect their brethren, said nothing. Often I wonder how these officers can sleep at night. After the 1992 Los Angeles riots and

Gates's comments following that tragedy, I now know why he wrote that letter following the MOVE incident. He thought what was done was right. I couldn't disagree more vigorously.

The press began to raise questions about a week after the fire: Why weren't the children evacuated from the house? Who gave the order for a helicopter to drop explosives on the house?

Caught between a supportive public and a critical media, I wanted to know the complete truth about what had happened May 13. I also needed to rally public support to bring about some reconciliation for the homeowners who had lost everything. We needed to rebuild that community. I wanted to fully understand what had happened. So I impaneled the Philadelphia Special Investigation Commission.

William H. Brown III, the former chair of the Equal Employment Opportunity Commission (EEOC) under President Gerald Ford, was one of my first choices. Bill was a Republican and an outstanding civil rights lawyer. In my careful selection of thirteen people for the commission, I didn't seek out friends or supporters but outstanding civic, business, community, and religious leaders. Charlie Bowser was the only member who could be characterized as a friend. Although I knew some might feel Charlie was appointed because of our political connections, I knew he would not let his past experiences with me stand in the way of work on the commission.

Such a panel would be independent seekers of the truth, I thought. The commission was truly a blue-ribbon panel with people such as: Henry S. Ruth, Jr., a lawyer and former Watergate special prosecutor; Father Paul Washington, rector of the Episcopal Church of the Advocate; the Honorable Bruce Kauffman, former justice of the Pennsylvania Supreme Court; Julia Chinn, president of the Cobbs Creek Town Watch, a community organization in the West Philadelphia neighborhood where MOVE was located; Msg. Edward Cullen, director of Catholic social services for the Archdiocese of Philadelphia; the Reverend Audrey Bronson, founder of the Sanctuary Church of the Open Door, located around the corner from Osage Avenue; M. Todd Cooke, chief executive officer of the Philadelphia Savings Fund Society; Charisse Ranielle Lillie, professor of law at Villanova University; Neil Welch, former assistant director of the FBI; Carl Singley, serving the commission as special counsel; William Lytton, the commission's staff director and counsel; and H. Graham McDonald, deputy staff director and counsel. The chief investigator was Neil Shanahan, a twenty-one-year veteran with the FBI.

My goal was to appoint a panel who would search out the truth, who would leave no stone unturned in finding out the truth. The people deserved to know who did what, when, and why. The people then could judge for themselves.

In making this decision I knew I was taking major risks. I knew that I would have absolutely no control over the outcome. But that's what democratic government is all about. It's about opening up our most difficult problems and letting the sun shine in even if it isn't flattering. I knew that this was why Sam Evans said bluntly, "To appoint a group of people to publicly rake you over the coals just shows you don't understand politics!"

I appointed the commission because I wanted the truth to be revealed. I firmly believed that the city could heal itself only if there were a complete airing of the facts. What I wanted from this commission was a thorough and complete investigation. I also envisioned a private, in-depth, exhaustive examination of all the facts and then the issuance of a public report.

I got a lot more than what I had envisioned. What I got was an $800,000 staff and a live television audience despite my strong reservations about this approach. I felt the commission was pandering to the public emotions. Indeed, some members of the commission, I felt, were more interested in that than in uncovering the real facts. Moreover I felt that the live television coverage would inhibit candid disclosure, especially by some of the police and fire personnel.

At that point I could see that the grand jury approach would have been more effective, but it was too late. I couldn't publicly express my views for fear of giving the appearance of interfering with the commission. I had no desire to do that even though I felt they were moving in the wrong direction.

My concerns were borne out by the commission's delay in producing a response. I had wanted the investigation to proceed immediately and for a report to be released by Labor Day. Instead, the commission didn't even get underway until October. They said they needed time to assemble staff and to coordinate the broadcast of the hearings with the local public television station, Channel 12.

Commissioner William H. Brown III, chair of the committee, opened the hearings with a statement of purpose for the press and the public:

> On May 13, 1985, years of conflict between the city of Philadelphia and a small, urban group known as "MOVE" ended in a violent day-long encounter between the group's members and the Philadelphia police.
>
> The confrontation began at dawn, when MOVE resisted an attempt by police, acting upon the order of the mayor, to serve arrest warrants on four MOVE members, who were barricaded inside a fortified row house on Osage Avenue on the city's west side.
>
> Eighteen hours later, at least 11 MOVE members, including 4 children, were dead. Nearly two square blocks of a comfortable residential neighborhood lay wasted by fire. Sixty-one families, some 250 men, women and children, were homeless, their achievements and aspirations consumed in the terrible fire that we all watched on our TV screens.
>
> It was one of the most devastating days in the modern history of this city.
>
> Soon afterward, this panel which sits before you today, the Philadelphia Special Investigation Commission, was directed to conduct a thorough, independent and impartial examination of the events leading up to and culminating in death and destruction on the 13th of May. We are to investigate the conduct of all city officials, agencies and departments. We are charged with the responsibility of gathering all the facts, searching them out wherever they may be, without regard to the personal interests of those upon whom responsibility may be placed, be it MOVE or officials and employees of the city of Philadelphia.
>
> This we have done, and continue to do as we open these hearings here today. . . .
>
> It is for you, the people of Philadelphia, that we have labored long and diligently, sometimes against powerful opposition, to piece together the full story of Osage Avenue. It is to you, the people of Philadelphia, and to you only, that we ultimately are responsible. Above all else, it is to you, the people, that we answer. We hope that you, the people of this city, recognize that what we do springs from an honest heart. It is to you, our fellow Philadelphians, that we now begin to present the facts of May 13th.[1]

Bill Brown's opening statement was eloquent and powerfully executed. I agreed with the basic thrust of his statement. He had captured my sentiments precisely.

I remember sitting in my office and watching Bill make the statement on television. Maybe I was wrong, I thought. This may be the best way to get the facts out. Perhaps I was worrying needlessly about the possible negative impact that a televised hearing could have.

But my worst fears were soon confirmed. As the commission brought in witnesses from various departments, it became clear to me that the operations of these departments were far from perfect. While I knew there had been major improvements since 1980, the public had nothing to compare the current situation with, except their own standards of perfection. Any department in any city would have fallen short when scrutinized under those conditions. Moreover, no department in any city ever had its operations examined so closely in a public forum.

This was the citizens' first glimpse of the inner workings of their government. I had succeeded in achieving a unique process—opening up government in a way it had never been before—but the process had a high price. As people glimpsed the inner workings of their government and saw it defending itself in these hearings, many citizens didn't like what they saw. The truth wasn't pretty.

Citizens saw, for example, a Licenses and Inspections (L & I) department with many inconsistencies in its enforcement of codes. Why didn't L & I investigate MOVE members as they built a bunker on top of their house in the middle of a residential neighborhood? No one had ever reported the bunker to me even though a Philadelphia police officer lived next door to the MOVE house.

The television drama raised many questions about the Philadelphia Police Department and its tactics. Why, for example, did the police use white intelligence officers to watch a predominantly African American organization that was known to have strong antiwhite feelings? Who developed the idea of dropping C-4 military explosives in the middle of a row-house complex? Or to use explosives on a street that was so narrow fire could jump from one side to the other and destroy building after building?

Other questions were raised: How did the police department obtain enough C-4 explosives to construct a three-pound bomb? Why did the police chief, Greg Sambor, tell the fire department to let the fire burn as Osage Avenue went up in smoke? What did the mayor know about the decision to drop the bomb? When did he know it?

And, finally, what occurred in the alley behind 6221 Osage Avenue between 7:30 and 8:00 P.M. as the fire burned out of control? Were police fired upon? Did they fire on MOVE members as they tried to escape the burning house? How many people tried to escape from the MOVE house? What happened to those who failed?

As the commission spent day after day listening to testimony, I was glued to my television set, often learning for the first time some of the facts about May 13. I had known nothing about the use of C-4 explosives until news reports revealed its use. There had never been any discussion with me about having a helicopter on stand-by.

As the hearings ferreted out the truth, they uncovered many of the inadequacies of city government. Unfortunately the investigation ignored the strengths government had gained. I had spent sixteen wonderful months as mayor and had continued the process of reform that had started with Bill Green. We had a long way to go yet, but I knew this city government was so much better than the one we had inherited from Frank Rizzo. It was more efficient, much better managed, more responsive, and more accountable. Watching the hearings, I was embarrassed. The questions asked dealt only with our weaknesses, not our strengths. Often as I watched I would yell at the screen, "Ask about the good stuff! Ask about the improvements!" None of that happened. The public was exposed only to our shortcomings.

Ramona Africa, the only adult survivor (one child, Birdie, also survived), refused to testify during the investigations. She later gave her account of the conflict in July 1991 pretrial testimony after she had served six years in prison for her role in the events of May 13, 1985.

She explained that MOVE had stored gasoline cans on the roof, in the shed kitchen, and down in the cellar to fuel their generator. But no weapons were in the house, she said.

With her long, thick dreadlocks framing her narrow face like a bushy veil, Ramona was intense and passionate during her interrogation. Her passion for the righteousness of MOVE had made her a dynamic spokesperson as MOVE's minister of communication.

Ramona described MOVE as a back-to-nature, spiritually centered organization that believed in living in harmony with the elements. Members ate raw food, mostly vegetables and fruit but also meat. They lived by the teachings of MOVE's founder, John Africa, who was killed in the fire. Despite longstanding hostilities with the police, Ramona said MOVE was not prejudiced against police officers.

> We have support from police officers. You know, before May 13, I walked the streets every day back and forth between 56th and Chester, Pentridge and wherever I had to go. I saw cops and I stood out there and talked to them, you know, gave them information about, you know, what was going on, you know, how we felt about our innocent family members being in prison. Right before May 13, I told Police Officer Ted Vaughn that we knew this city wanted to take action against us and wanted to kill us, wanted to kill all of us, and that if he ever heard of anything like that happening that, you know, we considered him like a brother, and that he really shouldn't get involved in nothing. . . .[2]

Most poignant was her view of the moral and social injustices against MOVE:

> This system is very prejudice against MOVE. I'm telling you right now, if it was anybody but MOVE people in that house, this City wouldn't have never, ever, did what it did. It wouldn't have burnt babies alive. It wouldn't have never shot 10,000 rounds of ammunition at a house knowing that there was men, women, babies and animals in that, in less than 90 minutes. They never would have did that. The City would have never dropped no bomb on a house containing white Irish Catholic men, women, babies. Now, I don't care if you admit it, accept it, deny it, or what, it's the truth and you know it. . . .
>
> I think they [the neighbors] violated their own rights. That's what I think. You know, it was their right to demand that the City resolve that issue peacefully, you know. That was their right. When they did not press that right and see that that right was, you know, fully—fully understood and acted on, they violated theirself. You know, we told those Osage residents that the City didn't care no more for them than

they did MOVE, and that if they came out there to kill MOVE, they
would give those residents no consideration at all. They would just do
what they wanted to do. We told them that. We told them that. That's
exactly what happened. The City didn't care about all of the houses
and belongings of neighbors surrounding 6221 Osage. They didn't
give a damn. They didn't give a damn at all, and we told those
residents that's what would happen. If the City had cared about the
Osage residents' complaints from the beginning, they would have
tried to resolve the issue in a way that was not a major confrontation
like that. The City didn't care about Osage residents, you know. What
does the City care about them? All they wanted to do was kill MOVE.
That's all. . . .

    I remember right before I was able to finally get out with Birdie.
I remember Conrad—that's who I remember—Conrad pulling the
cellar door open, finally getting the door open and us trying to come
out. Birdie and I tried about two times to get out. I went out first one
time and was met by gunfire, police gunfire, and had to push Birdie
back in and get back in myself. I tried again and again and the same
thing happened. At that point, it was so full of smoke down there that
I couldn't even see, and it was extremely hot. I couldn't see exactly
where the fire was coming from, but I knew at that point there was
a fire because I could see flames all outside the house when I tried
to come out.

    Finally, the third time Birdie and I, you know, made it out and
I could hear shots around me, but I just, like, made it up to the top
alley and Birdie was right behind me. . . .

    It was full of fire out there. Fire was everywhere. It was smoke
everywhere and all of the—at least most of the houses which would
be the back of the 6200 block of Pine Street, there were cops in all
those windows. . . . It was . . . a choice between being shot and being
burned to death.[3]

    After reflecting on the information from the hearings, I felt
that the real cause of the death of the eleven people was not the
dropping of the bomb but the fire. It could have been dealt with,
initially, by a few streams of water. The real cause for their deaths
was the stupid decision to let the fire burn combined with the
actions of renegade police officers in the alley, shooting to force
MOVE members exiting the house back inside.

    Following the tragedy of May 13, much emphasis was placed
on a city government dropping a bomb on a row house. I certainly never authorized the dropping of a bomb, and I really don't

believe that if Leo Brooks had known all of the facts, he would have done so either. I really don't know what was in the mind of Greg Sambor when he conceived this idea. He never discussed that with me. I don't know how he thought the plan would work. But whatever he thought initially, I feel he should have had enough common sense to know that you don't play with fire! We teach children early in life not to play with matches. We tell them that fire kills.

Did Sambor lose control? Did we have a police riot in the alley? As the facts unfolded, I saw that the MOVE tragedy was a time bomb waiting to explode on anyone's watch. MOVE and the police had been antagonists for years. No autopsy or ballistic tests were ever done to prove conclusively that a MOVE member had fired the fatal shot that killed Officer Ramp in 1978, but nine MOVE members were convicted and jailed for terms of thirty to one hundred years. Ever since that day, MOVE had vowed to wage war on Philadelphia until new hearings were held and its family members freed. Some members of the police department, I believe, had made an unspoken vow as well to avenge the death of the slain police officer.

The reason that Lucien Blackwell and I had stressed that none of the officers involved in the August 8, 1978, confrontation be involved in the May 13, 1985, confrontation was because we felt that those officers would be too emotionally involved. I knew some of them would seek revenge. The investigation was bringing it all out in the open.

Residents of Osage Avenue testified that the first assault on their peace came Christmas Eve 1983, when MOVE members unleashed a barrage of verbal abuse over loudspeakers.[4] Several neighbors tried to resolve the problem with MOVE members but were told that the attacks were part of MOVE's psychological warfare to force neighbors to complain to city officials who, in turn, would have to negotiate with MOVE to restore the peace. MOVE wanted to negotiate the release of their imprisoned family members.[5] That demand was later reduced to a review of the

trial record of the imprisoned MOVE members, testified Benja-
min Swans of the Crisis Intervention Network.[6]

Perhaps Bennie Swans's testimony was the most disquieting
of all. Bennie had been my point person on crisis intervention
among young people. The fact that Bennie was in active negotiation with MOVE members and had a possible solution was news
to me. The fact that he never sat down with me on this issue was
most disappointing. But Bennie was always a loner, never the
team player. Perhaps he was trying to get full credit himself for
the solution. Whatever the reason, he should be experiencing
some sleepless nights over not making it more widely known that
MOVE may have been more easily satisfied than we thought.

*During the hearing Charles Bowser stated that the response
of city officials to the MOVE crisis had contributed to the violent
confrontation:*
*"Police Commissioner Gregore Sambor revealed the confu-
sion which distorted the judgments at every level of government
when he testified that the residents of 6221 Osage could have
prevented the tragedy by a quick surrender," said Bowser.
"There was nothing to suggest a quick surrender was possible.
His own definition of the residents of 6221 Osage as violent
terrorists precluded any expectation of a quick surrender. When
questioned about his expectation he described it as his hope."*[7]
*During questioning of Brooks, he was asked what had been
done to protect the children. Brooks replied that he used "tear
gas and smoke as opposed to some more violent thing like the use
of the 50 caliber machine gun or something else."*[8]
*Both departments that were given the assignment to pick up
the children reported to Leo Brooks — the Department of Human
Services and the police department. The main function of the
managing director was to coordinate the departments under his
jurisdiction.*[9]

Throughout the week, the testimony grew uglier and uglier. The most damning testimony against the police involved the illegal use of C-4 explosives, weapons with silencers, and the order to let the fire burn.

At the time, there was much speculation that the large cache of C-4 held by the police had been sent to the Philadelphia Police Department as part of a sting operation to determine if Irish police officers in the department were smuggling explosives to the Irish Revolutionary Army (IRA) in Ireland. While there has never been any conclusive evidence on this issue, interestingly enough, all of the officers handling the C-4 were Irish Americans. In any event, there has never been a satisfactory explanation as to why the C-4 was sent to the Philadelphia police, and there was no reason to have had such a deadly explosive on hand.

It was also noted that two 22-caliber rifles equipped with silencers were issued for use May 13,[10] and reports indicated that 50 rounds of ammunition were expended from the silenced rifles[11] making it possible to fire on an enemy without his or her knowledge.

Police inspector John Tiers testified that the heavy weapons used at the scene were unauthorized. As "chief of the stake-out unit he did not know how they were obtained, and when he learned of the antitank gun he ordered it removed from the scene."[12]

It is inconceivable to me that the police commissioner and other commanders would allow police personnel to bring silencers and antitank guns to the scene. It's even more inconceivable since Sambor had assured me on at least three occasions that police would fire their weapons only at targets firing at them. Knowing that this kind of weaponry was used adds to my belief that Sambor deliberately deceived me and Leo Brooks. He knew all along what he wanted to do. He told us enough to get our approval, and then he proceeded to act on his "real" plan for the day.

The report of James R. Phelan, an explosives expert hired by the commission, "conclusively established that the bomb dropped on 6221 contained at least three pounds of a powerful military explosive known as C-4, that it would not perform the alleged objectives of making a hole in the roof of 6221 and also pushing the bunker from the roof, and dropping the bomb from the air was an uncontrolled use of explosives which should be expected to cause the greatest amount of random damage."[13]

Charles King, employed by the commission for his knowledge of the origins and causes of fires, established that the bomb was the cause of the fire, the same conclusion reached by the Philadelphia fire marshal.[14]

The bomb was dropped at approximately 5:30 P.M. and a fire that could have been easily extinguished developed, according to King and the fire marshal.[15] King testified that from the beginning of the fire until about 6:15 P.M. the fire could have been extinguished by the water hoses called "squirt guns" on the scene. But despite an order from the mayor and the managing director to extinguish the fire, it was left to burn.[16] Brooks said he told Sambor to extinguish the fire. Sambor claimed he told fire commissioner Bill Richmond about the order.[17] Richmond "'categorically' denied that Sambor told him of the order to extinguish the fire."[18]

The testimony of Charles King and the fire marshal clearly establishes that Gregore Sambor had control over the lives of the MOVE members. It was Sambor—not Richmond, not Brooks— who made a decision to let the fire burn. Sambor had forty-five minutes, according to expert testimony, in which he could have ordered the fire to be put out. As ill-advised as dropping the explosive device was, the public should not have been led to focus on that as the cause of the deaths of eleven people and the destruction of sixty-one homes. It was the decision made by the police commissioner to defy the order from Brooks to put the fire out that led to the deaths!

If the fire commissioner had known of Brooks's order, I believe he would have put the fire out. He did not do so because he was deliberately told not to by Sambor.

Among the most heart-wrenching testimonies delivered was that of the only child survivor, Birdie Africa, a child who seemed younger than his thirteen years in many ways. Birdie described their final minutes in the house:

> We was just sitting down there with the covers over our heads, and we had the dogs, and then we heard them putting gas, something, I think they was climbing up on the roof, then they started sticking gas in that pipe, they started sticking gas in there and Rad [Conrad] got up a log over and, near there, and blocked the gas out, and then they put a match in there, then that's how we knew the fire was, the house was on fire, and that they stuck a match in there and then all that smoke started coming in and we saw lights and stuff . . . We were still in there for a while, and we didn't say nothing, then they started yowling outside, "The kids coming out, the kids coming out," and the cops, they stopped shooting . . .
>
> . . . they wasn't shooting for a while and they was still yowling then the kids coming out, then Rad sticked his head out there and [they] shot, but they didn't get him. . . . he said, "the kids can't go out yet, 'cause they still shooting." . . . I was in the back, and all the rest of the kids was in front of me, and they was going, trying to go out and stuff, and then they started, Tomaso went to go out, and [he, they] shot it again, and then he went back in, and we had to wait for a while longer, that's how it started getting *real hot* . . . I think they got out, and then the thing was cleared and I just crawled out, I just crawled out and started running, and I keep falling in the fire and I was still running, and then I, Mona [Ramona] told, Mona got out, too, and she told me to climb up in the skinny alley, and I tried to and I couldn't, then I fainted.[19]

The final insult to the sordid situation was that the medical examiner's office was unprofessional and violated generally accepted practices for pathologists,[20] the commission said. As a result, the procedures used to recover the bodies included using a crane with a bucket to dig up debris and bodies, resulting in dismemberment, commingling of body parts, and the destruction of important physical and medical evidence.[21] *It was also found that some of the bodies contained metal fragments.*[22]

I had tried unsuccessfully for years to remove the medical examiner, Martin Aronson. In my view he was an apologist for the Rizzo administration and the police department. He had once declared a man legally dead who was, in fact, alive. The man, Greg Walters, was a reporter having an ongoing fight with Frank Rizzo.

I wanted Aronson out. I didn't trust him. The newspapers consistently called for his removal. Despite my best efforts, the civil service system protected him, and he could not be easily removed.

During my examination I faced the commission and stated my view of the happenings before answering any questions:

"For the past several weeks, this commission has heard testimony from most of the city officials, and from others, who were involved with the events which led to the confrontation on Osage Avenue on May 13, 1985. This confrontation, against a group of individuals collectively known as MOVE . . . represents one of the most devastating days in the history of our city. The pain and loss of this fateful disaster will be long in leaving us; some of us, including me, will never be free of its scars."[23]

I further stated that the goal of the commission was "to reveal the truth about that day and the events which led up to it, and through the examination of that truth, to insure that such a catastrophe never occurs again and that this goal had been fulfilled as almost everyone directly involved, who would or was able to testify, had testified."[24]

As citizens viewed the government's dirty laundry on television, they began to ask how this mayor, Wilson Goode, who was supposed to be such an efficient productivity expert, could let this happen. The investigation became a new vehicle for my critics' charges against me. That I had allowed MOVE to happen was, in some people's eyes, an example of my poor leadership ability. The press had a field day reporting every inefficiency and problem they could find, no matter how long it had existed or how prevalent the practice.

No one asked why the MOVE issues hadn't been resolved in the seven years since 1978. They focused only on my sixteen months in office. My administration was attacked as the one that made the critical difference in Philadelphia's history. Somehow as the city's first African American mayor, I was expected to maintain a standard and perform miracles that had never been required of my predecessors.

I knew that some people who never wanted a black mayor to begin with were now using these events as a new reason to challenge my competency. This, to me, was the most insulting challenge of all. I had a record of twenty years of topnotch performance, from my work with PCCA to the Public Utility Commission and managing director. I had demonstrated that I was not a paper tiger. I had built homes and regulated a $7-billion industry that won the praise of citizens and utility executives alike.

I was mayor because of my performance as managing director. I was not an unknown. I was crushed by the personal attacks from people who knew me, who knew my motives, my intentions, and my hopes for this city. Could anyone who really knew me, or who worked with me, believe that I could have allowed ammunition to be fired into a house full of children? Did they really think I was capable of deciding to drop a bomb on a home, leaving a fire to burn, and allowing police officers to use their guns to drive women and children back into a burning house?

I felt like Daniel in the lion's den awaiting my deliverance.

I drew my greatest strength from my faith in God and my faith in the grass-roots political machine of ministers, churches, and community leaders who knew me as one of their own and supported my ideas of reform for good government. I knew that the traditional politicians were fair-weather supporters. I knew that as soon as they saw a chink in the armor, they would run for cover. Others would be like buzzards circling in the air waiting to close in.

The big four—the mayor, the managing director, the police commissioner, and the fire commissioner—testified to a full audience. There were some inconsistencies in our testimony. The first was Greg Sambor's account of what he told me prior to May 13 about his plans. I was not told explosives would be used, even though Sambor testified that he had told me the insertion teams would use explosive charges to insert the gas. When he had explained the plan beforehand, he had used the term "small devices" to refer to the charges they would be using. When Leo used the word "explosive" on May 13, I certainly had no idea he was talking about a three-pound bomb made of C-4!

Other inconsistencies involved Leo Brooks's account that he did not tell me that the police were shooting over the heads of MOVE members as I had testified. Lucien Blackwell had been present during my phone conversation with Leo. I had relayed the information to him and the others as soon as I'd hung up. Lu · later repeated this conversation on television.

Leo also testified that he had told me that they planned to use a helicopter to drop an explosive device on the house. I was amazed at Leo's statement, since he had told me earlier it was possible that he hadn't remembered correctly. Leo never told me about a helicopter. That's why I was so stunned to see it on television.

There was another inconsistency about the actual time that Brooks called me. With all that was going on, I can't believe any of us could have accurately reconstructed the events minute for minute!

For the most part though, there was complete agreement on the major issues. Everyone agreed that Greg Sambor gave the order to let the fire burn. We agreed that the police had tried to use a crane to knock the bunker off the house. But the discussion that was highlighted in the media was, of course, about the inconsistencies. The media played it as if I was not being as forthright as I could be or was not telling everything that I knew.

As the hearings concluded and I reflected on the testimony and the media accounts, for the first time in my life I felt concerned about my own credibility. I was concerned because even though I had been completely forthright, there were suggestions by the media that I had been less than truthful. I really had no reason not to be truthful. Had Brooks and Sambor told me that they were going to use explosives to punch holes in the wall to put in listening devices, I'm sure I would have approved. And thinking back, I might have even approved a helicopter being used to help officials attach a small device to the bunker, if Brooks had assured me of its safe use. It was not my intention to avoid responsibility for the explosives used on the walls or the roof since it was my view then and now that the major failing on May 13 was the decision to let the fire burn. There was no reason, therefore, for me not to be forthright. More importantly, I would not lie just to be consistent with the others.

I had told the truth, but I felt that my words had fallen on deaf ears. I did not get my points across. The media believed the words of others. I thought about calling a press conference to protest the unfairness of it all, but that had never been my style. I knew I had told the truth. In the end God would be my judge. And as in all things in the past, God would be an impartial and fair judge of the truth.

CHAPTER FOURTEEN

Bruised Servant

United and determined, we all stood in my reception room one week after May 13—business, political, religious, and civic leaders. Some union leaders and developers were there also. We were there to pick up the pieces in the aftermath of the Osage Avenue tragedy.

Patrick Gillespie, president of the Building Trades Council, was the first to speak. "We are here to offer our support," he said. "This is not just the mayor's crisis. This is the city's crisis. We can't bring back those who died. We weep for them. But we can bring back the neighborhood. We can rebuild those houses. And we can do it by Christmas."

As Gillespie talked, I thought how wonderful it was that all these people were here ready to join in and help. I was a little bit concerned about Gillespie's statement that we would have the people back in their homes by Christmas. It was certainly my hope. But as a politician, I knew making that kind of promise this early in the process could be very problematic. But this was the day for the city to unify and pull together; so I didn't dispute Gillespie's pledge.

I had hoped that we could just let these developers get together and put the best people out there on Osage Avenue to get the job done. That would be wonderful.

No sooner had I thought we had an appropriate plan than lawyers reminded me that we needed a public competitive process if we planned to use public dollars. We couldn't just go out and place developers on jobs. We had to go through an appropriate process.

We concluded that the city's procurement process would be too cumbersome. So we decided that the Redevelopment Authority (RDA), a quasi-public agency with eminent domain authority, should be the one to accept bids. I requested that the authority conduct a fair, open process. They did.

The lowest bid was a joint venture between two minority firms, Ernest Edwards and Beverly Harper. They had won the bid fair and square. Frankly I had reservations about their ability to handle the project. They had had no prior experience on a project of this magnitude. But I couldn't legally interfere with the process. The bid was done. It was competitive. They'd won.

I had two options. I could accept the bids, or I could ask the Redevelopment Authority to throw them out and start the process all over again.

I decided not to interfere with the bid process. My decision was influenced by two factors. First, earlier that week Rev. Jesse Jackson had held a press conference on the site, calling for the rebuilding to be done by minority firms. Second, the residents who lost their homes wanted a black contractor to rebuild their homes. Despite my reservations, I knew I would have difficulty explaining why these two business people, who were black, could not do the job. The bid was accepted by RDA, and the project proceeded.

Julia Robinson, my housing czar, was placed in charge of the rebuilding efforts. Her job was to work with the Redevelopment Authority to get the job done.

The job was barely underway when we learned that Edwards had not obtained the necessary bonds to complete the job. It was also learned he had probably falsified records submitted to the Redevelopment Authority. Edwards was given a deadline to get his business straightened out or be removed from the job. He met the deadline. But the trouble with Edwards had just begun.

Things did go smoothly until about Thanksgiving. Edwards had promised to have the first group of houses ready by that time, but it didn't happen. Edwards's promises started to crumble one after another. By early December, two things were apparent. We would have only one or two of the residents back home by Christmas, and Edwards and Harper were incapable of completing the job. A second contractor was brought in to help. But soon Edwards was out all together, and the new contractor had to complete the job.

Before he left, Edwards had fallen behind schedule and run over budget, two of the worst things that can happen with a contractor. I had managed fifty jobs of this nature at PCCA and had never had a problem like this. Then I had personally been involved with the rebuilding projects, but quickly learned as mayor that I had to delegate responsibility. I had done so. I had assigned a cabinet officer to oversee the development along with an outside architectural firm and an outside management firm. I'm not sure what else I could have done. But despite all these people watching the store, Edwards ran behind schedule and exceeded his budget.

He refused to leave the job gracefully. He was acting as both developer and contractor and was only willing to relinquish the contractor role. He threatened to sue if we removed him as developer. I had no interest in a fight. I just wanted to get the houses finished for the homeowners. No purpose could be served by challenging Edwards in court. Additionally, we were paying daily relocation expenses for the homeowners. The best thing for the city was to get the houses finished and the people moved back in.

Finding a replacement contractor also proved to be difficult. After a period of time, we located George McCadden of G&V Construction Company in Virginia. He had been Virginia's minority contractor of the year in 1984, and he came with good credentials. But it was not long before McCadden parted with Edwards over contract disputes and late payments. We bit the bullet and removed Edwards from the job of developer as well. He threatened suit, but never did file. Edwards was subsequently convicted of fraud and sent to jail.

Despite a valiant attempt, McCadden soon ran into trouble

with cost overruns and was unable to finish all the houses. The city worked with him and hired other outside contractors to finish the houses; within a year after construction started, they were completed.

As the people began returning to their homes, I felt I had accomplished something good. Little did I know that this was the beginning of more very difficult days.

As we were in the midst of the controversy with Edwards and Harper, the public hearings on MOVE came to a conclusion. The hearings had been devastating for me. I had watched the government's inefficiency from a front-row seat. Now I had to get on with running the city and making the necessary cabinet changes. Leo Brooks had resigned back in July of 1985, and I had appointed James Stanley White to the managing director's post. The first thing White did was to have all the top managers trained in crisis management. He also worked on putting crisis management plans into place. Never again would a mayor or managing director be unable to quickly contact the police and fire commissioner during a crisis situation.

But there was other unfinished business. I had decided the day the MOVE hearings concluded that I would fire Sambor. I did not do so during the hearings because I did not want to compromise the work of the commission.

Barbara Mather, the city solicitor, informed Sambor's attorney that unless he resigned I would immediately terminate his tenure as police commissioner. He resigned, and I put Robert Armstrong in charge of the police department on an interim basis.

Now I had to find a new police commissioner.

Years of police brutality and the horror-filled images of the police confrontations with MOVE had created a picture of police authority that was both frightening and disturbing to most Philadelphians. I had personally been touched by the ugly image when police brutally beat my brother Alvestus during an altercation with an officer.

On April 26, 1977, a year before I became PUC chair, Al was beaten by seven Philadelphia police officers. According to Al and witness Eugene E. Johnson, an officer investigating a traffic violation blocked the service entrance to my brother's garage with his police car, preventing customers from entering or leaving.

"Al said he was going to ask the officer to move his car," Johnson reported. "I heard Al say, 'Would you please move your vehicle?' "

The officer responded, "Take your black ass in the station before I put a hole in you."

An argument ensued. Frustrated, my brother exclaimed, "Aah f—— it!" and reentered his station. He never touched the officer.

Shortly afterwards, several police cars roared up to the station from various directions. Officers jumped out of the cars and ran toward the garage, where they broke in the door and dragged Al out onto the concrete service bay. One officer grabbed Al's arms, apparently trying to handcuff him. Witnesses say Al never resisted arrest. Another officer jerked him to his knees.

The officers beat him unmercifully on his arms, legs, back, and head with nightsticks and blackjacks. Writhing in pain under the hail of blows, Al never fought back. Only after he lay prostrate, his face pushed into the concrete, was Al handcuffed and taken away to Philadelphia General Hospital for treatment.

His arrest charge? Assaulting police officers and resisting arrest. The district attorney conducted a two-week investigation and found no case. The charges were dropped. No disciplinary action was ever taken against the officers.

Fully aware of the Philadelphia Police Department's record on brutality, I decided to conduct a nationwide search for a new police chief. Web Fitzgerald, one of my assistants, on loan from SmithKline Beckman, was put in charge of the search process. He assembled résumés, did background checks, and set up interviews.

We interviewed the police chief from Seattle, as well as the police chief of Minneapolis. During the process, we learned that Kevin Tucker, the former head of the secret service in Philadelphia, was interested in applying for the job. His references were superb, his background spotless.

I interviewed Kevin, and minutes into the conversation knew I had found the right person. We spoke the same language and shared common goals. My mission was to restore credibility to the police department by rooting out corruption and Frank Rizzo loyalists. I wanted to give the police department back to the people by making it a system that all Philadelphians could feel was operating on their behalf and in their best interest. I hired Kevin Tucker to do just that. I told Tucker he had my full support and protection and directed him to "just get the job done."

Tucker needed my support as he faced strong opposition to his appointment from appropriations chair John Street. Street was relentless in attacking Tucker's residency status. While he maintained a permanent home in New Jersey, Tucker and his wife complied with the residency laws by renting an apartment in Philadelphia. That was not good enough for Street.

Street tried to make life miserable for Tucker. The attacks were a major reason for Kevin's untimely resignation two years later. He simply got tired of being badgered. But before he left, Kevin proved to be just as capable as I had felt he would be.

I had asked Kevin to reach deep into the organization and find police officers who had the talent, skill, and potential to one day become commissioner of the department. The primary candidate he identified was an intelligent, young black police captain named Willie Williams. Under Kevin's tutelage, Williams quickly rose through the ranks to become inspector, deputy police commissioner, and eventually the city's first black police commissioner. Williams instituted a series of reforms to help improve police morale and community relations.

While I was sorry to see Kevin leave two years after he began, I knew that in Williams he had found and helped groom a man who not only understood the needs of the rank and file of the police department, but who also had deep empathy and concern for all citizens of Philadelphia.

In his nearly four years as police commissioner, Williams perfected the community policing programs instituted by Tucker. Williams transformed the image of the Philadelphia Police Department from one of being brutal and corrupt to one that was a partner with the neighborhoods in reducing crime and solving community problems. He professionalized the department, and fought for and succeeded in promoting women and African Americans to high-level positions in the department. So effective was his tenure in Philadelphia that he became police chief of Los Angeles in June of 1992.

Although I drew tremendous criticism for hiring Tucker from outside, I'm proud of my decision. It laid the foundation for turning around the community's perception of the Philadelphia Police Department. Thanks to Kevin Tucker and Willie Williams, the police are now viewed as responsive, accessible, and responsible. None of this would have been possible if I had not gone outside of the department and recruited, appointed, and then supported Kevin Tucker's reform movement in the police department.

Ironically, in early 1992 I learned that John Street, now president of city council, had contracted Thomas Erekson as a legal adviser (instead of hiring him as an employee) in order to avoid residency law requirements. Erekson was not a Philadelphia resident. I remembered Street's treatment of Kevin Tucker and had to chuckle to myself at the irony.

Following MOVE, my tenure as mayor seemed to proceed as a slow-moving uphill battle. I was abandoned by many of the people I thought were loyal supporters. I felt abandoned by the business establishment, the political establishment, and the media as well.

On Sunday, December 29, 1985, Russell Cooke, an *Inquirer* staff writer, recapped my year in a story titled "Mayor Goode: After 2nd year, a dulled image":

> It was Goode's personal intervention last December that apparently kept former Eagles owner Leonard Tose from moving the team to Phoenix, Ariz. And it was at Goode's insistence that the crumbling SEPTA railroad bridge at Ninth and Columbia Avenue — whose sudden shutdown crippled the city's commuter rail system in November 1984 — was rebuilt in record time.
>
> But Goode's promise to have the MOVE neighborhood rebuilt by Christmas has not been fulfilled — a reminder that the promise of his first year in office might have been destroyed forever when the Police Department dropped a bomb on the MOVE compound at 6221 Osage Ave. . . .
>
> Indeed, a year ago, he was being hailed for singlehandedly boosting the spirits of Philadelphians, and as he put it then, for setting 'a tone' that government was working and someone was in charge. His first year ended on a note of hope, with the prospect of progress on critical public works projects, improving city services and a host of other ventures. . . .

The last 12 months, though, have been far less successful. Besides the MOVE confrontation, there has been the continuing police corruption scandal and the racial conflicts in the Elmwood section of Southwest Philadelphia.

Those two incidents, as well as the Easter Sunday window smashing spree in Center City by several hundred teenagers cast a pall over the city's image. . . .

In addition, Goode seemed to founder as he and city council could not reach an agreement on a new trash disposal system for the city while dumping fees increased millions of dollars and he failed to secure state funding for the proposed Center City convention center.

The mayor himself had to counter rumors of marital problems, finally making a remarkable address in his church in which he reportedly denied that he had physically abused his wife, Velma, or that his wife had a drinking problem.

Even what he paid for his business suits became a subject of controversy, when it was disclosed that the FBI was investigating a union leader who provided Goode and other city officials with suits at deep discounts.[1]

To say that 1985 had been a tough year is probably the essence of understatement.

The year had barely started when ten thousand young people paraded on Chestnut Street on Easter Sunday, showing off their Easter finery. A few hundred decided to go on a window-smashing spree. Only a few windows were broken, but for the first time since I had taken office, I started getting criticism for not doing enough about the plight of young people. In essence, I felt my critics were saying, "Why hasn't this black mayor done something to keep us from having to worry about black kids running up and down the streets here? Aren't there some recreation programs that could prevent this sort of thing?" I think some people figured that because I was black, I should be able to keep all black folks in line, especially these kids who were wrecking their neighborhoods. I had been in office for about fifteen months. No one could have turned around decades of neglect in just fifteen months.

Soon after this came MOVE and the investigation. Things had gone from bad to worse.

Then came the worst lie of all. During my campaign, Frank Rizzo had circulated lies about me being a spouse abuser and had gotten someone to doctor a police report to make it appear as if

I had broken my wife's jaw. This was a typical Rizzo smear tactic. I thought the nonsense had died away with my election, but apparently the MOVE incident gave Rizzo new hope that he could once again become mayor. He started the rumors again, and this time he had help. Mary Mason, a WHAT radio personality, allowed a caller to put the misinformation on the air.

Mason could have kept the call off the air. The fact that she did not do so made me wonder whether she was part of a Rizzo plan to spread these vicious lies about me and my family. Everyone who knew the family knew that these were lies, but it hurt deeply nonetheless.

Velma and I publicly denied the ludicrous accusations at a special service our church held to show their support. The media was invited; none of them came. Someone did, however, write a newspaper story and referred to the church service as a "confessional."

While this was going on, I was also getting threats against my children. The *Daily News,* in a July 19, 1985, article, reported it this way:

> In remarks at First Baptist, Goode blamed the attacks on his family on "people who are intent on evil, and nothing else but evil."
>
> Supporters "ought to know basically what the mayor has to put up with," he said, which includes "people who have threatened my children."
>
> He did not detail the threats, but said police officers were required, for the last three months of the school term, to "follow my daughter around everyplace she went in school."
>
> The mayor was referring to his youngest daughter, Natasha, who attends public school.
>
> Goode told the church audience he draws strength from God to endure the burdens of office.
>
> He got a standing ovation . . . when he declared he would remain as mayor and would run for a second term.
>
> "I would not be your mayor if I did not believe that a long time before I was born, God ordained at a given point in time that I would be your mayor," he said.[2]

I had barely finished reeling from the controversy over the lies spread about my wife when another controversy ensued. This time it was about suits.

The first union that endorsed me after I decided to run for

mayor in 1983 was the Amalgamated Clothing Union. Nick DiPiero was the union head. Nick was a very influential union leader, and his early endorsement had paved the way for many other endorsements.

I told Nick that as a candidate, and as mayor, I wanted to wear as many items as I could that were manufactured in Philadelphia.

"Just imagine, Nick, how good it would be for me to stand up at a rally and say, 'Buy Philadelphia. Everything I'm wearing was made in this city.' What do you think? Can I do that, Nick? Can that be done?"

"Yes, Mr. Mayor. That's a wonderful idea! Let me take you to some companies so we can get the ball rolling."

The only requirement I had, however, was that I had to pay for the clothes.

"I don't want them any other way, Nick," I said. "I have to pay for this clothing."

"Mr. Mayor, we know how you operate," he replied. "But let's just get the ball rolling. We'll arrange for the companies to bill you."

I knew Nick to be an honorable man, so I didn't worry about the billing details. I felt he had understood me and had done me a great service with his endorsement. Now both of us were working hand in hand to try and rebuild the dying clothing industry in Philadelphia.

I felt that some people would respond to the advertising well, sensing that if the mayor felt the quality of the clothing was high enough to wear, so would they. That's all I wanted.

My conversation with Nick took place during my 1983 campaign. I went to Stanley Blacker on Lehigh Avenue and purchased four suits, paying cash. The suits were all identical and navy blue. When I arrived home that night, Velma asked, "Why in the world would you buy four identically cut suits in the same color? No one will know when you change suits."

My response was, "Bill Green always wore a suit, and I could never tell the difference."

"You are not Bill Green," Velma said. "You need to vary your color schemes, show some creativity in style."

Before the inauguration, Nick made arrangements for me to

buy several other suits. Each time he did, I reminded him, "Nick, I need a bill. Will they remember?"

"Yes, Mr. Mayor. They'll bill you. I won't let anything happen to you. You're the first mayor to show any interest in our problems in the clothing industry."

A month later, I still hadn't received any bills. I turned the matter over to my chief of staff, Shirley Hamilton.

"Shirley, I don't know what has happened to these bills," I said, "but would you get on Nick's case and get these bills in here? He may think he's doing me a favor, but tell him I pay my own way."

Shirley was usually excellent with details like this. But after a few more months, and a few more suits, I was now very, very concerned. As I kept protesting the lack of bills, I finally got one sent to me. But I couldn't make heads or tails of it.

I asked Shirley to check to make sure she received a bill for every suit I bought. I was now immersed in politics and had little time to go track down clothing bills.

Before I knew it, the suit situation had emerged into a controversy. Russell Cooke, the *Inquirer* reporter who had written the 1985 summary about me, called me to ask about reports he had received that I was getting suits from local manufacturers. He wanted to know how many I had received. I really wasn't sure. But instead of putting him on hold and getting the facts, I pulled a likely number out of the air. I didn't have anything to hide. I was trying to be responsive, trying to be open.

As soon as I said a figure, I knew I should have waited and gotten my facts together and questioned Cooke a bit more. But I was anxious to demonstrate that I had nothing to hide, so I told him what I thought. That was an absolute mistake! I had given him the wrong number of suits, and he also had the facts wrong.

The story presented was that I was getting all of these free suits from local manufacturers, but it sounded as if I was trying to hide something. I was not. All I had done was to try to help a failing industry. In the process, I had not followed up on some details appropriately.

Nick DiPiero was eventually placed on trial for these and other charges. The jury found him innocent. I thought that was the end of the matter until I learned that the Pennsylvania Ethics

Commission was investigating the case. I believed their investigation of me was political. Most people did. But how could I prove it?

A few days after the investigation got under way, I received a call from a noted defense attorney, A. Charles Peruto, who told me of a conversation he'd had with two investigators from the commission. "They are really after you," Peruto said. "I'm calling because they seem so hellbent on nailing you. You should know that one of the investigators is a former police officer. These guys really don't like you, Mr. Mayor. I didn't like the way they sounded. So I just wanted to alert you."

For a few days I did nothing. Later I shared the conversation with my attorney, Nolan N. Atkinson, Jr. He proceeded to contact the ethics panel. I didn't understand why this was still an issue because I had paid the bills directly to the companies. John "Jay" Flaherty, my deputy mayor, had worked out the details for payment. As far as I was concerned, my slate was clean. But the ethics commission persisted.

After months of investigation and interrogation, the state ethics commission issued a ruling clearing me of any wrongdoing other than a technical violation for not filing the disclosure forms promptly. Of course, since I had always intended to pay for the suits, I felt there had been no reason to disclose the suits as gifts.

The investigation was a witch hunt and a ploy to smear my reputation for the upcoming election and to put doubt in people's minds about my qualifications as mayor.

Before the year was out, I had another shocker. On November 20, 1985, about four hundred white residents demonstrated outside the home of a black couple who had just bought a row house in the all-white Elmwood section of Southwest Philadelphia. The next night, November 21, 1985, a smaller crowd gathered outside the home of a newly arrived interracial couple, demanding that they move out. The first couple did move out, but the second couple stayed. The first house was heavily damaged by arson despite a police detail placed there for protection.

I declared a state of emergency and banned the gathering of more than four people at a time. The incident in Southwest Philadelphia was deeply disappointing and discouraging. I had worked hard to improve racial relations in the city. I had fought hard all my life to remove barriers that separate people by race, religion, gender, and ethnic background. I believed that any person should be able to live in any house, on any block, in any neighborhood in the city. No one had the right to tell others where they could live. I would not tolerate a group of neighbors banding together to tell others they couldn't live in the neighborhood because of their color or family composition. I was determined to be a leader who stood for what was right.

But no matter what I did in that year, everything I touched seemed to fall apart. No matter which way I turned, I was being battered and bruised by some of the same people and organizations that I once thought I could trust. It was a rude awakening. The deepest blow was yet to come as we drew closer to the mayoral primary.

Everywhere I turned, someone was looking over my shoulder. The district attorney opened a state investigation of MOVE. I had set up my own panel. There was a D.A. investigation of the rebuilding process. Altogether three grand juries were investigating issues related to MOVE.

My focus was to keep the city running and to complete major projects, as I had done with the rebuilding of the Osage Avenue houses. Constructing a new convention center and criminal justice building, balancing the budget, and getting a trash-to-steam plant built were also high on the list.

I never lost sight of the fact that the government had to continue to function well. Therefore, I was amazed at the news stories that described government as paralyzed and stalemated. The complete opposite was true. The media couldn't see, or refused to see, how strongly and efficiently government continued to operate following MOVE. It had apparently decided that there was no way I could concentrate on four investigations, rebuild sixty-one homes, and still keep the city functioning.

Even the *Philadelphia Inquirer* had to conclude in its 1985 year-end review: "These problems have worked to obscure some important progress in the city during Goode's two years, especially the creation of 17,000 jobs, the continuing boom in downtown investment and a drop in major crimes of about 8 percent."[3]

This was one of only a few media references to the positive events that took place during the year.

I was glad to see 1985 end. It was one of the toughest years of my life.

The year 1986 started out with my son, W. Wilson Goode, Jr., being suspended from school for a brief period of time on Friday, January 17, 1986. I never expected to be proud to see one of my children suspended. Steve Lopez, in the Sunday, January 19, 1986, issue of the *Philadelphia Inquirer,* wrote:

> W. Wilson Goode Jr., the other politician in the family, was suspended from college for a short time Friday during a sit-in at the University of Pennsylvania.
>
> He and his colleagues refused to leave the office of the president until they got what they had come for. After 12 hours, they got it, or at least a step in the right direction. And the suspension was revoked. . . .
>
> Goode, a senior majoring in political science, had participated in several demonstrations at Penn, and played a major role in Friday's. After graduation, he plans to enter law school. And after that, professional politics.
>
> Before answering questions, he organizes his thoughts and measures his words, his deep eyes framing the right construction. The result is a delivery that sometimes sounds like his father's.
>
> "I'd like to effect change," he said. "Leadership is not my ambition. . . . But I think that because I have the characteristics of leadership, my responsibility is to lead. . . ."
>
> Goode is discussing the university's refusal to drop its $92 million investment in companies that do business in a country where racism is protected by law. Apartheid is a system that repulses Wilson Goode, Jr., on two levels—as a black, and as a human.
>
> "I can relate to apartheid in South Africa the way I relate to slavery in our country," he says.
>
> He understands that university trustees must make prudent financial investments, but he thinks they have a higher responsibility—moral integrity.
>
> "An investment in South Africa," he adds, "is an investment in racial abuse, hatred and murder. I see that as incorrect, and my goal is to effect some change. . . ."
>
> "I don't see it as a victory yet," Goode says. "It was a victory in one battle, but there are more battles."
>
> Goode won't say why he called his father when it was over, but it is clear by his comments that he admires W. Wilson Goode, Sr., and that his father's political difficulties in the past year have strengthened the bond.
>
> "We went through a lot," he says of the Goode family.[4]

My son continues to fight for basic principles of right and wrong. It's kind of eerie, but as he fought his political battles, I saw myself twenty-five years earlier.

Having put one major problem behind me with the hiring of a new police chief, I faced a major contract battle with city service workers. Earl Stout, my nemesis from my managing director days, was head of the blue-collar workers union.

Stout was a medium-sized man with a booming, commanding voice. He was always animated, waving his hands and arms or pointing his finger as he made a point in the most profane way possible. But he was charismatic, with an engaging personality and plenty of street smarts.

The city had had an ongoing fight with Stout for years. The battle centered on three basic issues. Stout had filed suit to get the city to pay back money for health and welfare benefits he claimed to have negotiated in contract talks with Frank Rizzo as far back as 1975. The contract stated that the city had to reimburse the union for whatever they spent in providing these benefits. No audit. No reviews. The city was obligated to pay, he asserted. When we went to court on the case, Frank Rizzo testified in court that he had intended to offer these benefits to the union. Now Stout was holding the city to Rizzo's promise.

Stout wanted $48 million, the amount he said was owed him in back payment for these benefits. He wanted no discussion. No negotiations. "Just bring me the check, Mr. Mayor, and then we will talk. And by the way, Mr. Mayor, make it certified. I don't trust you."

Stout also had been pushing the city to allow his son Billy's company to provide a landfill for the city. I told him this was a clear conflict of interest. He saw none, and said he took it personally that I would not help his son.

Lastly, he did not want to submit to an audit of his health and welfare benefits payments. The John F. Kennedy Memorial Hospital, owned and operated by District Council 33, was involved in providing most of the health and welfare benefits to the workers. I felt that I could not adequately assess Stout's real costs until I looked at the hospital records. Stout was adamant. "No looking at hospital records. No audit. Just bring the check, Mr. Mayor, and make sure it's certified."

Stout didn't want to even begin the contract talks until we gave him the check. For the entire month of June he refused to return my phone calls. Finally on the afternoon of June 30, he agreed to a meeting at his offices.

We arrived at 4:00 P.M. but were made to wait several hours before the face-to-face negotiations started.

The atmosphere in the meeting room was a combination of a circus and a kangaroo court. The negotiating team, laughing and talking loudly, exhibited no decorum, no respect—just rudeness and cockiness.

Sitting down at the table, I started to very formally present our position. Stout interrupted. "Wait a minute. I don't want to hear all that stuff." The other members of his team laughed derisively. Some even taunted, "Respect this man. After all, he *is* the mayor—for now."

Their sharp tone and abrupt manner were humiliating. There I was, the mayor of the city, with a team of advisers preparing to negotiate, and Stout looked me in the face laughing and encouraging those around him to also laugh as he continued to make outrageous statements. I believe Stout had made a deal with Frank Rizzo to make me look bad as mayor in preparation for Rizzo's run for the mayor's race. His refusal to negotiate was a clear sign that he intended to strike. There were several points during his ridiculous behavior at which I wanted to walk out— just to leave him there ranting and raving. I did not, because he then would have an excuse to strike. I was not going to be that excuse.

Stout continued, "I have told you over and over again that I want my money!" he bellowed, waving his arms. "I want $48 million in cold cash. Do you have my money? Do you? Because if you don't, you are wasting my time. Answer me! Do you have my money? Just tell me, is the check in your briefcase or did you bring me cash? Do you have it?"

"Mr. Stout, you know I don't have the money."

He stood up.

"Good-bye, Mr. Mayor. Bye-bye. We are leaving."

"But aren't you going to listen to our position?"

"I have it. You have mine. Good-bye. See you in the streets."
They left laughing, cocky and disrespectful.

At 12:01 A.M. on July 1, 1986, about fourteen thousand blue-collar workers went on strike. The city was closed down. Stout's strategy was working.

The greatest impact of the strike, with the most serious consequences, was made by the sanitation workers. We made out all right the first week, but two weeks of uncollected garbage in the hot sun was about as much as anyone could endure. As the smell of garbage grew stronger and stronger, so did the tempers of Philadelphians. During this whole episode, I was visible throughout the city, talking directly to people. But this strike situation was new to me. I needed help.

I remembered that Maynard Jackson, the former mayor of Atlanta, had faced a similar problem a few years ago and had successfully navigated it. I called Maynard and asked his advice.

"Set up dumping sites where people can come and dump trash," he advised. "That way, at least, you can get the trash out of the neighborhoods. Don't give in, whatever you do. In the end, the majority of the people will support you. Keep the faith!"

We set up the dumping sites around the city, but that did not eradicate the smell or the poor health conditions created by the garbage. After another week, I felt we had a health emergency on our hands. I went to court. The judge ordered the sanitation workers back to work, but the sanitation workers were adamant: "We are not going back to work." By now I was just as adamant. I had a new weapon to use—a court order.

My attorneys advised me that I was on solid legal ground in firing any worker who failed to return to work. At the same time, I checked with the city's personnel department and learned they had more than two thousand people waiting on the sanitation worker civil service list. I had what I needed to take them on. I called a press conference.

"I am demanding that the sanitation workers return to work immediately. I want them back on the job. And I am issuing a clear warning now that any worker who won't return will be fired."

A reporter stated, "They don't believe you will fire them, Mr.

Mayor. What do you have to say to them about that?"

"Try me," I said. "Just try me."

The next day, headlines blared the words *"Try Me."* My actions brought Stout back to the bargaining table and his workers to the streets to pick up trash. The situation concluded with us getting a cap on the health and welfare package, the right to audit, and some other work-rule changes.

Stout remained leader of the union for another two years before being defeated. Eventually he was indicted for misusing health and welfare money, among other funds. He's now serving time in prison.

During the summer of 1986, Rev. Louise Williams Bishop provided me with sorely needed inspiration by organizing a series of prayer vigils at churches around the city. The services were billed as healing services for the community. These prayer vigils were a tremendous solace for me at a time when I felt alone and misunderstood, and they became the key to rebuilding the public's confidence in me. The primary election was that next spring, May 1987.

There were about six or seven prayer vigils in all. They were attended by more than three thousand people. The media even gave the vigils coverage.

The campaign started immediately after the vigils. Ed Rendell had lost the primary for governor, and word was out that he would run for mayor. I asked Rendell about this, and he told me as well as the black clergy that he would not run. Still, people continued to come to me, declaring, "Ed Rendell will run against you for mayor."

"But I have the man's word that he won't run against me," I said. "Rendell is an honorable man, and he assured me that he would not run." The rumors persisted. Sam Evans told me that Rendell was planning to run against me.

"Wilson, you're a fool," Evans said, shaking his head. "Ed Rendell will run against you. He planned to do it even before he ran for governor."

"No!" I protested. "In exchange for my supporting Rendell for governor against Casey, Ed has said he will not run for mayor."

"You may be operating in good faith," my friends said, "but everybody is not as honorable as you are."

I knew Frank Rizzo would run, though it was not yet clear whether he would run as a Republican or a Democrat. During the year he had hosted a local radio program and had spent much of the time disparaging me and my administration, bringing up MOVE and all of the problems I had encountered as mayor. I wasn't worried. I felt I could beat Rizzo. Within the Democratic party, I knew that I was a sure winner against him. Despite whatever problems I had and how people felt about me, I knew most folks disliked Rizzo more.

The media was having a feeding frenzy with all of this fighting. Each day a story seemed to appear that a new candidate had declared. Ed Rendell held his cards close to his chest.

During my election campaign in 1983, I had hired a man named Neil Oxman as my media adviser. Oxman was a good friend of Rendell. I knew that, but couldn't accept rumors I'd heard that Oxman, who was now working on my reelection campaign, was going to abandon me for Rendell.

"That's not honorable," I said.

I wouldn't listen to the folks who told me, "There's no honor among rogues and thugs. Why can't you understand that?"

It wasn't too long after that that Oxman called and asked if he could stop by my house.

"Sure, Neil. I'll see you around seven this evening."

When Neil arrived, I noticed that he was a little fidgety and seemed to want to get something off his chest. Finally, he blurted it out.

"I can't work for you any longer."

I asked him why.

"I can't do it in good conscience," he said. "Ed and I have been close for years. I really don't know what Ed is going to do," he said.

"Well, I certainly hope that you don't work for him if he runs," I said. "You know all my secrets."

"No, I don't think so. I'm going to take some time off," he said.

Despite what he said, deep down inside I felt that if Rendell ran, Oxman would be there. Not long after that, Rendell announced that he would run, and soon after that I learned that Oxman would indeed help Rendell.

I was disappointed in both Rendell and Oxman. Rendell had given me a solemn pledge when I supported him for governor that he would not run against me. He went back on his word. Oxman's decision to work for Rendell was unethical in my opinion. He had held at least two campaign meetings with me. He knew my structure and my strategy. To work for the other side was not honorable. But this was politics.

I recruited Reynard Rochon, an accountant and former city administrator of New Orleans, as my campaign manager. Rochon was an expert in getting out the black vote in reelection campaigns. The firm of Doak and Strum replaced Neil Oxman as my media advisers. I used Paul Maslin as my pollster, and together we created a local campaign structure that I felt pretty comfortable with. The goal was to form a cohesive organization so that we could increase voter registration. The key to winning the election was to turn out the same number of black voters as white voters.

Just as the campaign was getting under way, my father, who was eighty-four, became critically ill. I was attending the mayor's conference in Washington when the call came from Shirley Hamilton.

"Mr. Mayor, call your mother. It's urgent."

I hurriedly hung up and called my mother.

"Yes, Mom, what's wrong?"

"Your dad has taken for the worse. You should call and talk to the doctor."

I did, and I was on the next train home. My sister Mary arrived from California later that evening. We spent the next twenty-four hours by Dad's bedside. On January 22, 1987, we had a big snowfall. My father died about six o'clock that evening.

As I stood there at my father's bedside watching him struggle to breathe, watching him fight death, I could see his strength. It was as if he were fighting against all those landlords on all those farms down South. But just as with the farmers, he lost the struggle.

I had forgiven my dad for all the pain he had caused us over the years. In spite of it, I loved him deeply. As my mother started to cry, I did also.

I delivered the eulogy at his funeral: "Dad would be proud tonight with all this fuss being made over him. But he would also be angry—angry at a system that denied him an education and called him a boy until he was sixty years of age. But, Dad, we make a pledge to you tonight that we will work to make sure that every barrier is broken down that denied you your rightful place."

The next day Ed Rendell asked for the removal of Jim White as managing director and Harry Perks as streets commissioner because they had not gotten the snow up quickly enough. City services became the campaign issue. I ran a strong campaign highlighting my record. I published an impressive brochure listing all my accomplishments. I closed most of my speeches by asking, "If they could not deliver perfect city services in 302 years, how do you expect this mayor to do it in three?" My mother provided the theme for my campaign when she reminded me of an old hymn, "May the Work I've Done Speak for Me."

Those very simple words provided me with a focus to get people to look at my record so they could make a realistic determination of my achievements in office. Having Rochon on my team also made a tremendous difference. Since he was an outsider, I didn't have to worry about him shifting allegiance to one of my opponents. Also, Rochon had marvelous insights and could often pick up on issues I had overlooked.

Early in the campaign we agreed to a televised debate with Ed Rendell. I could hardly wait. I'm sure some people were surprised to see me coming out so aggressively as I attacked Rendell as "Fast Eddie," charging that he played fast and loose with the truth.

"He professes to be some kind of budget expert," I said. "Then why did his budget increase over a hundred percent while he was district attorney?" I then produced the figures to show how his spending had swelled.

I was like a hungry dog with a bone as I charged into Rendell and attacked his credibility. He was shocked. This was a side of me he'd never seen before and an aggressiveness he didn't know how to fight against in a campaign. His previous campaigns had always been very low-key and pleasant. Not this one. I knew I had to come out strong because many people perceived Rendell as a tough attorney and prosecutor. They thought he would eat me up. Instead the tables were dramatically turned.

As we neared election day for the primary, Rochon declared, "It's in the bag. We're going to win this election and win it handily."

It rained election day, always a bad sign, because it was generally believed that black voters didn't vote when it rained. The results were shocking and deeply gratifying as another myth bit the dust. The results showed that 2 percent more black voters came out than white voters.

I beat Ed Rendell by 14 percentage points, a decisive win by sixty thousand votes, as I captured 97 percent of the black vote and 12 percent of the white support. Frank Rizzo went on to win the Republican primary against John Egan. All of my advisers were elated, stating, "Yes, you want Frank Rizzo as your opponent." Only Rochon dissented.

"Mr. Mayor, you don't want Frank Rizzo as your opponent," he said. "You wanted John Egan. Rizzo is going to mean a lot of problems for you."

Reynard Rochon felt that my advisers were setting me up for a loss. "They should know that Rizzo is a more difficult candidate than Egan. Why are they telling you that? I don't trust them. You watch them, Wilson. You watch them."

Rochon said that it was his view that they believed that Frank Rizzo was going to beat me and they had already given up the campaign.

In fact, Rochon came to believe that William Batoff, my chief fund raiser, and Doak and Strum, the media advisers, were either explicitly or implicitly cooperating with the Rizzo campaign in some way to ensure my loss. Batoff was another former Rizzo supporter. Rochon didn't feel that Batoff was putting forth his best effort in fund raising. He had similar feelings about the media advisers.

As the campaign progressed, Rochon became more suspicious and more vocal.

"These people are not working in your best interest," he said.

"They're trying to get you to spend more of your money on needless media interests now so that you won't have any money left for election day."

I didn't know whether Rochon was right or not, but I knew the strategy and had succumbed to a ploy that put a dent in my campaign chest back in 1986. Then, too, the culprits were people who claimed to have my best interests in mind.

It happened about six months after the MOVE disaster. The city held a race for district attorney. I favored Lynne Abraham. The party leaders, including the black leaders, wanted Robert Williams, a black commonwealth court judge. Strategically, it was a bad idea to run Williams for several reasons. I felt that most of the white community would not stand for having a black mayor and a black district attorney. Secondly, I suspected that the people attempting to draft Williams for the seat knew he couldn't win but wanted to push him out front and then blame me for his defeat, further weakening my chances for reelection in 1987.

The campaign manager for Williams was Marty Weinberg, my nemesis during the PUC confirmation hearing days, who had tried to block my confirmation. Weinberg was Rizzo's campaign manager and solicitor.

I had a pretty strong campaign war chest at the time, close to $200,000. About a month before the 1986 election, I was visited by a committee that included Bill Batoff, Lucien Blackwell, Joe Smith (Democratic party chair), and John F. White, Jr.

"Bobby Williams is dragging far behind in the polls," they explained. "We want you to loan Williams $100,000 of your campaign fund because his loss would affect you."

They looked me in the eye and added, "If you loan him this money, we will guarantee you that we will raise it back for you if he can't pay it back."

Wanting to be supportive of my party, I lent Williams the money. To this day I've never received a cent of it back. To put it bluntly, I was had. I pumped $105,000 into the Williams campaign.

The election was held and Williams lost. What did he do? He blamed me for his defeat. He didn't even speak to me on election night. The press also used Williams's defeat as an indicator that my influence and popularity were so weak that I couldn't even deliver Bobby Williams as a candidate. The Williams fiasco also gave Frank Rizzo much encouragement. If Williams, a black Democrat and well-known commonwealth judge, could be defeated by Ron Castille, an unknown white Republican, then Rizzo figured as a Republican he could beat this Democratic mayor who had been so heavily damaged by MOVE.

I don't think Frank Rizzo ever understood how I beat him in the first election, and he was determined to come back and defeat me one day. I believe he only attempted to work with me occasionally to protect some of his interests and friends, like Marty Weinberg, who had the legal contract for the gas works, and his brother, Joe, who was fire commissioner when I took office. Rizzo wanted to see how much influence he could have with me. When it became clear that he had none, Rizzo was determined to regain his position as mayor. That's why during the MOVE confrontation I felt that there were Frank Rizzo loyalists among the police officers on the scene, and they saw May 13 as an opportunity to rid the city of both MOVE and Wilson Goode.

The Bobby Williams story immediately crystallized in my mind as I now talked to Rochon about what Doak and Strum were suggesting. I decided to follow my instincts and hold on to enough of my funds for my get-out-the-vote effort on election day.

We went into October leading handily in the polls, which showed a 20 percent margin between myself and Rizzo. It also showed a 15 to 16 percent undecided group. My experience with Frank Rizzo was that all the undecided votes would become his. These were the closet Rizzo supporters who fully supported Rizzo but were ashamed to admit it in public.

What I did not anticipate and was completely unprepared for was a preelection media blitz by Rizzo. A savvy politician, Rizzo understood some critical things. He knew that my basic support in the white community came from liberal Jewish voters. So he created a media spot that linked me with Louis Farrakhan, the national spokesman for the black Muslim organization, the Nation of Islam. The link was weak, but that didn't matter as long as it provided the right psychological impact of fear and racism.

The campaign spot said, "Charlie Burris brought Louis Farrakhan into Philadelphia. Burris is a supporter of Wilson Goode, and Wilson Goode allegedly bought a ticket to this Muslim affair." The camera then panned a board with photos of me, Burris, and Farrakhan. It was a stretch, but the subtle racism and fear implied in the message worked well enough to significantly erode my support in the liberal Jewish community during the last couple of weeks of the election. What had once appeared to be a sure election had suddenly turned into a cliff-hanger.

Amazingly, my media advisers never analyzed this shift in public opinion for me to let me know what was happening. Rochon, who has an uncanny sixth sense about these things, uncovered it and told me we had to use all of our money to turn out the vote for election day.

Despite strong evidence to the contrary, some of my advisers were still insisting that I had nothing to worry about. "This is in the bag for you," they said. "Frank Rizzo can't go anywhere." This advice came from people I had trusted. Now I knew they were trying to lull me into a sense of complacency. Even leaders of the Democratic party sought to mislead me with overly optimistic forecasts of my strengths and Rizzo's weaknesses.

Early election morning I combed the city, talking to supporters and ward leaders. Even they said, "Go home and go to bed, Mr. Goode. Your base is turning out two to one against Frank Rizzo's support."

One of the wards I visited, the Fortieth in Southwest Philadelphia, was led by ward leader Bobby Avellino. I expected honesty from my own party. The party had endorsed me and was now supporting me. What I got from Avellino was deception. He told me flatly that there was little interest in Rizzo and the turnout of my supporters was outnumbering his two to one. This was just not true, and Avellino should have known that.

About 2:00 P.M., I talked with Rochon.

"How's it going?" I asked jovially.

"Well, the turnout in the Northeast (a Rizzo stronghold) is equaling or surpassing our turnout," he said. "But we are going to be all right."

At the same time this was happening, Larry Kane, the Channel 10 news anchor, called to offer me congratulations.

"Mr. Mayor, congratulations! This is Larry Kane."

"What happened, Larry?" I asked.

"We just got the exit polls. They show you are ahead twelve points."

I passed the news on to Rochon. He said nothing, thanked me for the information, and went to work.

During this election day, Rochon was working in seclusion out of a private room in the Adams Mark Hotel with Bill Josephs, my son, and four or five other people and lots of charts and telephones. Every two hours from 10:00 A.M. to 6:00 P.M. the number of votes from targeted wards and divisions would come in. The key to our election-day strategy was not only to track voter turnout but to redeploy our field people to bring turnout to its highest potential in areas that were most favorable to my candidacy.

At 10:00 A.M. there was a mysteriously high morning voter turnout—votes for Frank Rizzo. By 12:00 noon, that trend was continuing, and there were no encouraging signs in our key wards. Our projected numbers had been too high, we realized. By 2:00 P.M. seven hours of voting had passed and only six remained. If the trend continued, we would lose. There were divisions in the Rizzo stronghold where there was already 60 percent turnout. Within my strongest area, there was only 34 percent turnout at best.

Then it happened—as I am told. At 4:00 P.M. a call came in from West Philadelphia, from the Fifty-second Ward, home of the Fattah organization led by then state representative Chaka Fattah. After hours of bad signs, second-guessing, emotional anxiety, and depression, the Fifty-second Ward reported a turnout of around 50 percent. There was optimism. There was hope for a win.

We did a lot of quick planning for a good old-fashioned street fight for after-work voters. The race would be won by maximizing turnout in key wards while not neglecting other wards. It would take more than a blitz for the turnout; it would take a strategic attack—a targeted blitz. As the numbers came across the screen that night, it read just as our projections had indicated. As daytime turned into evening and the polls closed, we knew what to expect. We knew that Rizzo had made a strong showing and had maximized his support with over 300,000 voters. We also knew that we had caught up and beaten him. It was only a matter of time before the public knew what we knew. I had won the election!

Rizzo refused to concede and even asked for a recount. Amazingly, the press went along with this, implying that Rizzo could emerge the winner in a recount. I remained confident, knowing that if anything, my 18,000-vote lead was probably an undercount. During the recount, we found some places with as much as a 500-vote difference in my favor. Within a few hours I had picked up another 2,000 votes. So Rizzo's people called off the recount, saying, "We're satisfied."

Again, an effective campaign organization gave me the victory, allowing me to become the only person ever to defeat Frank Rizzo — not once, but twice.

I was glad that I had used my basic instincts in the campaign, but I couldn't have done without the invaluable advice and guidance that I received from Reynard Rochon. At the conclusion of the campaign he let me know in detail about the uneasiness he'd felt about some of my advisers. Essentially, he believed they were playing both sides of the fence.

I thought back to one of the most memorable situations in the campaign — the debate that I had with Rizzo. Without planning to, I found myself attacking on his level after he attacked me for being a liar, stating that I was not telling the public the truth about the budget.

"You are the liar, and a certified liar at that," I countered, to Rizzo's surprise. "You're probably the only certified liar around town because you have lied, claimed that you have not lied, taken a lie detector test to prove your claims, and then failed the test, which makes you a certified liar. So don't stand here and call me a liar."

In retrospect, that probably was not the most dignified approach to his charge. But it worked.

As I approached my second term, I became reflective about the many things that had been accomplished, but worried about many of the new politicians.

Over the years black politicians had gained significant power. Bill Gray was now majority whip in Congress. Robert N. C. Nix, Jr., was the chief justice of the Pennsylvania Supreme Court. Joe

Coleman was president of the city council. Our reform movement had broken down the racial barriers, but it was threatening
to create others as these new "bosses" sought to solidify and hold
on to their power, not through merit, but by political control.

Among themselves they decided something that should have
been the decision of the voters: Who was going to be included
in the next level of leadership? Essentially, they were saying they
didn't like the way the first wave of reformers had played the
political game. It was too altruistic. They didn't like this "common good" stuff—working primarily for the best interests of the
community rather than themselves. Basically, they wanted now
to play politics the same way the "old boy" establishment had
played. Their goal was not to reform politics, but to change the
complexion of who was in charge.

Realizing this, I knew the only way I would get some things
passed by the council in my final administration would be to
work on behalf of their interests. I was out of the equation. So I
started strategizing, doing things like getting Blackwell to see that
by supporting some of my reforms he wasn't helping me, but
painting a favorable portrait of himself as future mayor in the eyes
of the people and the business establishment. I made similar
suggestions to Street as he pursued his desire to become council
president.

Early in my second administration I realized my reforms
would never be fully realized because I couldn't get the support
I needed from the city council and other leaders. With support,
many things could have been done. We could have upgraded our
financial bond rating had council supported my budgets. We
could have had our financial system in better shape. We could
have gotten a trash-to-steam plant. But I saw that the political
clock was being turned backwards. True, many of the leaders
were black, and many had come up through the activist ranks of
the streets. The only difference now, though, between them and
a James H. J. Tate or Frank Rizzo was the color of their skins. The
more I realized this, the more heartsick I became about Philadelphia politics and its future.

A system that manipulates the control of power by rewarding
friends and punishing enemies sometimes demands a flexibility
of conscience. People who are your friends today can turn out to

be enemies tomorrow. I learned that truth in some very hard, brutal situations during my last term.

The first year of my second term I worked with John Street and Lucien Blackwell in an attempt to make peace. The budget was coming up, and I needed $148 million in new taxes. I told them, "John, Lu, we can do what is necessary now in order for you all to go through the next three years. We can deliver the community services that are needed and do so without another tax raise if I can get this $148 million approved."

They agreed to go out and get the support for the tax increase for the city. I knew that if they supported it, it would happen. But somewhere within the next forty-eight hours, Street and Blackwell did a complete about-face. I discovered their change of heart by watching them announce it on a local television show, stating that only half of the $148 million was really necessary to provide city services. For some reason, Blackwell and Street had decided that their future interest was not best served by working with me. It would have helped had they leveled with me up front. But I also knew that without Street and Blackwell, chances for my budget were nonexistent. They held the cards with the white conservatives and Republicans.

While this was going on, another group of council members led by George Burrell and including Marian Tasco, Augusta Clark, and Ángel Ortiz, met with me and also opposed the $148 million. At least they were willing to support a $120-million budget which was more than Street and Blackwell were now saying they would approve. These were the so-called reformers on council, but they were not real reformers. They were really politicians first, supported by Congressman William Gray and pledged to support George Burrell for mayor the next time around. What they wanted was for me to side with them against Street and Blackwell. But all they had were their votes, with little possibility of expanding it beyond another vote or two. What Street and Blackwell had was the potential to put together an alliance of white conservatives and Republicans. I had received very little support from white conservatives and Republicans in my campaigns for mayor. John Street knew this well. And because Joseph Coleman, the president, had abdicated his leadership to John Street and Lucien Blackwell, they knew how to form the alliance for Street's future as a council president candidate and Blackwell's future as a candidate for mayor. Coleman's leadership grew weaker month after month until no one in council would move until they found out what Street wanted.

Simultaneously, the school district was seeking a multiyear funding package. Blackwell and Street panned that also, basically because Connie Clayton, superintendent of the Philadelphia School District, was a potential candidate for mayor, and they didn't want to help her win any support.

In the end the city ended up getting a $73-million tax package on paper and only $50 million in actual funds. I had gotten $98 million less than I had asked for, a situation that I feel eventually drove the city into a $200-million deficit.

As a politician, one of my greatest strengths was in delivering votes on election day. One of my greatest weaknesses was that I had not put together a ticket of people who shared my values, my goals, and my mission.

The one thing that has maintained some semblance of balance for me is the fact that I have great public appeal. I also have the organizational know-how to put together a winning campaign. Why? Because despite the consequences of MOVE, I still prefer to operate in good faith. I know that if I do the right thing and maintain the right motives and have good intentions, I will attract people of similar faith and values. The fundamental mistake I made as mayor was to believe that most, and to hope that all, people also operated this way.

I learned the hard way that I can't assume or expect that everyone else will act in good faith. For those people lacking this kind of consciousness there must be a mechanism to motivate them to stay in line politically. Perhaps our greatest reward is public praise. Conversely, our greatest deterrent to bad behavior is public criticism. It seems that the only way to keep politicians accountable for their behavior today is to show their wrongdoing in the glare of the public spotlight.

I strongly resisted doing that. I did not want to be an African American mayor who was constantly fighting other African American leaders in public. In Philadelphia, we had three African Americans in leadership at the top of the city council. I didn't want to fight them in public. Black Philadelphians had waited a long time — 302 years — to see blacks rise to the pinnacle of power in Philadelphia city government. I was not going to be party to creating a public display of disunity, even if failing to do so jeopardized my own career. That was a game I never played. I didn't want to damage morale within the black community.

To people who don't understand racial pride, I may sound completely illogical. But as Philadelphia's first black mayor I did not want to take part in publicly attacking black leadership.

All ethnic and racial groups must have pride in themselves. Blacks have endured slavery, reconstruction, segregation, Jim Crow, and discrimination. It has taken a long time for us to reach the mountaintop. I wanted more than anything else for black people to feel proud, especially those blacks who have migrated here from the South.

For those who came from the cotton, tobacco, and peanut fields; for those who never had a chance to vote until they left the South; for those in this city who felt they had no one to vote for as mayor until I ran for office; for those who stood in line three hours just to be able to tell their grandchildren that "I voted for the first black mayor of Philadelphia" — I wanted black people to feel proud.

So I willingly carried an extra burden. I carried the legacy of my African ancestors who ran cities before there was a Philadelphia. I carried the legacy of all those who resisted slavery, those who would rather be "buried in my grave before I'd be a slave." Yes, I had a higher purpose in my office. And, yes, I allowed black politicians to attack me without responding. If I had to do it all over again, I would do the same thing, because I left political office as a proud and unbowed African American man.

I'm sure some people in leadership thought my reluctance to engage in public battle to be sign of political weakness. Privately I had tried to explain my views, but most people never believed me. They couldn't accept that I didn't want to exploit a black opponent's weakness. They wondered, Why are you in this business if you're not willing to go for the jugular? Why are you in this business if you're not willing to engage in public fights? Why are you in this business if you're not willing to go into the back rooms and break someone's leg or twist their arm to get the job done? You've got to play the brutal game the way it has always been played!

I refused to play dirty politics. My decision, however, did not stop others from playing hardball.

Later in the summer of 1988, I faced another union battle. Earl Stout was gone now, having lost his seat to Jim Sutton. My mission was to negotiate a long-term contract that would enable us to work our way out of some of the problems we were having providing health and welfare support. I also wanted to get some givebacks from the unions and to halt the unions' veto powers over purchasing equipment like trucks.

The negotiations rapidly focused on three issues: reducing the work force, placing a cap on health and welfare costs shared by the city, and freezing the benefits until a new system could be negotiated. We wanted to change work rules on crew size, and we wanted to remove the unions' right to veto what size equipment we could purchase to pick up trash. Amazingly, we got most of what we wanted without a strike.

At the same time some council members were circumventing my successes by charging: "The mayor is crying wolf. There's enough money here. We don't have to reduce the number of employees. You don't have to lay off these people."

I knew they were wrong, wrong, wrong! Budget constraints dictated that we had to close firehouses and lay off some two thousand people. We had to cut service programs and generally reshape the whole face of government.

My administration developed a five-year financial strategic plan that identified areas we needed to revise, such as property tax assessments, where there was a disparity between what we thought real estate taxes ought to be and what the state thought. As a result of the state's plan, we were losing substantial amounts of money and had the potential of losing over $300 million over the next five years.

Secondly, we had to streamline the work force and bring it down to about 24,500 and keep it there. We did, reducing it from

26,500 to 24,400. We also enacted management savings by getting the state to assume more responsibility for programs they mandated. I had outlined the basic principles of this plan and said that we needed $65 million in taxes that next year. I appointed a tax policy and budget advisory committee and took the plan on the road to win public support.

The first two meetings I held were hotbeds of hostility. The first one was in the Northeast at a firehouse. I encountered one of the worst mob scenes I'd ever experienced. The audience was white, ill mannered, and extremely disrespectful. It was as if I had been invited to a lynching and I was the guest of honor.

Throughout my presentation, people shouted, hissed, called me names, and lambasted me as inept for the MOVE disaster. They called me incompetent and said I should resign from office.

"Why are you coming out here?" someone yelled. "We're going to impeach you!"

"Don't talk to me about taxes," someone else snarled, "especially when I'm paying more taxes than ever before."

I maintained my cool and refused to leave. Somehow in the midst of all this, I managed to make my presentation.

The next morning, Blackwell and Street came to ask me to halt the town meetings.

"They're destructive!" Blackwell hissed. "You're going to destroy every Democrat that ever runs for office."

My next town meeting was in a black neighborhood in West Philadelphia. It was much better. Only about 10 percent of the people attending the meeting booed and hissed me. The ward leader in this community was Ella Dunn. I had closed a firehouse in that neighborhood as part of the process to reduce the budget. Ella had asked me to reopen the firehouse for her, and I explained why I couldn't do it for her or anyone. I was unprepared for her venomous attack.

"I was here when you needed me and I voted for you," she said. "And what do you do? You repay us by closing down our firehouse. We don't like what you've done to us."

Despite Ella's attack, the majority of the people who attended were supportive. I eventually held twenty-four town meetings in all. Most went very well and were uneventful, but the media only fully covered the first two, playing up the attacks and the hostility. They came to a couple more later, but when nothing negative happened, they left.

I felt as if I was fighting for Philadelphia all by myself. In the spring of 1989, I postponed the tax increase until the next year, trying to buy some time and work out differences with city council. The olive branch did not help. Council, led by John Street as its appropriations chair, would simply not face reality.

The financial pressure continued to build throughout the summer. By fall, there was even infighting in my inner circle. Betsy Reveal was now my finance director. She had been an associate dean at Harvard. Ernest Barefield was my special counsel. He had been the chief of staff for the late Harold Washington in Chicago. Reveal and Barefield had been the point people on the budget plan. In the process they had caused major morale problems throughout the government.

Other cabinet members and commissioners claimed that they were being intentionally excluded from the process. My office was constantly flooded with complaints.

Reveal and Barefield had been effective in pulling together a strong strategic plan. They were professionals, but I had a problem. The best way to solve it was to bring them face-to-face.

The meeting was intense; I was actively involved. We made some real progress, but that night I ended up in the emergency room of Lankenau Hospital with a rapid heartbeat. It was the first time I had been sick in thirty-five years. The doctors, however, gave me a clean bill of health.

After that, the staff's working relationships improved. They proceeded to fight the financial challenges, not one another.

By the time 1990 rolled around, it was clear that we would not get the additional tax money and I would have to make major cuts in city programs. Much as I hated to, I reduced spending for the homeless, AIDS, every single thing I could.

John Street now had full control of the appropriation process in council. He seemed to enjoy taking my budgets and proposals and redoing them so that they would not work. I have often stated that the budget crisis was caused in large part by John Street. I still believe that's true.

As 1990 came around, it became apparent to me that we were running out of time. For the first time our cash flow was projecting a deficit by December. We had to do some short-term borrowing. This had been a tradition since 1972, but this time it was really needed. We decided to go to market.

Everything seemed fine at first, but then something very strange happened. Jonathan Saidel, the city's controller, held a press conference and stated that we should not be borrowing the money. It wasn't needed. Saidel clearly did not understand the city's financial situation or history. This kind of short-term borrowing was not an unusual tactic.

But Wall Street took Saidel seriously. His comments sent shock waves through the money markets, and he almost single-handedly killed the deal. Then Speaker of the House Robert O'Donnell said the same thing. The statements of these two, more than anything else, killed chances for a bond sale. Without their irresponsible comments, I believe the bonds would have been sold.

After the bond sale's failure, Saidel and O'Donnell joined with other elected officials to put the pieces back together. Eventually, these efforts led to the creation of an oversight board that will guide the city through its financial difficulties.

In the midst of all this bad news, there was good news. In December of 1989, Muriel Lynette, my oldest daughter, announced that she would be married on August 25, 1990. She was to marry Rev. Anthony Trufant, the pastor of the church of Christian Compassion in Philadelphia. The wedding was a beautiful one held at the Mount Carmel Baptist Church. The Reverend Amos Brown, the groom's uncle and pastor of the Third Baptist Church in San Francisco, performed the ceremony. Muriel was as beautiful a bride as she had been a baby. When the minister asked "who giveth this woman," Velma and I stood and said in unison, "We do." We were proud parents.

After the loan failed, I had no choice but to find another way to keep the city afloat. By December of 1990 we were literally running out of money. Our bills were as much as 150 days behind, and I feared we wouldn't make the payroll.

The only option that eventually presented itself to me was a loan arrangement through CoreStates; we took it. I personally worked with the bank officials to conclude the loan. This gave us enough cash flow to finish out my term.

Although we were successful in getting the necessary cash to carry us through 1991, the damage was done. The bond sale failure had caused Wall Street to downgrade the city's bond rating to junk-bond status. This prevented us from entering the money market without the assistance of some external entity. The financial collapse was brought about primarily by political issues. Saidel's and O'Donnell's statements had caused Wall Street to lose confidence in Philadelphia's ability to implement its financial plan. John Street and other council members had refused to take the necessary steps to send a message to Wall Street that there was political consensus on solutions to this problem. I wished Gov. Robert Casey would have been willing to give a signal to Wall Street that the commonwealth would assist the city in the ways it eventually did.

All the rating agencies confided in me that they had no problem with Reveal's financial management and her financial plan. What they had a problem with was the lack of consensus by the governor, the Pennsylvania Senate and House of Representatives, the mayor, and council members. This consensus was made impossible because of other political agendas. Robert O'Donnell wanted to be governor. He did not want to appear to be bailing out Philadelphia. Lucien Blackwell and George Burrell, council members, wanted to be mayor. They did not want to support any plan that had taxes or major cuts. John Street was campaigning for council president. He and his supporters wanted to put the whole issue off until after the general election. In fact, about two weeks before the general election in 1991, John Street; Vincent Fumo, the state senate minority appropriations chair; Robert Brady, the party's chair; and David Cohen, Rendell's campaign manager (not the David Cohen I had worked with on city council), met with me in my office to plead with me not to publicly release my five-year plan until after the election. They all felt that the release of the plan would be harmful to their election chances. I did not want to be blamed for the defeat of any Democratic candidate in the upcoming election, so I concurred with the request as long as we could release the plan immediately after the election. Not surprisingly, after the election, Rendell asked that we defer the matter of the five-year plan to him and his incoming administration. I agreed for two reasons: one, the operative state law gave the incoming administration authority immediately upon assuming office to revise the five-year plan proposed by me; two, I wanted to do whatever possible to guarantee success of the financial recovery plan.

I had worked hard to avoid the financial problems, but I learned the hard way that personal political agendas will always supplant the common agenda. But the facts have now spoken for themselves. Since John Street had achieved his goal of becoming council president, Rendell was able to get the five-year plan approved without delay from council. As president, John Street could now work in harmony with a new mayor to start to solve Philadelphia's long-term financial problems. He could now look like a hero in helping to solve a fiscal crisis that he, more than anyone, helped to create.

Nineteen ninety-one was also an election year. As the election unfolded, there were three black candidates and two white candidates running for mayor. The favorite was Ed Rendell. The Republicans had endorsed district attorney Ron Castille, but there were two other candidates: former mayor Frank Rizzo and financial adviser Sam Katz. The Republican race was a tossup, with Rizzo given a slight edge.

On the Democratic side, in addition to Rendell, Peter Hearn, a very popular attorney, was also running. The three black candidates were council members Lucien Blackwell and George Burrell and the former managing director, James Stanley White.

My sentimental favorite was James White. He was one of the most loyal and dedicated people I had ever met. But White, in my view, couldn't win. Additionally, I kept getting information that he would eventually drop out and support Blackwell.

I could not support Blackwell because I felt that he really couldn't do the job as mayor. I did not feel he was the right person to be mayor. I felt that he was influenced too much by John Street.

And then there was George Burrell. Burrell had the ability. He was smart and articulate and had a passion for governmental service. I knew he would stay in the race, and I sincerely thought at one point that he had a shot at winning.

I was inclined to endorse Burrell, because I thought that between Blackwell and him, he was the better of the two. I did not think White would stick it out until the end. But there were lots of rumors about Burrell allegedly not paying his taxes. The rumor was that as soon as I endorsed Burrell, the *Inquirer* would run a story on his taxes.

Before I endorsed Burrell for mayor, I asked him directly about the rumors of tax delinquency. He assured me that he had no problem that was going to interfere with the campaign. To confirm this I also consulted his law partner, Rotan Lee. He too assured me that I could be comfortable in endorsing Burrell. I did. A few days later the *Inquirer* ran the tax story. Burrell came in third behind Rendell and Blackwell in the election.

In retrospect, I should have endorsed James White. He had been a loyal and committed managing director. I should have, as I have done with many other things, followed my gut instincts. It would have felt right to endorse Jim White. It was not one of my proud moments. Jim White had earned my endorsement and my support. I will always deeply regret that I did not support him.

While the Democratic party candidates were going through this upheaval, Frank Rizzo was running against Ron Castille and Sam Katz in the Republican primary. I correctly predicted that it would become an Ed Rendell/Frank Rizzo race for the general election. But no one could have prepared me for the surprise that followed.

Following the primary I got a call from Sam Evans who asked me to come to his office for a brief meeting. That was July 1991. I have always respected Sam and valued, if not always followed, his advice. I went to his office not knowing what to expect.

"I want to make you a proposition," Sam was now saying. "I want you to talk your police commissioner, Willie Williams, into running for mayor as an independent candidate in the fall election. His running will pull votes away from Ed Rendell and assure Frank Rizzo's victory.

"If Rizzo wins, he has promised to give you anything you want, Mr. Mayor. He has also agreed to appoint Willie Williams as the police commissioner. Other black leaders and I have already talked to Willie Williams about this. I want you to convince him that this is the thing to do, because Ed Rendell is not going to be mayor of Philadelphia. We're going to see to that."

I made sure that I recorded this conversation in my mind with as much exactitude as I could muster. Returning to my office, I even wrote it down to make sure I had gotten all of the pieces. Then I called Willie Williams and asked him to come and see me.

I met with Willie later that afternoon, repeating what Sam had said. He confirmed that Sam Evans and another black leader had told him the same thing.

"When I walked into Sam Evans's office, I felt insulted," Willie said. "He was asking me to run for mayor with the thought that I was automatically going to lose, as if I was nothing, a nobody."

"Willie," I said, "you can never allow yourself to get caught in a situation like this. It will lead you nowhere fast."

"Mr. Mayor, before you even talked to me, I had made up my mind I was not going to do this. I was not going to be a part of this."

After that conversation with Sam, I was reminded of the sentiment that politicians have no permanent friends, no permanent enemies, only permanent interests. All Evans and his friends knew was it appeared they could make a better deal with Frank Rizzo than Ed Rendell. It didn't seem to matter that they would have to get in bed with the enemy to do it.

But life is strange. Before this deal or any other could be made, Frank Rizzo suddenly died.

During the general election, Sam endorsed Ed Rendell and served on his inaugural committee. Sam even had a place on stage. And so it goes.

CHAPTER FIFTEEN

In Goode Faith

On inauguration day, Monday, January 6, 1992, as I sat on stage with the other participants, I watched the clock move quickly toward twelve noon. In a few minutes Ed Rendell would step up to the podium and take the oath of office to become the 128th mayor of Philadelphia. This was the changing of the guard. My heart pounded with uncertainty as he started to take the oath of office. This is it, I said to myself. It's really over.

"I, Edward Rendell, do hereby . . . so help me God." The audience burst into applause. It was now Mayor Edward Rendell and former mayor Wilson Goode. The ceremony ended after a brief speech by Rendell. Ironically, John Street, the incoming council president, had taken twice as long as the mayor to make his speech.

I walked out of the Academy of Music, where Ricardo Muti had brought so much pleasure to tens of thousands of music lovers with his conducting of the Philadelphia Orchestra. It was over now. I had cleared out of the mayor's office on Friday, so I headed straight for my new office—with no secretary, no assistant, no staff clamoring for my attention. I was alone in my job for the first time since leaving college almost thirty years before—alone in an office with only a portable phone and a desk that had been left there by the previous occupants.

But for some reason I was content. I was happy. I had been to the mountaintop as mayor of one of the largest and most historically significant cities in the United States. I was now ready to move on with my life, to do something different: to help African American males, to rescue our children, to help build support systems for those most at risk in our society. I was ready to leave the job of mayor behind me.

Unfortunately, as with many former politicians, the media wouldn't let me go peacefully out of office. They dug up stories—some just plain ridiculous—to try to paint a picture of me as a prima donna who wasted the taxpayers' money on excessive security and perks.

To their charges I can only say that I believe I never spent the city's money frivolously. Any extra security to protect me or my family was assigned because it was felt to be necessary. Sadly, racism is still alive and well in this country and in this city. Our already higher-than-normal security risks as Philadelphia's first African American First Family were further increased after the MOVE tragedy.

Another criticism I found ironic was the charge that I inappropriately depleted the city's supply of gifts for visiting dignitaries and retiring executives. I don't understand the logic that approves of giving a four-hundred-dollar engraved bowl to a cabinet member but criticizes giving an inexpensive magnifying glass (engraved with my name and of no further use to the city) to lower-level personnel for years of loyal service.

Though the media's nitpicking was disheartening, I was focused on some unfinished business at the Philadelphia Housing Authority (PHA). I had appointed myself to the PHA board with the expectation of becoming an active member following my term as mayor. While in office, I had not been effective in turning PHA around the way I had wanted. Now was my chance to make up for that.

Over the years, the agency had progressively worsened, as conniving public servants used it to advance their own goals and possibly to pad their pockets. Reform was further hampered by politics, as Housing and Urban Development (HUD) officials claimed their jurisdictional authority over the agency and, in the process, unwittingly aided abusers in their schemes.

Early in my first term I had appointed Garfield Harris, a longtime housing activist, as executive director and Julia Robinson as my housing czar and directed them to clean up PHA. They had begun to reform the agency when Kenneth Finlayson, the regional administrator for the HUD office that funded PHA, told me to see that the programs were stopped. He personally instructed me to stay out of the day-to-day operations.

"Since the city has not put money into PHA, the city should not be meddling in its operations," he said. Finlayson also characterized my attempts to clean up PHA as political and threatened to take whatever steps were necessary to make sure I didn't interfere in the agency. Evidently I was interfering by seeking accountability for PHA's actions.

Since HUD funded PHA, I backed off and let Finlayson handle it himself. Finlayson remained regional director and kept tight control of PHA's reins until he was transferred elsewhere after the election of President George Bush.

By this time I was into my second term and immersed in the fiscal crisis of the city. PHA was still a real concern for me, but my hands had been tied by Finlayson. I didn't feel that an all-out war was wise while I struggled with the MOVE aftermath and the city budget and financial problems.

After Jonathan Saidel was elected controller, he approached me about his becoming chair of PHA. I thought this at least offered an opportunity to get things moving. I had never been impressed with Saidel's accomplishments, but he did seem honest and hard working.

"My only interest, Mr. Mayor, is to get in there and help these poor tenants," Saidel said. "I don't have a whole lot to challenge me as city controller and I need a challenge. PHA will be my challenge."

Saidel's argument was persuasive and sounded sincere. I trusted his words despite the impression I'd had of him. Maybe I'd been wrong about him; maybe he really was committed to the improvement of the authority for the benefit of the tenants. So I didn't try to block his election as chair of the board.

Within months Saidel had removed top staff people and

replaced them with people who had political connections. It wasn't a good sign.

During my last six months in office, the issue of patronage at PHA reared its ugly head again. This time the favor seekers were state senators Hardy Williams and Vince Fumo, who each lobbied me to appoint one of their friends to the PHA board when a term expired in September 1991.

Hardy was lobbying for one of his close aides to be appointed. I liked the person, but he was not my idea of someone who was qualified to sit on the PHA board. This was not the Hardy Williams I had worked for from 1969 through 1972. This one was different. He had become totally political, but I wasn't surprised. I had watched Williams change while I was in the mayor's office. He was chair of the Senate delegation from Philadelphia. In our weekly meetings he would complain that I was not using my office to help him make money through legal contracts with firms he was associated with. (He rarely asked what he could do to help me carry out my agenda as mayor.) I had campaigned for a Hardy Williams who was interested in the community. I was now talking to a Hardy Williams who was concerned mostly with himself and what I could do for him.

Fumo's actions were predictable. He was known for using his position to help his friends and supporters.

I didn't fully know the extent of Saidel's mismanagement until I appointed myself to the PHA board. I was reluctant to appoint myself, but with the shape PHA was in, I wanted to have more control over seeing that things got fixed.

Before doing so, I checked with the secretary of HUD, Jack Kemp; HUD regional administrator, Mike Smerconish; and David Cohen, now Rendell's alter ego and chief of staff, to make sure there were no conflicts. They all signed off on the appointment.

My first PHA meeting made me realize that the abuses at PHA were worse than I had dreamed. Several board members joined with me in challenging the way things were being done. When we realized how entrenched the problems were, we called for Saidel's resignation, along with a thorough housecleaning. I was amazed by the political maneuverings this prompted.

The immediate response was from Saidel himself, who started spreading rumors that black elected officials wanted to take over the patronage at the authority. He convinced Mayor Rendell, Senator Fumo, and Democratic party chair Robert Brady to join with him in working out an arrangement with Michael Smerconish to have HUD take over the Philadelphia Housing Authority. The purpose of the city's political leadership was two-fold: They would keep John Paone, executive director, on the payroll for six months, thereby protecting their patronage and contracts and they would keep a black takeover from happening. All the concern over a black takeover of the board was interesting given that 85 percent of PHA tenants are African American.[1]

Smerconish bought the arrangement because it made him look as if he were doing something about one of the worst-run housing authorities in the country. But it really was a political deal that kept those in control who had been there all along, while showing a face of apparent reform to the public.

On Monday, June 1, Saidel announced that he was resigning as chair and leaving the PHA board. Ironically, while the public was being presented with an image of collapse and reform by Mayor Rendell and HUD officials, those of us on the board knew that deals were still in the works to keep in place some of the worst abusers of PHA.

The more things change, the more things stay the same, I thought to myself. Even out of office, I found that the wheel of patronage continued to turn, presenting itself as a wheel of fortune for whatever politician or friend had the chance to take advantage of it. The only losers, of course, were the unsuspecting citizens — in this case, the tenants.

I find it disturbing that many of the people I thought to be at the forefront of Philadelphia's political reform movement have sold out to the expedient and convenient way of running government. They divide the spoils and favors among the few who "get things done" and in the process forget the people who need to have things done for them.

But patronage politics will continue only as long as we fail to push for real reform. Philadelphia is now pushing hard to reform the 1951 Home Rule Charter. There is no question that the charter needs reform, but the major problem with the government is not the charter. It's our acceptance of the way the political game is played. It's our acceptance of politics as usual. It's our caving in to power politics and our glorification of politicians who use political clout as if that were the same as practicing good government.

If we continue in this way, government will eventually function only through those few people who have amassed political favors. And we will be headed for another era of bossism.

In my two terms as mayor, I found few elected officials with a clear vision for the city or workable solutions for the problems they were elected to address in their districts. Instead, they were content to operate as "peddlers of petty influence," abdicating the potential they had to influence change.

A politician must feel the pulse of the people and read the signs of the times to be a good leader. Sadly, neither the Democratic nor the Republican party in Philadelphia has that awareness. The Democratic party continues to hold a "ward leaders mentality" in selecting candidates to run for office. Candidates are selected for their loyalty to the party leadership and their willingness to share patronage and maintain the status quo.

Despite numerous opportunities to break away from the mold, both parties often run mediocre candidates even when superior candidates are available.

In 1985, for example, despite my advice, party chair Joseph Smith pushed Robert Williams as the candidate for district attorney. I supported Lynne Abraham because I felt she was a far superior candidate. Robert Williams was crushed by Ronald Castille.

In the 1991 election, Lynne Abraham was so popular that both the Democrats and Republicans supported her. But only after Bob Brady and Vincent Fumo tried unsuccessfully to get the Board of Judges to select Russell Nigro as the candidate. Again, quality was not the issue; party loyalty was.

Robert Brady, the Democratic party chair, is an effective and dedicated party leader. He is the best party chair since William Green, Jr., the former mayor's father. He has mastered the traditional party game. He plays it as honorably and fairly as anyone can. And by so doing, he has earned the respect of party members. The only problem is that the traditional party game is the wrong one. There is a big difference between learning *to do things right* and *doing the right things*.

Today I believe both parties remain out of touch with the changing sentiments in the city, state, and nation. Despite the fact that voters often reject these hand-picked, mediocre candidates, the parties continue to run them. In the recent primary for U.S. senator, the state's Democrats selected Lieutenant Governor Mark Singel. The people chose Lynn Yeakel to face Arlen Specter after Specter raised the ire of many voters by his insensitivity in the Anita Hill/Clarence Thomas hearings. The Ross Perot phenomenon was a direct result of party politics as usual. The people are saying that we are tired of it, but the politicians still are not listening.

I believe that government must exist to serve the people if our ideals of democracy are to remain and grow. Government is a service corporation whose product is public service and whose consumers are the voters. Each citizen has a right to expect that the government will deliver quality services on an equal and unbiased basis. Each citizen has a right to expect that these services cannot be bought with political favors or friendship.

Therefore, when well-meaning people and media representatives suggested to me that I should "stop delivering services to the Fifth District if city councilman John Street won't act right," I let them know that the people of the Fifth District should never be punished for the sins of John Street.

Good politicians must hold fast to their beliefs, even when those around them say they are wrong. The minute you change, you become someone else.

The public must not be confused by words like *reform* when actions point to more of the same. Many politicians will talk about reform, but few will ever embrace it in a significant way.

I ran for the office of mayor to make a difference. My goal was to bring people into the government who I believed would be enforcers of good government. I wanted to open up the system, break down barriers, and break up the old boys network.

But despite my best efforts and good intentions, many of my real plans and motives were obscured by events beyond my control. I regret that my administration was bombarded with so many issues that my vision of political multiculturalism got lost. Or maybe the media and my critics just didn't want to promote it.

I had a clear vision for the things that I did. My appointment of blacks and women to nontraditional jobs was to send a clear message that no qualified candidate for any top-level job would be excluded because of gender, race, religion, or sexual orientation.

My compassion for the disenfranchised was the motivation for the policy changes I made in the early years of my administration. The life of a homeless person was as important to me as the life of any other citizen in our city. It didn't matter to me whether or not the homeless voted. As Philadelphians, they were my concern and deserved the benefits of good government. We are all the same in the eyes of God. We are his children. Why should we be any less equal in the eyes of politicians?

As mayor, I sometimes confronted controversial issues that put me in no-win situations. But I tried to always stand for the right things, even if I stood alone.

As mayor, I sometimes made mistakes, but I have tried to own up to them. I made one of the biggest mistakes of my political life when I appointed Gregore Sambor as police commissioner. We did not share similar philosophies on the operation of a police department.

An unwritten bond exists between the people and government officials. People seek to put individuals in office who they hope will uphold the public trust and defend the human rights of all citizens. When that bond is violated, the trust broken, the betrayal cuts deep, wounding the soul. I believe such was the betrayal felt by Philadelphians following the MOVE incident. Many people felt betrayed by the brutality the police used against MOVE.

The MOVE crisis also taught me that it was impossible for anyone inside the Philadelphia Police Department to wrest control of that department away from Frank Rizzo and his loyalists. As I have said, I failed mightily in appointing Greg Sambor as police commissioner. He was the wrong man. And after MOVE, I was politically weaker for that decision. That's why I made the decision to go outside of the department to find the next police commissioner. It was not a popular decision, but a necessary one.

My years in Philadelphia and my tenure in office have made

me especially sensitive to concerns about police brutality. When the people who are hired to protect citizens become the enemy, the sense of betrayal cuts deeply. I believe that betrayal was the spark that ignited the 1992 riots in Los Angeles and elsewhere following the acquittal of four police officers in the Rodney King case.

Those officers were not the first to be acquitted of police brutality, nor will they be the last. Regardless of what the jury saw, the shame of that case was the message it sent to the public—that police officers can be caught on videotape brutalizing and taunting an unarmed man and still walk away free, retain their police jobs, and, maybe, brutalize someone else.

The message delivered in that verdict brutalized Rodney King and all citizens who expect police protection but fear brutality because of age, sex, or the color of their skin.

Thus, I understand the fear some people have of the police. That, again, is why MOVE remains such a devastating experience for me.

The MOVE incident was the darkest hour of my Christian experience. The ghosts of the MOVE tragedy haunt me daily. The deaths of those children, of those people, continue to haunt me. My God, how I wish I could bring them back!

I wish I could have one more chance to relive May 13, 1985, to save those lives, those homes, and those memories that were burned to ashes. No matter how I view others' responsibilities, I cannot escape the fact that the MOVE bombing happened on my watch. That will always be with me and I am deeply sorry.

I ask all of the members of the MOVE organization and their supporters to forgive me. God knows I had no malice in my heart toward anyone in that organization, and God knows that, in many ways, I too was a victim of May 13.

When I left office, I left behind official responsibility for dealing with MOVE. But there is at least one overriding issue of unfinished business that caused the tragedy on May 13 and that continues now to pose major problems for the city: the trials and convictions emanating from the August 8, 1978, confrontation between MOVE and the city. There is enough uncertainty about the murder and conspiracy convictions of the nine MOVE members that a special investigative panel should be set up by the governor and the mayor, with cooperation from the state's attorney general and the city's district attorney. This investigative panel should be granted subpoena powers and access to all records and files. No stone should be left unturned in searching for the truth.

I don't believe that we now know the truth. I don't believe that there was sufficient evidence to prove that these nine people conspired and then killed Officer Ramp. In fact, I don't believe that there is evidence that any MOVE member killed Officer Ramp.

The conflict with MOVE will be resolved only when the whole truth is known.

When I first came to my conclusion on this matter in 1990, I called for the chief justice of the Pennsylvania Supreme Court to convene a special panel. I spoke with him privately about this at first, and later publicly made the request. After about a year of going back and forth with staff at the chief justice's office, I concluded that he was not going to appoint the panel. At that point I wanted to establish the panel myself. I received names from a variety of people. However, I concluded that it was inappropriate for me to make such major appointments two months before I left office. Nonetheless, with Ramona Africa now released from jail, the timing is right for establishing such a panel. Africa is moving throughout the community and around the nation pushing for the release from jail of her brothers and sisters. There must be an orderly process to achieve that. The panel is that orderly process.

As I prepared to leave office, I wondered where I would go next. I had many choices to make. Do I use the power of my office and leverage to make a quick buck in corporate America? I chose another way.

God has not given me all that he has merely to enrich myself and my family. During my eight years in office, I saw thousands of African American males who did not have the advantages my children had. I saw young men wasting their lives away. Some were dying of AIDS, and others were languishing idly in prison.

I saw black men shooting down their brothers in the streets. I saw them standing on street corners, unemployed, unemployable, and hopeless about the future.

I saw some turn into old men before they were forty, their bodies wrecked by the ravages of drugs and alcohol. I saw them drop out of schools as functional illiterates. And I saw mere boys fathering babies that they lacked the financial or moral resources to provide for. I saw black males at risk simply because they were alive.

I spent two summers as mayor in my mobile office traveling from neighborhood to neighborhood. As I talked with young black men standing on street corners, I found they'd lost their sense of values. I saw many crying out for attention.

At a dedication ceremony for a mural erected at Twentieth and Federal streets in South Philadelphia, I looked at the wall that was a tombstone to the young boys and girls who had died violently. Reading the names I asked, "Why? Why? Why?" and finally, "What can I do to help?"

Youth at risk is a problem that has become bigger than life itself, but it is a problem that can be resolved. Looking at the bright-eyed, eager young men I see in church, I thought how wonderful it would be for them to reach out and come back into our cities to help heal the crisis confronting black youth.

Goode Cause, Inc., was born out of that vision. It is a vehicle to bring problems and resources together to attempt to find solutions that will mend our broken cities.

Through Goode Cause, I want to become a catalyst of change by matching children in need with the adults who want to help them. I want to challenge my church brothers and sisters to move beyond the comfort of their sanctuary walls and get the church involved in the streets. We can save souls, but first we must save lives.

I want to challenge the lay leadership in the black church to do more, to get more involved in our communities so that they can bring a new spirit of hope and reform to our communities.

Guided by my faith in God and my love for Philadelphia, I persevered in my reforms despite frequent criticisms by the media and political foes that my values and philosophy didn't belong in government, much less in the mayor's office. Before I left office, one newspaper declared that I was "too good to be mayor." I rejected that notion as ludicrous. The faith, self-confidence, and strength of character that guided me as a man more than adequately served me in public office.

But my basic philosophy, approach, standards, and sense of morality are in complete opposition to the direction in which the city is moving politically. Today, I can do more, I feel, in helping to shape public policy and opinion than I could have as mayor. As mayor, I had opinions that were contrary to the city council's and were played up by the media as a power struggle between me and John Street or Lucien Blackwell. Diversity does not have to create hostility. I feel I can be a lot clearer with my comments now than before.

I feel that I can now explain my differences with John Street and Lucien Blackwell without the black community seeing these differences among us as disunity among their elected black leadership. Street and Blackwell embraced the traditional school of politics, while I sought reform. Our differences were never personal, but philosophical. Consequently, our different approaches were bound to lead to the conflicts we had.

My life in politics is over now. But I believe the best is yet to come. The victories of my tenure in office, as well as the tragedies, have sensitized me to the deep needs of the people living in our cities, and to our young people in particular.

With God's help, I took the ashes of a childhood of poverty and insecurity and traded them for a faith and determination that catapulted me to the highest public office in one of America's major cities. Becoming mayor was not the climax of my dreams, but another stepping stone in a lifetime of experiences and wonders that I cannot yet fully fathom.

EPILOGUE

A Letter to My Children

Dear Muriel, Wilson Jr., and Natasha,

I write to you now because you, my children, are the keepers of my torch. You will carry it until you pass it along to your children. I have shared what I have learned about people, about government and politics, about church and religion, about faith in God.

I have done this in the hope that you can avoid some of the pitfalls I have encountered in my life; that you will be able to better understand the people who run the government that serves you; that you will look twice at what you read in your daily newspapers or see on your televisions.

My greatest hope is that you will always seek the truth even when it's painful; that you will never lose sight of who you are, what you stand for, and what you want out of life; that you will always stay close to God; and that whatever you do, you will do it in good faith.

Despite the frustration and discouragement I endured while in public office, I hope that you will see politics as a noble profession where leaders who seek to do the right thing for the people can succeed. And even if you don't succeed, you will gain strength in knowing you have done the right thing. That's most important above all else.

As I look back at my life, I am reminded of the words of that favorite hymn, which says, in part:

> May the life I live speak for me, . . .
> When the best I try to live, my mistakes He will forgive,
> May the life I live speak for me.
>
> May the service I give speak for me, . . .
> When I've done the best I can and my friends don't understand,
> May the service I give speak for me.
>
> The work I've done it seems so small,
> Sometimes it seems like, seems like nothing at all,
> But when I stand before my God,
> I want to hear Him say, "Well done,"
> May the work I've done speak for me.[1]

It's a passionate, moving hymn that touches my heart as it speaks of a sincere effort to do what's right throughout one's life. I've tried to live my life that way. Many times along the way I have stumbled, but my human failings have always occurred while trying to give my best effort to doing the right thing.

I have tried to live my life in good faith and by doing good deeds. Values instilled in me as a child have reaped a solid foundation of faith, trust, hard work, integrity, and determination. Your mother and I have tried to instill these same values in each of you. At age fifty-four, I know that the seeds of character sown in my childhood have blossomed and flowered into mighty oaks at various stages of my life. They have shaped my character, formed my personality, and inspired my life philosophy. You have been surrounded with love and understanding. And I have tried to be a good example for the three of you.

I have lived my life secure in the belief that if I perform a task with earnestness and sincerity, I will be rewarded with success. But my foray into elective office has seasoned me and taught me a bitter lesson. For a long time, I believed that most of the people who entered politics did so to work for the common good.

After fourteen years I must unhappily conclude that the overwhelming majority of people in elective office are there to serve themselves, not the public. Few are interested in reform if it does not benefit them personally. Their primary interest in getting reelected is to use elective office to help themselves, their friends, and their supporters.

If you should journey through the political wilderness, people will ask you, "Why shouldn't politicians have personal ambition or use their office to help their friends?" My reasoning remains as clear today as it was in college when I formulated it.

No one lives in a vacuum. I want you to always remember that every act you commit as adults with free will affects someone else. No matter how high or how low your station in life, your individual decisions touch the cosmos.

Buying political favors is a common occurrence. Yet, that does not change the fact that every time the governmental process is circumvented to help a private-interest group, a financial contributor, or a special supporter, the citizens who are forced to go through regular channels are bumped from their place in line. In essence, they are displaced and denied equal treatment under the law.

As you walk through life, you will find that some people are rewarded for doing wrong, while others are attacked for the good they do.

You know the media in recent years has not been kind to me. I don't know why. Some people suggest that the media had unrealistic expectations of me. Others have said that the press never figured out how to deal with a black mayor, especially one whom they saw as being too religious, too moralistic, and too rigid in his views and beliefs. They said my style of leadership was out of touch with what was needed in the eighties and nineties, that the values that had made me a good church deacon were inadequate for the office of the mayor.

Children, don't ever let anyone's opinion compromise your values or your internal strengths. For you know as well as I do that the faith, self-confidence, and strength of character that have guided me as a man, father, husband, and community leader have more than adequately served me in public office.

I tried hard to balance the obligations of being an African American politician breaking new ground with that of being the proud father of three wonderful children. Thank you for being there—so loving and supportive—and always cheering me on.

So, Muriel Lynette, you must carry on the dream of building a better world. You have chosen a lofty profession in law. Always use it to seek justice and freedom and equality. As the First Lady of one of the nation's great congregations, you have the obligation of being a role model for many young women in your church and community. Remember that the harvest is plentiful but the laborers are few. Continue to be a laborer for God's kingdom here on earth.

And to my son and namesake, W. Wilson Goode, Jr.—you will carry both the burden and the gift of my name. I have tried to make you proud of me. I have tried to teach you by example. I am pleased that you have chosen a life of public service. I can see in you real passion for the underdog, for those struggling to make it. I see your caring attitude, your high moral standards, your faith in God. Continue to use your special gifts in the passionate way you have done thus far. You will change much if you do.

And to Natasha Patrice, my baby—decide now how you will use the special gifts that you have. They have been given to you not only to enrich yourself but to help others. Reach out and help. Think about how you can use your skills to help alleviate some of the suffering and misery in the world. Your intellect and interpersonal skills will take you far. Your love for children will shape your character.

This has been a long letter, but I had a lot to share with you. Now take the torch and go forth into a world that awaits you. Remember above all, whatever you do, do it "in Goode faith."

I love you,
Daddy

Notes

Chapter Eight

1. In 1979, the assets of the combined utilities of the Pennsylvania Commonwealth totaled $7 billion. As commissioner of PUC, I oversaw the agency that regulated the utilities.

Chapter Nine

1. Tom Masland, "A group that chose to live on the very brink," *Philadelphia Inquirer,* August 9, 1978, 7-A.
2. Ibid.
3. Ibid.
4. Ibid.
5. Larry Eichel, "MOVE Members Speak Out—Loudly," *Philadelphia Inquirer,* April 21, 1975, 3-B.
6. Ibid.
7. Ibid., 1-B.
8. Bob Frump, "The Mayor: Grief Filled with Rage," *Philadelphia Inquirer,* August 9, 1978, 1-A.
9. Ibid., 5-A.

Chapter Ten

1. Acel Moore, "Goode now is free to make his run," *Philadelphia Inquirer,* November 4, 1982.

2. Roger Cohn, "Goode views city's problems, vows to be 'tool for unification,' " *Philadelphia Inquirer,* November 7, 1982, 1-B.

3. Carolyn Acker, "Wilson Goode: He Transformed the Job," *Philadelphia Daily News,* November 30, 1982, 6.

4. Ibid.

5. Ibid.

Chapter Twelve

1. "The Findings, Conclusions and Recommendations of the Philadelphia Special Investigation Commission," *Temple Law Quarterly* (vol. 59, no. 2), Summer 1986, 347.

2. Charles W. Bowser, *Let the Bunker Burn: The Final Battle with MOVE* (Philadelphia: Camino Books, 1989), 16-17.

3. Ibid., 17.

4. Ibid., 38.

5. Ibid., 39.

Chapter Thirteen

1. "MOVE Commission Hearings—Day One"; October 8, 1985; 3-4.

2. City of Philadelphia Litigation re Ramona Africa, 87-2678; Master File 85-2745; U.S. District Court for the Eastern District of Pennsylvania, Philadelphia, Pa.; July 11, 1991; 116.

3. Ibid.; 115, 117-118, 131, 132, 138, 140.

4. Mrs. Mapp, Oct. 9, 1985, p. 5; "The Philadelphia Special Commission Investigation Commission: Report of Commissioner Charles W. Bowser," *Temple Law Quarterly* (vol. 59, no. 2), Summer 1986, 382.

5. Mrs. Wilson, p. 87; *Quarterly,* 382.

6. Mr. Swans, N.T. Oct. 10, 1985, p. 104; *Quarterly,* 382. (Note: "N.T." refers to the commission's notes of testimony as cited by Commissioner Bowser; the first page reference indicates location of testimony in those notes.)

7. *Quarterly,* 384.

8. Brooks, N.T. Oct. 16, 1985, p. 186; *Quarterly,* 388.

9. *Quarterly,* 361.

10. Ibid., 393.

11. Stewart, N.T. Oct. 31, A.M., p. 120; *Quarterly,* 394.

12. Tiers, N.T. Oct. ————, pp. ——; *Quarterly,* 393.

13. Phelan, N.T. Nov. 1, P.M., pp. 93-94; *Quarterly,* 397.

14. King, N.T. Nov. 5, A.M., pp. 83-85; *Quarterly,* 398.

15. Richmond, N.T. Oct. 30., A.M., pp. 30-31; *Quarterly,* 398.

16. Brooks, N.T. Oct. 16, P.M., pp. 67-70; *Quarterly,* 399.

17. Sambor, N.T. Oct. 18, A.M., p. 80; *Quarterly,* 399.

18. Richmond, N.T. Oct. 30, A.M., pp. 78-80; *Quarterly,* 399.

19. "Transcript of Fire Marshal's Interview with Birdie Africa," May 25, 1985.

20. "The Findings, Conclusions and Recommendations of the Philadelphia Special Investigation Commission," *Quarterly,* 369.

21. Ibid., 370.

22. Ibid., 369.

23. "Opening Statement of W. Wilson Goode, Mayor, before the Philadelphia Special Investigation Commission"; Wednesday, November 6, 1985; 1.

24. Ibid.

Chapter Fourteen

1. Russell Cooke, "Mayor Goode: After 2d year, a dulled image," *Philadelphia Inquirer,* December 29, 1985, 1-A.

2. Carolyn Acker and Ron Goldwyn, "Goode rips 'lies' about family life," *Philadelphia Daily News,* July 19, 1985, 3.

3. Cooke, "Mayor Goode," 14-A.

4. Steve Lopez, "Mayor's son mum on talk after sit-in," *Philadelphia Inquirer,* January 19, 1986, 2-B.

Epilogue

1. From "May the Work I've Done Speak for Me," written by Sullivan Pugh. Courtesy of AVI Music Publishing Group, Inc.

Index